The Emergence of Agriculture

THE EMERGENCE OF AGRICULTURE

Bruce D. Smith

SCIENTIFIC AMERICAN LIBRARY

A division of HPHLP
New York

Library of Congress Cataloging-in-Publication Data

Smith, Bruce D.
    The emergence of agriculture.
    Includes index.
    1. Agriculture—Origin.   2. Agriculture, Prehistoric.   3. Plants, Cultivated—Origin.   4. Domestic animals—Origin.   5. Man—Influence on nature.   6. Paleoethnobotany.   I. Title.
    GN799.A4S52   1994   630′.9—dc20   94-22833

ISBN 0-7167-5055-4

ISSN 1040-3213

Printed in the United States of America

Scientific American Library
A division of HPHLP
New York

Distributed by W. H. Freeman and Company
41 Madison Avenue, New York, New York 10010
20 Beaumont Street, Oxford OX1 2NQ, England

1 2 3 4 5 6 7 8 9 0 KP 9 8 7 6 5 4

This book is number 54 of a series.

To my mother and father

Emily Bateman Smith
Goldwin Albert Smith

CONTENTS

PREFACE

For several million years or more, our human ancestors survived by hunting wild animals and gathering wild plants. Then, between 10,000 and 4500 years ago, hunter-gatherer societies in at least seven different regions of the world independently domesticated selected species of plants and animals and developed agricultural economies. This transition from a foraging to a farming way of life was a major turning point in the long evolutionary history of our species.

Why did agriculture emerge independently in some regions of the world and not in others? What led hunter-gatherer societies from south China to the south-central Andes to make the transition to an agricultural way of life? Answers to these and other questions have been sought since the 1930s by biologists studying present-day species and by archaeologists analyzing plant and animal remains excavated from ancient settlements. In just the past decade, a number of new approaches for collecting and analyzing information have emerged, and, as a result, our understanding of this revolutionary development in human history has increased dramatically.

For a number of reasons, what we now know about the emergence of agriculture has been partitioned along geographical and scientific disciplinary lines. Books and articles written on the topic, whether for professional or general audiences, have focused on only one region of the world, or on the domestication of either plants or animals, but not both, or on the research of biologists only, or archaeologists only, without providing a balance between the two complementary perspectives.

In this book, all these parts of the puzzle are pieced together—my goal has been to integrate the discoveries of the past several decades, achieved by biologists and archaeologists working in both hemispheres, into a comprehensive consideration of the origins of agriculture.

My own research on this topic had its start in the early 1980s, when I began to consider the possibility that eastern North America was an as yet unrecognized third center of domestication in the Americas, along with Mexico and the south-central Andes. This theory was contrary to the scientific consensus of the time, which held that the first domesticated plant, along with the concept of agriculture, had arrived in what is now the eastern United States from Mexico. That view has now been overturned as the result of discoveries made possible by a number of innovative approaches in biology and archaeology, and eastern North America is now recognized as one of the world's seven known independent centers of domestication. As I hope to show in the chapters of this book, many of these new approaches are now being widely adopted in other regions of the world, and have helped scientists immeasurably in their efforts to understand the emergence of agriculture.

This volume benefited greatly from the advice and corrections of a number of scholars, including Mark Aldenderfer, Ofer Bar-Yosef, Kent V. Flannery, James B. Griffin, Christine Hastorf, Richard S. MacNeish, Ramiro Matos, T. Douglas Price, Jeremy Sabloff, W. H. Wills, and Melinda Zeder. I wish to thank all of these individuals for their invaluable insights and numerous suggestions for improvement.

Considerable credit also goes to Jonathan Cobb, of the Scientific American Library, who helped to shape the book early in its development and shepherded it through the first draft. The photographs in this book clearly illustrate the remarkable skills of Travis Amos in seeking out difficult-to-acquire images and then identifying the best of these to illuminate key points of the text. Susan Moran deserves my special thanks. Although I thought it would be difficult indeed to improve on the text of my first draft, Susan and the copy editor, Barbara Salazar, sympathetically but firmly transformed what I had written, page by page, line by line, from a manuscript into a book. During this transformation process my appreciation of Susan Moran's remarkable and varied talents steadily grew, and I gratefully acknowledge all of the ways in which her ideas and expertise are evident in this volume.

Finally, I want to thank my family for enduring all of the vacation time, evenings, and weekends lost to the writing of this book over the past three years.

Bruce D. Smith
Washington, D.C.
August, 1994

A Note on Radiocarbon Dates

To begin to understand the emergence of agriculture, it is necessary to know when different species of plants and animals were domesticated in different regions of the world. Radiocarbon dating of early domesticates, as discussed in Chapter 3, provides this essential information, but radiocarbon dates, and the ages of early domesticates, can be reported in different ways. Because of past variation in the amount of carbon-14 in the earth's atmosphere, the carbon-14 determined age of a specimen can diverge from its true calender age, and conversion or correction formulas are sometimes applied. In this book, all radiocarbon dates are uncorrected, and all considerations of the timing of domestication and the emergence of agriculture are expressed in uncorrected radiocarbon years before the present (B.P.).

The Emergence of Agriculture

1

IN SEARCH OF ORIGINS

This fresco by Diego Rivera illustrates the culture of corn and the preparation of corn pancakes. Maize was first cultivated, and ways to prepare it first developed, more than 4500 years ago in what is now Mexico. Biologists and archaeologists seek to gain a better understanding of such processes of domestication, using evidence such as the chipped stone hoes on the facing page, dating to between about A.D. 1000 and A.D. 1100.

Fourteen miles north of the modern city of Jericho, in the Jordan Valley, lies the ancient city of Jericho. This older Jericho is a "tell," a large mound built up of the discarded mud bricks of layer upon layer of houses constructed over thousands of years. Near the bottom of this tell, buried beneath more than twenty-five layers of construction, archaeologists have unearthed the earliest evidence of agriculture in the world: a farming village that is 10,000 years old. Underneath this evidence of the world's first agricultural settlement, an earlier settlement was also excavated, where a hunter-gatherer group had camped to take advantage of the spring nearby. Like most camps of hunter-gatherer groups, this settlement

The Jericho Tower. With the formation of permanent agricultural villages came a willingness to invest in community building projects such as this 3-meter-high circular stone tower. The tower was erected 10,000 years ago at the edge of the farming settlement at Jericho, and is shown exposed where two large excavation trenches intersect. Reached by an internal staircase (covered by the square metal grate), the top of the tower would have provided a vantage point for villagers to gaze out on a rapidly changing world.

was likely less than a thousand square meters in size (0.1 hectare); its remnants today consist of a scattering of circular house floors, discarded tools, and the remains of wild plants and animals.

The world's first farming village, found in an overlying layer, was dramatically different from this small hunter-gatherer camp. Covering an area of almost 2.5 hectares (6 acres), this early agricultural settlement contained larger mud-brick houses, and may have had a population of 300 people or more. Its growth was clearly supported by the harvest from nearby fields of recently domesticated barley. Even more striking than the dramatic population increase, however, were the various signs of a growing organizational complexity. Large-scale construction projects at Jericho attest to the marshaling of considerable manpower. An elaborate system of ditches and walls was built, not for defense, but to divert floodwaters away from the expanding village. A large circular tower of unknown purpose, along with a variety of ritual objects, including plastered human skulls, reflect efforts to organize and unify a settled community of a size far beyond what the world had previously seen.

Ten thousand years ago, at the edge of this spring-fed oasis at Jericho, the world changed forever. The farming community established there foreshadowed the massive process of transformation that was to come. There were a few other small farming communities in the Jordan Valley around Jericho, and soon others would appear in similar lake and riverside settings near the present site of Damascus and along the Euphrates. Over the next thousand years in the Near East, domesticated plants and animals would provide new, reliable food sources, shattering the total reliance on wild species that had defined the nature of human existence for millions of years. Created by humans, these new food sources could be stored, on the hoof and in silos,

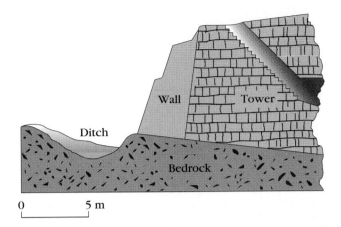

Shown in cross section, the Jericho Tower and staircase, along with an adjacent stone wall and ditch, were once thought to have been built for defense. More recently, Ofer Bar-Yosef of Harvard University has determined that the walls and ditches of Jericho were designed to protect the settlement not from invaders but from floodwaters.

against future need, and had the potential of ever-expanding yields, the limits of which are only now coming into view.

When these new agricultural economies emerged, they didn't just allow human population growth, they also fueled the creation of ever larger and more complex human societies, far beyond what had developed in hunting and gathering times. Large farming villages appeared as people were able to live permanently in higher densities. Such settlements were continuously occupied for thousands of years, and their remains often provide detailed archaeological records of the expanding complexity and scale of agricultural societies. Villages turned into towns, cities and city states gained control of growing agricultural landscapes, and empires emerged as our ancestors became more and more successful at organizing agricultural production and the populations it fed.

Although the Near East and China have yielded the earliest evidence of agricultural societies, these early farmers of Asia were the source of only some of the other farming societies that developed later in various regions of the world. Agriculture emerged not once or twice but many times, as quite different species of plants and animals were domesticated separately and independently in different regions. From each of these separate starting points, the first farming societies and their food-production economies developed along separate pathways up to the present day. Moreover, these early farming societies expanded into adjacent regions, where distinct agricultural landscapes in turn emerged and newly formed farming societies also began their separate historical pathways of development, each responding to changing local challenges and opportunities, both natural and cultural. It is the initial emergence and early expansion of this agricultural way of life, and the transformations in human society they made possible, that will be explored in the pages that follow.

The spread of agricultural landscapes is now approaching an endgame as farmers encroach on zones of marginal productivity and ever-escalating potential costs. Each day, satellites passing over the Amazon rain forest of Brazil record the smoke plumes drifting up from piles of newly cut trees and other vegetation. Most of this land is being deforested so that it can be permanently converted to farmland. Using satellite imagery of these smoke plumes, a team headed by Alberto Setzer of the National Space Research Institute of Brazil estimated that 8 million hectares—about 20 million acres—of forest had been cleared in 1987 alone, at an annual deforestation rate of more than 2 percent. New satellite data have also provided startlingly high estimates of deforestation in India, Cameroon, Myanmar (formerly Burma), and Costa Rica. If these new studies are correct, the world is losing up to 20 million hectares (almost 50 million acres) of tropical forest annually.

The clearing of tropical rain forests represents just the most recent chapter in the long, complex, and still unfolding history of agricultural expansion. Each year more of the earth's land surface is transformed into cropland or pasture to feed a rapidly growing world population. In the Near East and North Africa 97 percent of the available arable land is now under production, while throughout Asia the agricultural frontier has expanded until now more than 80 percent of the potential cropland is being cultivated. In other regions of the world where land is still available for agricultural expansion, primarily sub-Saharan Africa and Latin America, relatively poor soils hold only limited promise as future farmland.

The increasing mechanization of farming since 1950 has accelerated our approach to the limits of agricultural expansion, but from a longer-term perspective we are seeing the continuation of the process that first began 8000 to 10,000 years ago in Asia and about 6000 to 5000 years ago in the Western Hemisphere, when human societies first domesticated plants and animals.

In view of the importance of the agricultural transformation of the earth, it is not surprising that scholars have long been interested in the origins of agriculture. The questions to be answered are numerous and diverse. How did agriculture begin? In what sequence and in what combinations were different species of plants and animals first domesticated in different parts of the world? Why were certain plants and animals domesticated and not others? What were the wild ancestors of these domesticates? Where, specifically, were certain plants and animals first domesticated? Why did agriculture emerge in some regions and not in others?

Answers to these and other questions are being sought by a broad spectrum of biologists and archaeologists. No one approach can uncover all of the relevant information, so scientists in many areas of biological and archaeological research are engaged in the quest for answers. Each of the various approaches holds the key to some answers, and together they can often produce impressive insights into this major turning point in human history. Two men, Nikolai Vavilov and Robert Braidwood, played central roles in establishing the biological and archaeological approaches to the origins of agriculture.

Nikolai Vavilov and the Biological Approach

It may seem surprising to learn that some of the most interesting insights into the origins of agriculture have come not from investigation of archaeological sites, but through research on living organisms. The first concerted attempt to understand agricultural origins through this kind of research was undertaken in the 1930s by Nikolai Ivanovich Vavilov, a Soviet biologist and geneticist. Vavilov's efforts came to an end prematurely when he was imprisoned by Stalinist authorities in 1940 for his defense of genetics and opposition to T. D. Lysenko's teachings on the heritability of acquired characteristics, but before then he had visited fifty-two countries in a search for seeds of crop plants and geographical patterns of genetic diversity. He and other scientists from the All Union Institute of Plant Industry mapped the distribution and degree of genetic diversity of numerous crops throughout the world, and observed that some regions of the world exhibited extremely high levels of variation while

Nikolai Ivanovich Vavilov, Russian plant geneticist, began the search for agricultural origins through the study of modern plants.

others were relatively impoverished. In a small, isolated pocket on the Ethiopian Plateau, for example, Vavilov discovered hundreds of varieties of ancient wheat. He reasoned that since diversity in cultivated forms results from experimentation and deliberate human selection over time, the high degree of diversity in Ethiopian wheats indicated that this crop had been cultivated in the region for a very long time. The longer a crop had been grown, he reasoned, the more uses for it would have developed, and a variety of uses would be reflected in a variety of forms: corn for popping and for roasting, for use in medicine and in ceremonies, for example. More textures and colors could have evolved, as well as greater resistance to more pests and diseases.

It seemed reasonable, almost inescapable, therefore, that the area where a crop plant had the greatest diversity of forms would also be the place where it was first domesticated. Vavilov proposed that by locating the center of a crop's genetic diversity, one pinpointed its origin. As he mapped the centers of diversity of more and more crops, he found that

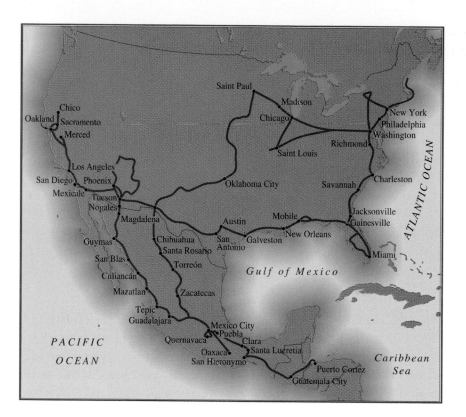

Vavilov traveled widely throughout the world collecting seed and plant specimens and searching for centers of plant diversity. His route of travel during a 1930 expedition to North America took him to many regions of the United States and Mexico.

many overlapped. The Near East center of diversity of wheat, for example, overlapped the centers of barley, rye, lentils, peas, flax, and other crops. From 1926 until 1940 Vavilov was continually revising and updating his findings, and in 1940 his last synthesis outlined seven overlapping areas of maximum diversity for a variety of crop plants, and he identified these seven regions as the world's major centers of origin for cultivated plants.

Vavilov's central assumption—that the location where a crop plant was first domesticated is today marked by its geographical center of genetic diversity—has since been shown to have a basic flaw. Domesticates can, and did, originate in one region and then develop much of their diversity in another. Although Vavilov's centers of origin have been sub

jected to considerable rethinking, his work marks an important beginning in biological research on the origins of agriculture. Vavilov forcefully put forward identification of the centers of origin of the world's crop plants as a goal of biological and genetic research on domesticated plants. In so doing he staked out an area of inquiry that has proved very productive for later generations of plant geneticists and biologists. Vavilov also demonstrated the importance of active field research. Scientists continue to collect seeds and map the geographical ranges of crop plants around the world.

As we will see, later generations of scholars have expanded their mapping to encompass the wild relatives of domesticated crops—species that may have been the progenitors of the first domesticates. If the wild ancestor of a domesticate could be identified, and if it is assumed that the geographical range of the ancestor is the same today as it was at the time the plant was first domesticated, then the present-day range of the wild progenitor should define an outer boundary wherein to look for the area where it was first domesticated. The center of origin of a domesticated plant or animal could thus be established through the seemingly simple and straightforward process of mapping the present-day distribution of its wild progenitor. The value of such an approach of course varies with the size of the

geographical range of the suspected wild ancestor. The small geographical ranges of the wild ancestors of domesticated sheep and goats, for example, help to define their areas of initial domestication, but cattle and pigs have such broad distributions that their ranges provide little help in establishing where they were first brought under domestication. In addition, the geographical ranges of wild plants and animals have changed, sometimes substantially, over the past 10,000 years, often as a result of expanding agricultural landscapes. Scientists can address the possibility of such changes over time, however, by

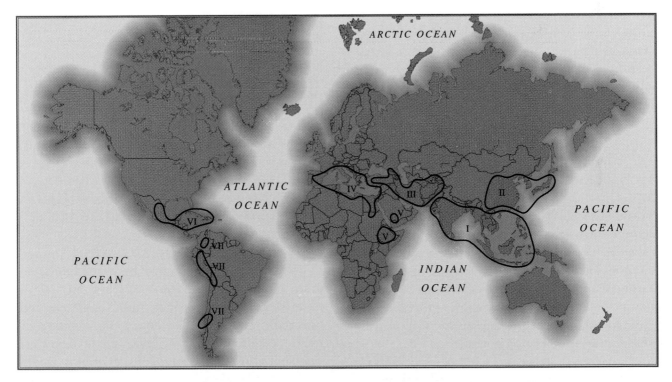

Vavilov's final map, published in 1940, showed seven centers of origin of domesticated plants: I, the tropical south Asiatic center; II, the east Asiatic center; III, the southwestern Asiatic center; IV, the Mediterranean center; V, the Abyssinian center; VI, the Central American center; VII, the Andean (South American) center.

establishing the presence of potential ancestor species in archaeological sites of different time periods and at different locations. In this way, they can chart the geographical range of a species in the past.

Another problem is how to identify the wild ancestor of a domesticate. It is seldom easy to establish which of several possible progenitor species actually gave rise to a present-day domesticate, given the long and complex intervening history of genetic manipulation and diversification. Remarkable strides have been made in this area, however, with the development of powerful new procedures for directly comparing the genetic composition of domesticates and their wild relatives. As a result it is possible to identify wild ancestors with confidence. When biological investigators pair this new and rapidly expanding genetic research with their continuing efforts to map the present-day distribution of domesticated plants and animals and their potential wild progenitors, they are able to throw increasing light on the origins of agriculture.

Robert Braidwood of the Oriental Institute, University of Chicago, who pioneered the archaeological search for the origins of agriculture in the 1950s.

Robert Braidwood and the Archaeological Approach

A parallel scholarly tradition of concerted archaeological inquiry into the origins of agriculture can be traced back to the 1940s and Robert Braidwood of the Oriental Institute, the University of Chicago. During World War II, Braidwood began to formulate an interdisciplinary research program that would focus on the beginnings of the early agricultural revolution in the Near East:

> *What would we learn,* we wondered, were we to concentrate on the threshold of cultural change that must have attended the very earliest use of effectively domesticated plants and

animals. . . . What fascinated us about all this was that excavated traces of the *beginnings* of this early "agricultural revolution" had not yet been recovered. Thus our field research goal in 1947 was to try to find the traces of such a "threshold."

The research program that Braidwood initiated in the Near East in the late 1940s and early 1950s established the origins of agriculture as a broad and important new field of inquiry in archaeology. Braidwood also provided a clear example of how archaeological research on agricultural origins should be structured and carried out. The basic strategy he used so successfully in the Fertile Crescent was quickly adopted and applied in other regions, and today provides the basic approach employed throughout the world by archaeologists studying agricultural origins.

What were the key elements of Braidwood's approach? First, he reasoned that the best place to attempt to find archaeological evidence of the transition to an agricultural way of life in the Near East was in the "natural habitat zone for all potential domesticates." This reasoning led him in the late 1940s to the remote Chemchemal Valley of northeastern Iraq, near the southern margin of the Zagros Mountains, and well within the geographical range of all the wild ancestors of the seven major Near Eastern domesticates (barley, emmer and einkorn wheat, goats, sheep, pigs, and cattle).

The Chemchemal Valley also clearly contained the second key element required by Braidwood's approach—ancient settlements that seemed to span the transition from a hunting and gathering way of life to the establishment of early farming villages. Braidwood's research team selected for initial investigation two archaeological sites that met this criterion remarkably well. Located only 2 kilometers apart, the sites of Karim Shahir and Jarmo were perched on the edge of flat-topped grassy plateaus, looking down a steep slope onto the Cham-Gawra, a seasonal stream meandering some 40 meters below.

When excavated by Bruce Howe of Braidwood's team, Karim Shahir turned out to be a small (500 square meters) seasonal settlement that had been occupied for a short period of time more than 9000 years ago by a hunting and gathering society. Discarded flint tools, some of which were manufactured at Karim Shahir, had been used to hunt and butcher wild animals, mostly sheep and goats, judging from the animal bone fragments recovered during excavation. Other stone tools attested to the pounding and grinding of seeds and other wild plant materials. A few small fire hearths and cooking pits and a

pavement of river cobbles provided the only other evidence of the activities of the small group of hunter-gatherers that briefly lived at Karim Shahir. Their movements tied to the seasons, to the annual ripening of wild wheats and barley at different elevations, and to the corresponding movement of wild herds of sheep and goats to higher pastures as spring turned to summer, hunter-gatherer societies on the margin of the Zagros Mountains would have occupied a number of settlements like Karim Shahir in any given year.

Located 2 kilometers downstream from Karim Shahir, and dating perhaps 500 to 1000 years later, the site of Jarmo hosted a way of life that was worlds apart. Here, in the early 1950s, Braidwood encountered clear and convincing evidence of a very different way of life—a permanent farming village.

These foundation walls supported some of the contiguous rectangular mud-brick houses of the farming village at Jarmo about 8700 to 8000 years ago. This remarkably preserved community plan of an early agricultural settlement was uncovered at a depth of more than 2 meters during Braidwood's excavation.

Excavation down through more than 5 meters of deposits uncovered the history of this agricultural community recorded in a vertical sequence of rectangular mud-brick houses.

The early farming village at Jarmo was likely occupied for anywhere from two to seven centuries somewhere around 8700 to 8000 years ago, and appears to have had, on the average, perhaps twenty-five households and a population of 150 to 200 people. Careful excavation up through the successive building layers at Jarmo provided considerable information about the way of life of these early agriculturalists: what their houses looked like and how they were arranged in a community plan, how large the settlement was and the size of its population, what tools they manufactured and used, how and where they prepared and cooked their food, and what materials they traded for and from where. All this information about the people of Jarmo provided a human, cultural context for considering the central questions of agricultural origins and the initial domestication of plants and animals.

This then brings us to the third key element of Braidwood's research strategy: he included scientists from the biological and earth sciences in a coordinated interdisciplinary approach to the question of the emergence of agriculture. Specialists in their fields were asked to seek evidence of what the climate was like when Jarmo flourished, to reconstruct the environment around the settlement, to identify and analyze the animal bones and plant remains recovered during excavation, and to look for ways to distinguish the wild from the domesticated in the scattered and fragmentary bits of bone and seeds that had survived 8000 years in the ground.

These were not easy tasks in the early 1950s, for little was yet known about how the seeds and bones of domesticates preserved in archaeological sites could be distinguished from those of wild plants and animals. Braidwood's pioneering interdisciplinary approach addressed this critically important challenge, and as we shall see, the analysis of plant and animal materials from archaeological sites has now matured into two well-established disciplines, and clear criteria for identifying domesticated plants and animals have been developed.

In the four decades that have passed since Braidwood's landmark project, the search for agricultural origins in the Near East has expanded to encompass much of the Fertile Crescent. As more sites have been excavated and more information recovered, sites such as Jarmo and Jericho have become part of a much larger and more complex story, as their study has become integrated into that of the entire region. But Braidwood's emphasis on an interdisciplinary approach and on establishing a human, cultural context can be seen today wherever archaeologists search for the beginnings of a farming way of life.

We can see, then, that the archaeological approach to agricultural origins in large measure complements biological research focused on present-day populations of plants and animals. Archaeological research not only offers independent confirmation and an often tighter geographical delineation of the areas of initial domestication; it also provides a date for the origins of agriculture and reveals the pace at which agriculture emerged.

Archaeological excavation of early farming settlements in various regions of the world is the only means of directly observing the economic and cultural context of domestication and the transition to farming. It is this social and economic background that provides a basis for understanding not only when and where plants and animals were domesticated but the process of domestication itself—how and why human societies initiated new relationships with certain wild species and began to intervene actively in their life cycles. What kind of human societies first domesticated plants and animals, and what prompted them to do so? How large and how permanent were these early agrarian settlements? Which species of plants and animals did these people use for food before they began to domesticate some of them? What attributes or characteristics, if any, may have preadapted some wild food sources to human manipulation and domestication? Were different species brought under domestication together as part of an integrated economic strategy? What kinds of changes can be seen in these human societies once they began to invest time and energy in managing domesticates and producing their own food? Did domesticates quickly occupy center stage in rapidly expanding farming economies, or was agriculture slow in developing? Such questions can be answered only through archaeological investigation of human settlements and by careful analysis of the human societies that first developed farming long ago.

The two parallel scholarly traditions of research on agricultural origins, one focusing on present-day populations of domesticates and their wild relatives, the other directed toward archaeological evidence, thus offer solutions to different parts of what is a large and multifaceted problem. In the decades that have passed since Vavilov and Braidwood laid the foundation for the biological and archaeological approaches to agricultural origins, a number of advances in knowledge and available technology have been made, the most important of them coming in the 1970s.

Advances in Theory and Technology

Researchers in both the biological and archaeological sciences have dramatically improved our understanding of how plants and animals were actually domesticated—the specific human actions that resulted in the creation of domesticates. They have also come to a clearer understanding of the motivation that led human societies to embark on courses of action that led to domestication, as will be discussed in some depth in the next chapter. In part, they owe their success to remarkable improvements in their ability to recognize the actual physical changes that indicate domestication in plants and animals—changes that can be observed in the animal bones and plant remains recovered during archaeological excavation and that are also described in Chapter 2.

Today biologists and archaeologists also bring to the search for agricultural origins an impressive array of technological innovations, the most important of which are described in Chapter 3. New dating techniques have greatly improved our ability to establish when various species of plants and animals were first domesticated. New methods of excavation have substantially increased the amount of plant and animal remains recovered from archaeological sites. New microscopes have made it possible to identify extremely small markers of domestication in plants. Similarly, an array of new biochemical techniques have made it possible to identify with considerable accuracy the wild populations that gave rise to different species of plants and animals. These tools of the trade have been successfully employed in different parts of the world in the search for the origins of agriculture.

Archaeological and biological research on the emergence of agriculture has not progressed uniformly around the world. In some regions, such as the Near East (discussed in Chapter 4) and eastern North America (Chapter 8), the two approaches have given us a good outline of the transition from hunting and gathering to a farming way of life. The small area of the Near East known as the Fertile

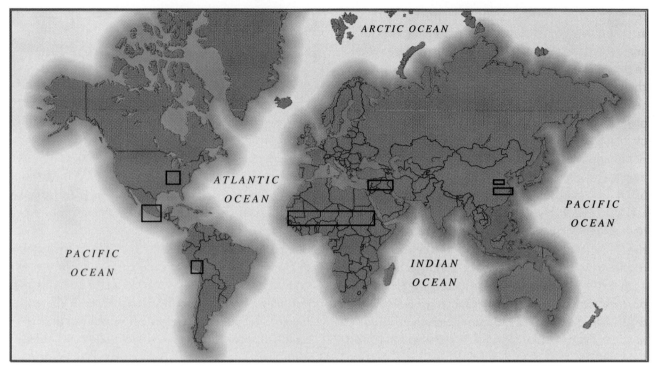

The seven areas of the world where the independent domestication of plants and
animals led to the emergence of agriculture.

Crescent witnessed the earliest development of an
agricultural economy in the world, about 10,000
years before the present (B.P.). When it was fully
formed, about 8000 years ago, this first agricultural
economy was remarkable for its inclusion of a large
number of both plants and animals that would become important in agricultural economies throughout the world (barley, wheats, lentils, sheep, goats,
cattle, pigs). We now have a clear general picture of
the domestication of all of these species and the development of agricultural economies in a complex
process that spanned 2000 years.

In China (Chapter 6), on the other hand, considerable analysis of plant and animal popula-

tions, both past and present day, is still to be done.
Moreover, despite the long and detailed archaeological record of agriculture in China, we still lack
evidence of the initial transition from a hunting-and-
gathering way of life to a farming economy. The
earliest known farming settlements, along the
Yellow River in the north and the Yangtze in the
south, are clearly many centuries past the initial
transition to agriculture.

Sub-Saharan Africa (Chapter 5) stands in dramatic contrast to China. Here the archaeological record is rather limited; what is known about
the emergence of uniquely African agricultural economies is the result of extensive biological

research on modern plant populations, both wild and domesticated. Similarly, in Middle America and South America (Chapter 7), remarkable advances in biological research have dramatically changed the picture of agricultural beginnings in both the central highlands of Mexico and the central Andes of Peru and Bolivia, pointing to the need for archaeologists to focus on new areas and new time periods.

Very little is yet known about the early history of food production in either Southeast Asia (Chapter 6) or the lowland rain forests of South America (Chapter 7), although there is considerable speculation regarding the great age of root-crop agriculture in the tropics.

To a considerable extent, then, this book has been shaped by the level of success of archaeological and biological research carried out in different regions. Its emphasis is on those regions of the world—China, the Fertile Crescent, central Mexico, the central Andes, sub-Saharan Africa, and eastern North America—where wild species were independently domesticated and distinctive agricultural economies emerged, and on the two regions where agricultural expansion is best documented: Europe (Chapter 5) and the southwestern United States (Chapter 8).

Before agriculture came to these various parts of the world, all were inhabited by groups of hunter-gatherers who relied on the hunting of animals and the collecting of wild plants. How did these groups transform themselves into tillers of the earth and husbanders of animals? Part of the answer rests in an understanding of how efforts leading to the domestication of wild species could have emerged out of a wider class of human behavior common to all hunter-gatherers.

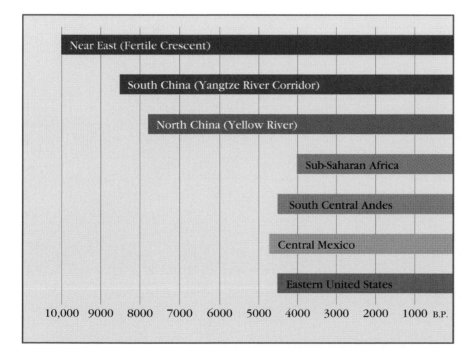

The approximate time periods when plants and animals were first domesticated in the seven primary centers of agricultural development.

2
CREATING NEW PLANTS AND ANIMALS

 An old man with a donkey cart, China. Created by human societies in different places at different times over the past 10,000 years, domesticated plants and animals have provided a reliable source of food, clothing, and pulling power. Artifacts such as the 6400-year-old spade on the facing page, excavated at the Ho-mu-tu site in China, provide evidence of early rice farming economies.

The changes brought over the past 10,000 years as agricultural landscapes replaced wild plant and animal communities, while not so abrupt as those caused by the impact of an asteroid at the Cretaceous-Tertiary boundary some 65 million years ago or so massive as those caused by advancing glacial ice in the Pleistocene, are nonetheless comparable to these other forces of global change.

Though the "agricultural revolution" exhibits some basic similarities to the major "natural" forces of global change, it differs dramatically in being a uniquely human creation, and, unlike these natural changes, it cannot be traced to a single causal event or process. The agricultural transformation had a series of isolated, independent beginnings involving different peoples, different areas of the world, different time periods, and different animals and plants. All of these separate beginnings, however, seem to have come about in generally similar ways, in response to a similar motivation.

Manipulating the Environment to Reduce Risk

I think that the motivations that eventually led our ancestors to domesticate plants and animals can comfortably be included in a much broader class of behavior: efforts by hunter-gatherer societies to increase both the economic contribution and the reliability of one or more of the wild species they depended on for survival, and thus reduce risk and uncertainty. Hunter-gatherer societies that survive today attempt to reduce risk in a variety of ways, from storing food against hard times to maintaining far-reaching kinship networks. These networks serve as a kind of insurance policy that enables family groups to survive lean years by temporarily moving in with distant relatives in regions where food is more plentiful. More interesting for our purposes, present-day hunter-gatherer societies also reduce

In Australia, hunter-gatherer societies "domesticate" the landscape, burning off vegetation to encourage the growth of valued plant species.

risk both by deliberately manipulating the habitats of plants and animals they rely on for food and by actively intervening in the life cycles of those species. Both these types of activities are undertaken to increase the yield and dependability of wild food sources. Together such activities represent a deliberate effort to modify the environment and make it more to the liking of these species—in a way to domesticate it.

In Australia, for example, where hunting-and-gathering groups have lived without agriculture for at least 20,000 years, Aborigine societies burn vegetation to encourage some species of grasses they depend on for food at the expense of other plants that do not fare so well in the burned-over areas. They also increase the yield of some food plants by intervening directly in their life cycles. After they dig out the tubers of the wild yam *Discorea,* for example, Aborigine foragers replace the stem-attached top of the tubers so that more yams will grow to be dug up another time.

The Kumeyaay Indians, a hunter-gatherer society of southern California, made even more extensive efforts to reduce risk by "domesticating" the landscape. By interviewing Kumeyaay elders and studying historical documents, Florence Shipek, a historian at the University of Wisconsin at Parkside, has been able to document a range of activities that encouraged the growth of desirable wild plants.

Straddling the border with Mexico, the coastal valley area of the Kumeyaay was not naturally rich in plant foods, and was subject to frequent droughts and floods, along with considerable variation in rainfall and temperature from year to year. Yet when the Spanish entered coastal California in 1769, they encountered relatively large Kumeyaay populations, which they described as subsisting not on agriculture but on wild seeds and other foods. The

Kumeyaay thrived in this erratic and inhospitable environment as a result of very intense and far-reaching experiments in transplanting food plants across the full range of micro-habitat zones.

From coastal sandbars and marshes up through floodplains, valleys, and foothills, to high mountain deserts, the Kumeyaay had made experimental plantings of a variety of food and medicinal plants. They created groves of wild oaks and pines producing edible nuts at higher elevations and established plantings of high-desert species such as desert palm and mesquite along the coast. They planted agave, yucca, and wild grapes in various micro-habitats. They also planted cuttings of cacti and other succulents near their villages. They carefully burned many of the groves and other plantings of wild species to keep yields high, and by regularly burning off chaparral they improved the browse for deer. In early summer they harvested large stands of a wild grain-grass, now extinct, by hand stripping seeds from the stalk. Then they burned off the stands and broadcast a portion of the harvested seed across the burned areas. This highly modified and carefully "domesticated" landscape of the Kumeyaay, a complex mosaic of manipulated wild plants, disappeared with the coming of European settlers and their crops, and survives today only in the memories of Kumeyaay elders, in early Spanish documents, and in Shipek's writings.

Thus hunter-gatherer societies of the past and present, to varying degrees and in a wide variety of ways, have reshaped their environments to make them more to their liking. Across the full course of human history, societies dependent on wild plants and animals for their survival should not be seen as passive participants in the ecosystem who simply conform their lives to a rigid, unyielding natural environment. These societies have actively and continually experimented with manipulation of plant and animal communities to reduce risk in their own lives.

It is from such efforts that domesticated animals and plants were initially created. The likelihood that any plant or animal will actually be domesticated, however, is not the same in all situations. The opportunities for experimentation that could lead to domesticates varied widely. Many habitats and many species of animals and plants held only limited potential for manipulation, while others held great promise. Such promising species can be considered as preadapted to domestication. And just as some species are more likely candidates for domestication than others, some types of human intervention in the life cycles of species are more likely pathways to domestication than others.

What Is Domestication?

Scholars have been providing definitions and descriptions of "domestication" from various perspectives for more than a hundred years. Debate continues today on the fine points, but there is considerable agreement on a good starting definition: domestication is the human creation of a new form of plant or animal—one that is identifiably different from its wild ancestors and extant wild relatives.

Differentiation within wild species—the emergence of new forms of plants and animals—has of course occurred innumerable times in the earth's history without any human assistance at all. One of the most common ways in which such "natural" episodes of differentiation occur parallels the process by which humans create domesticates. First, a physical barrier of some sort separates a species into distinct reproductive groups within its geographical range. Over successive generations the groups on the two sides of the barrier begin to diverge as they respond to different sets of environmental forces or Darwinian selective pressures (differences in climate, habitat, predators and competitors, and so on).

Domestication is similar to this natural process, except that human societies set up the physical barrier and determine the selective pressures. A new set of selective pressures comes into play when humans intervene in key aspects of the life cycle of the now "captive" population, creating new rules for survival and reproductive success. Only those individuals able to survive and produce offspring under the new rules contribute genetic information to the next generation.

Over generations, in response to the new rules for survival, the captive populations change in a number of ways, some deliberately caused by the domesticators, others incidental and automatic. Taken together, all of the adaptations or adjustments made by a captive population can be collectively described as that species' "adaptive syndrome of domestication."

Many of the changes that occur as part of the adaptive syndrome of domestication are "phenotypic," or observable (larger seeds on a food plant, say, or smaller size in a herd animal), and it is such observable changes that often enable us to determine that the species has been domesticated. Associated with these observable changes, of course, are changes at the molecular level, in the genes themselves. The ratio of female to male, or young to old, in a population of domesticates may also serve to distinguish them from wild populations. Defining domestication in terms of either phenotypic or genotypic changes in individual animals, or changes in the composition of their populations, while certainly appropriate, is at the same time somewhat misleading. Although such measurable changes are often

Seeds of wild and domesticated marsh elder (top), sunflower (center), and squash (bottom) differ considerably in size, allowing archaeologists to recognize the presence of domesticates in ancient settlements. The wild marsh elder seed is modern; the domesticated marsh elder seed is from the Turner site, in southeast Missouri, which has been dated to A.D. 1300. The wild and domesticated sunflower and squash seeds are from the Cloudsplitter rock shelter in eastern Kentucky, and are more than 2000 years old.

the goal of domestication, they are at the same time symptomatic of an underlying change in the relationship between human societies and plant and animal communities. Domestication is not simply an observable end product—physical changes in plants and animals. It also reflects a revolutionary change in the relationship between human societies and the species they have domesticated.

When we take into consideration this new relationship between humans and other species, we have to expand our earlier definition of domesticates as human-modified plants and animals to include this essential attribute: they have been changed so much that they have lost the ability to survive in the wild. Corn (*Zea mays*), for example, is by almost

any measure one of the most successful plants in the history of the world, occupying as it does vast areas of the earth's land surface. Yet any cornfield left untended will simply cease to exist within a few years. Long-term human selection has produced in *Zea mays* a plant incapable of dispersing seed that can survive to the next growing season, germinate, and successfully compete with the variety of aggressive intruders likely to invade any uncultivated cornfield. Human societies long ago intervened in the life cycle of teosinte, the wild ancestor of *Zea mays*, and selected for plants with reduced ability to disperse their kernels, and these kernels themselves were less able to delay sprouting until the following spring. At the same time humans took over responsibility for the dispersal and germination of seeds by harvesting and storing kernels and then planting them in cultivated fields at the start of the next growing season. Human beings have similarly intervened in the life cycles of many plants and animals, so that after thousands of years of selection and sheltered existence, these organisms have been transformed into a rich variety of domesticated species that are highly successful in agricultural landscapes and at the same time incapable of surviving without human help. In the same way, the survival of human societies has come to depend on domesticated food sources.

How do such relationships of increasing mutual dependence get started? Within the general pool of hunter-gatherers' efforts to manipulate their habitats, what particular types of intervention in the life cycles of target species precede and precipitate domestication? And why are some species and not others drawn into such revolutionary relationships?

Researchers have identified a logical sequence of human activities that give us ever-increasing levels of control over wild plants and animals, culminating in the specific actions that result in domestication. Some scholars have proposed that these increasing levels of intervention represent a continuous and gradual developmental pathway leading up to domestication. Let's look at possible pathways to the domestication, first of seed plants, then of animals.

The Domestication of Seed Plants

Most of the major crop plants grown today are seed plants. The pathway leading to the domestication of seed plants might have begun with the encouragement of wild plants that grew outside of any human-made environment. While such human efforts as the Australian Aborigine's burning of the landscape can increase the number and size of wild stands, and hence their yields, even intensive harvesting will have no appreciable genetic effect on the wild plants in that stand, because it is the seeds that *escape the harvester* and are exposed to the full set of natural selective pressures that become the next generation of plants.

Another form of human intervention, however, does represent a step toward domestication: the disturbance of the soil and associated disruption of existing plant communities that accompany a wide range of human activities, particularly around settlements. People disturb plant communities by clearing away vegetation, building houses, excavating pits for storage and cooking, and piling up refuse. These activities have little lasting impact on plant communities if the people move on fairly soon. Hunter-gatherer populations that move their settlements frequently produce a series of temporarily disturbed patches that soon return to the original vegetation cover after the people have left. When people maintain their settlements over a number of

years, though, a new human-created plant habitat becomes more permanently established.

Such relatively permanent disturbed habitats have three important characteristics. First, being comparatively clear of preexisting vegetation, they are open to colonization, particularly by pioneer plants and other plants adapted to any similar naturally disturbed habitats that may exist in the wild. Second, they are in close proximity to human settlements, where hunter-gatherers could accidentally drop seeds they had harvested from wild stands and thus inadvertently introduce colonizers. Third, these disturbed habitats bear some resemblance to the broken ground of seedbeds prepared for cultivated plants. Thus by producing habitats where soil was disturbed, sedentary hunter-gatherers inadvertently created experimental quasi-garden plots that a variety of wild plants, some of economic importance, had an opportunity to invade and colonize.

Plants that are successful in such disturbed habitats, particularly those created by human action, are usually called "weeds." As Edgar Anderson, a botanist and director of the Missouri Botanical Garden, pointed out in the 1950s, some natural forces—most notably rivers, which constantly rework floodplain soils—create zones of permanently disturbed soil that typically are inhabited by a range of weeds, long adapted to the open floodplain. Anderson argued that the weeds of natural open habitats were preadapted to colonizing human-created open habitats, and in this respect were excellent candidates for eventual domestication. Representing in many respects a new niche, the patches of soil that people inadvertently disturbed around their settlements not only offered excellent opportunities for weeds to invade from their natural habitats but also provided a place where weedy adaptations by other colonizing wild plants, particularly those of economic importance, could develop.

The attitude of hunter-gatherers toward the weedy plants that colonized the ground they had disturbed could have ranged from dislike and active eradication, through simple toleration, to various degrees of encouragement and use. Those weedy colonizers with a history of having been harvested as wild food sources were the most likely to be actively encouraged, perhaps by people removing competing plants or expanding the disturbed soil area.

In sum, disturbed soil settings close to human settlements were similar in some respects to the prepared seedbeds of garden plots. They were open to colonization by weedy species preadapted to growing in such settings and offered opportunities for first attempts to encourage and control weedy "camp follower" plant species. As a result, they may well have provided the context for a logical next step that led directly to plant domestication: the deliberate planting of stored seed stock.

No matter where they were carried out, the first experiments with planting could well have consisted simply of efforts to enlarge stands of wild or camp follower food plants by broadcasting some of the harvested seed over a wider area, as the Kumeyaay did. The hunter-gatherers could have later elaborated the process by minimally preparing the soil to receive the wild seeds and then "weeding." These initial experiments with planting, seen as a logical extension of hunter-gatherers' efforts to increase the yield and dependability of wild and weedy species, would not lead to true domestication, however, unless people isolated the plants in question and intervened in their reproduction. They could have done so easily enough. All they needed to do was set aside some seeds of target species after they had harvested them, and then plant those stored seeds the following year in a prepared area, or "seedbed." When sown with part of the previous year's harvest, such planting areas would have provided substantial genetic isolation from populations of wild relatives.

Over time, the practice of planting stored seed stock would produce domesticated plants—plants that had responded and adapted to the newly created human environment, and in doing so had undergone a series of changes in their "morphology," or outward shape and form. At first glance, planting might seem a simple and logical extension of hunter-gatherers' manipulation of food plants. In fact, however, it marks an essential change in the relationship of human societies to their environment.

Unintended Benefits: The Consequences of Seedbed Competition and Human Harvesting

By storing and planting harvested seed, hunter-gatherers assumed control of the life cycles of the now isolated target plants, shielding them in many ways from the competition and pressure of the natural environment. But at the same time that this protective relationship released the plants from one set of selective pressures, it subjected them to another. As the now "protected" plants adjusted to this new set of selective forces, their morphology changed, and many of these changes were advantageous to the human harvesters in ways the harvesters had not foreseen. Jack Harlan, an evolutionary biologist, and his co-workers first outlined many of these unintended changes.

Where plants grow in the wild, only the seeds that escape human harvesting and are dispersed on the ground have a chance of sprouting and growing to form next year's stand. Just the opposite is true, however, once humans begin to store seed stock to

The compaction of seeds is a good indicator of domestication. In the wild *Chenopodium* plant known as lamb's-quarters, on the right, seeds are distributed in numerous small clusters. On the left, in contrast, the seeds of a domesticated *Chenopodium* plant are tightly compacted at the top of the main stem.

plant the following year. Now the seeds that are collected have a better chance of contributing genetic material to the next generation's prepared seedbed than those that are lost. And harvesters are less likely to miss seeds that are conveniently packaged in terminal clusters at the ends of stalks. Over time, plants that retain their seeds long enough to be harvested and that package them in convenient clusters both contribute more seeds to next year's seed stock and generate a larger harvest. Harvesting, then, coupled with storage and deliberate planting, inadvertently encourages plants to increase their harvest yields as they respond to the newly imposed selection guidelines for reproductive success.

These two automatic responses by plants to the harvesting of stored seed stock—retention of seeds and their packaging in terminal clusters—also result in recognizable morphological changes in the plants, changes that serve as markers of domestication. These are the markers that archaeobotanists look for in the fragmented seeds and other plant parts they recover from archaeological sites. When they compare plant assemblages from different time periods, for example, they look for a stronger attachment of seeds to stalks that indicates an increased retention of seeds.

Several other important morphological markers of domestication are the result of the intense competition among plants that sprout in prepared seedbeds. Seedlings that sprout quickly, grow rapidly toward the sun, and then shade nearby seedlings with their spreading leaves have a distinct advantage. Young plants that can literally put their neighboring competitors in the shade markedly improve their own chances of surviving to harvest and contributing seeds to the next year's planting cycle. Over time, such pressures strongly favor plants whose seeds have both greater start-up food reserves within and substantially reduced inhibitions to rapid sprouting.

The seeds of wild plants commonly remain dormant in the ground for months until winter is over, the rains come, or conditions are otherwise suitable for germination. Thick impermeable seed coats are often essential in the seeds of wild plants that have to survive, exposed to the elements, from one growing season to the next. Once humans take over the responsibility for safely storing seeds away from moisture and predators, however, thick seed coats are not necessary. Since any delay in germination after the seed is planted will often, in the face of competition for nutrients and sunlight, reduce a young plant's chances of contributing to the harvest (and

the next year's planting), its seeds lose much or all of the ability to lie dormant and sometimes acquire a thinner seed coat. Similarly, by favoring seeds with greater start-up food reserves, seedbed competition selects for larger seed size.

Like plants' automatic responses to harvesting, the two automatic responses to seedbed competition (larger seeds, thinner seed coat) thus inadvertently make the harvest both larger and more easily processed. A thinner seed coat and a larger seed size are key morphological markers of domestication that investigators often look for in seeds recovered from archaeological sites. They provide clear evidence of deliberate planting. With the aid of scanning electron microscopes and light microscopes, archaeobotanists patiently examine and measure ancient seeds, looking for the morphological characteristics that indicate whether or not domesticated plants were yet present at particular settlements of known age.

In sum, a few seemingly simple steps brought remarkable changes to the relationship between human societies and particular plant species. When human beings took control of the reproductive cycles of some populations of certain species by harvesting, storing, and planting their seeds in prepared areas, they effectively created a separate and parallel world for these plants. Populations of the same species that grew beyond the human realm continued to be shaped by the rules of reproductive competition and survival in the natural world, but those plants now controlled by humans became subject to new rules for success. These new rules favored plants with larger seeds that could sprout quickly and that were retained on the plant at harvest and packaged in terminal clusters for easier collection. These changes, rather than being deliberately caused by humans, were probably in large measure unintentional and automatic responses to

In a timeless tableau, women harvest grain. A several-thousand-year-old cave painting from Tassili n'Ajjer, Algeria.

human planting, part of the adaptive syndrome of domestication.

These changes made crop plants dramatically more important as sources of food than wild stands. Such plants would produce larger and more dependable yields than wild ones, and they would lose substantially fewer seeds at harvesting. Their seeds were larger, and thinner seed coats made processing easier. This serendipitous response to planting, so advantageous to the planters, is one of the most interesting and perhaps most important elements in the process of plant domestication. Among all the various human efforts to reduce risk by manipulating resources, the planting of stored seed stock would have yielded very rapid and dramatic benefits, and the results would have encouraged further experimentation. It is likely that human societies also began to deliberately select plants for other

characteristics soon after they first undertook intentional planting, adding to the list of morphological markers of domestication.

What attributes in a wild plant would have made it a likely candidate for deliberate planting? Obviously a wild plant that hunter-gatherer societies already relied on as an important food source would have been a prime candidate for experimentation. In general, one could expect successful domesticates to have those attributes that would make them able to thrive in the environment that humans had created and now controlled. "Generalist" plants that could do as well in disturbed soil as in the wild would be better able to make the transition to the human environment than plants with more stringent habitat requirements. Species adapted to growing in dense stands would be better candidates for domestication than those that grew in more dispersed patterns. Similarly, species able to tolerate the moisture, temperature, and other conditions of storage would be good candidates for domestication, as would those whose rates of mutation and genetic variation enabled them to adapt rapidly to the new selective pressures.

The Domestication of Animals

Just as some wild plant species are more predisposed than others to respond rapidly and successfully to human planting, so too are some species of wild animals clearly preadapted to domestication. As early as 1865 Francis Galton proposed that almost all animal species had at one time or another been "auditioned" by human societies for possible domestication. While many may have been called, few species of animals have in fact been chosen to fill the new role of domesticate. Galton suggested that the reason was that the role was difficult to fill. To negotiate the transition from the wild to a domesticated life, he argued, animal species had to meet a particular set of behavioral and physiological requirements:

> 1, They should be hardy; 2, they should have an inborn liking for man; 3, they should be comfort loving; 4, they should be found useful to the savages; 5, they should breed freely; 6, they should be easy to tend.

Many of the inherent aspects of physiology and behavior Galton pointed to are today recognized as important elements of preadaptation to domestication. His criterion that candidates for domestication "should be found useful" reiterates a basic point already made in regard to plants—that wild species that were already important sources of food would be particularly likely candidates for efforts to domesticate them. Galton's other five aspects of preadaptation all have to do with the relative ease with which wild animal species would be able to respond to and survive in the human environment. As in the case of plants, there were two key elements of the initial domestication of animal species: some individuals were separated from populations in the wild, and then humans made a concerted intervention in the life cycles of the now captive populations. Once these individuals were brought under control, human societies assumed responsibility for managing the size and location of the area the animals occupied, their food supply, and their successful reproduction. These three dimensions of human management—space, feeding, and breeding—define in large measure the elements of preadaptation Galton recognized.

Specialized feeding habits, for example, represent a major barrier to domestication. Flexible feeders such as pigs and goats would be far better able to adjust to the feeding opportunities offered under human control. In addition, species better able to adjust to new conditions of disease, temperature, and confinement would be good candidates for domestication ("they should be hardy").

Similarly, animal species vary considerably in the number and narrowness of the behavioral, physiological, and situational cues that are necessary preconditions for successful reproduction. Obviously, those species with the fewest and least constraining sets of cues are good candidates for domestication ("they should breed freely"). The ability to reproduce in crowded conditions, for instance, could be an essential attribute for successful domestication.

Crowding under human management represents a formidable barrier to domesticating species that are largely solitary in the wild. Species vary considerably in the size and composition of the groups they form at different seasons of the year, and in the size of the "home range" that those groups typically occupy. Relatively solitary and strongly territorial species that defend their territories against intruders would be incapable of easy group interaction. Even in the wild species whose females and young live in groups through part or all of the year, the males' territorial behavior and patterns of reproductive competition can make breeding and control in confinement impossible. Species that in the wild form gregarious and highly social groups comprising both sexes, on the other hand, are good targets for domestication. Similar behavioral barriers to domestication exist in species such as antelopes and gazelles, which are adapted to escape from fleet-footed predators. They can run extremely fast and are skittish or high-strung in temperament. Sophisticated fencing is needed to contain them, and they often panic when they are so constrained. As a result, they are difficult to feed and to breed under close control ("they should be easy to tend").

Finally, and perhaps most important, highly social and gregarious animals whose behavioral patterns are based on a dominance hierarchy are strongly preadapted to domestication. Groups that have a dominant leader are predisposed to submit to a human herdsman who steps into the position of the lead male. Thus, to become domesticated, a wild animal species should have a preexisting capacity for submissive behavior. Such a predisposition also dramatically increases the ability of human herders to communicate commands to their captives ("they should have an inborn liking for man").

In sum, the ideal candidate for domestication would be a wild animal that is already an important food source, does not depend on rapid flight to escape predators, is a placid dietary generalist, is highly social and gregarious, has an established pattern of social interaction based on a dominance hierarchy, and tolerates breeding and feeding in close confinement. It is no accident, then, that when we examine the origins of agriculture in the Near East, we find that the goat and sheep, two of the first an-

Kurdish sheep herders drive their flock, in Turkey. Sheep were excellent candidates for human control and domestication because of their social and submissive herd structure.

imal species in the world to be brought under domestication, fit this profile quite closely. Both species are relatively placid and slow-moving foragers. Neither species is territorial, and both sheep and goats form highly social groups having a single dominant leader. In addition, such groups maintain small home ranges, and thus are predisposed to human constraint.

The Transition to Domestication

Given this general profile of preadaptation, what progression of increasing intervention in the life cycles of preadapted wild species leads human societies to the critical point of domesticating them? Scholars have proposed various stages of human manipulation that might develop into full captivity and control, from random hunting through intentional specialized hunting to following herds of animals, enclosing them in pens, and keeping them as pets. As with efforts to "improve" the environment by intervening in the life cycles of selected plant species, some forms of manipulation point to domestication, others don't.

Human beings could try to enhance the habitats of hunted species by eliminating either their predators or their competitors or by burning the landscape or clearing woodlands to encourage the growth of the food plants. Efforts of both kinds could well produce an increase in the animal populations and make for good hunting, but they will not lead to domestication. Similarly, specialized hunting strategies targeted at free-living animal populations would not significantly shift an essentially predator-prey relationship toward domestication. Such efforts do not lead toward the three elements essential to animal domestication: constraint of the movement of target pop-

ulations, regulation of their breeding, and control of their feeding both to ensure and to shape successive generations.

These three elements are the core of the conceptual shift that marks the transition to domestication. Richard Meadow, director of the zooarchaeological laboratory at Harvard University, has insightfully described this conceptual shift as a change in focus from ensuring the deaths of living animals to ensuring their survival—more particularly, to ensuring the creation of progeny. To manage captive populations a society must master an entirely new set of tasks and develop complex new areas of knowledge. No longer do the skills of stalking and killing wild animals determine a dependable meat supply, but rather the knowledge of how to sustain, manage, and regenerate animal populations largely or entirely under human control.

Any efforts to manipulate wild animal populations that would contribute to this newly required body of knowledge could contribute to their initial domestication. For example, the practice of capturing young wild animals and rearing them to adulthood, which is widespread among hunter-gatherer societies today, could certainly have provided auditioning opportunities. During such episodes of captivity, the captors could have assessed the predisposition of species to captivity and learned many aspects of their management, from food requirements to breeding patterns. The rearing of wild youngsters as pets would not easily lead to their successful breeding as adults, but it would still provide considerable insight into the skills necessary to manage captive populations.

Hunter-gatherers might have attempted the partial management of wild animals that were already important food sources and were preadapted to domestication—social herds with a dominance hierarchy and small home ranges. A herd of such

A child and his pet. Hunter-gatherer societies would have consistently brought home young wild animals to raise as pets, becoming familiar with their habits and needs, and learning about their potential for control and domestication.

animals might have been kept in a compact group to be preyed upon whenever meat was required. Humans might have constrained the movement of wild species within a small area with a favorable habitat and a supply of water. The habituation of these animals to human herders/hunters could have been an important early step along the pathway to domestication.

Markers of Animal Domestication

The critical point on the road to the domestication of seed plants is the deliberate planting of seed stock in prepared seedbeds, and the associated separation of these plants from wild populations. The analogous point that marks the transition to the domestication of animals was reached when humans isolated a herd or flock of animals and undertook to control their reproduction. Like seed plants, animals responded to the new set of selective pressures they encountered, to the confinement and crowding of the human environment, and underwent a variety of morphological changes. In many cases, however, these morphological markers of domestication are not so uniformly present in individual organisms as those that appear in plants. As a result, the evidence of early domestication is easier to read in ancient seeds than it is in bone fragments excavated from ancient settlements. Unlike seeds, individual bones only rarely carry clear structural changes indicative of initial captivity and domestication.

For a time in the 1970s it was thought that such a basic structural signature of animal domestication had been found. After analyzing the microstructure of bones from the sites of Suberde and Erbabain in Turkey, Dexter Perkins of Columbia University and Patricia Daly of the University of Pennsylvania believed they had found clear and consistent differences between the bones of wild and domesticated sheep and goats. Bone consists of crystals of calcium phosphate (hydroxyapatite) deposited along long fibers of the protein collagen. According to Perkins and Daly, hydroxyapatite crystals were oriented perpendicularly to the long axis of collagen fibers in the wild animals, whereas they were more randomly oriented in the bones of animals thought to be domesticated. If Perkins and Daly were correct, a simple microscopic examination of a thin section of bone could establish whether an animal was wild or domesticated.

To test the validity of the proposed marker of animal domestication, Melinda Zeder of the National Museum of Natural History, Smithsonian Institution (then an undergraduate at the University of Michigan), looked for differences in the bone structure of modern wild and domesticated sheep from the Near East. Four wild sheep killed in the Tarus Mountains near the Caspian Sea were found to have the expected perpendicular orientation of crystals. A dozen domesticated sheep acquired from traditional pastoral societies in remote rural areas of Iran, however, also had hydroxyapatite crystals oriented perpendicular to the long axis of collagen fibers, contrary to what Perkins and Daly predicted. It was later found that the random orientation of crystals Perkins and Daly observed in some archaeological bone samples had been caused not by domestication but rather by chemical processes that took place long after the bones had become buried in the ground. Since Zeder showed the crystalline

structure marker to be invalid, no other clear micromorphological marker of domestication in animals has been proposed.

This is not to say, however, that no morphological changes associated with domestication can be observed in animal bones recovered from archaeological sites. On the contrary, a variety of changes in skeletal elements have been employed to distinguish domesticated animals from wild individuals of the same species. Such morphological markers provide a valuable way of recognizing the presence

Melinda A. Zeder, Smithsonian Institution archaeologist, excavating a small domesticated donkey at the site of Tel Halif in the southern Levant.

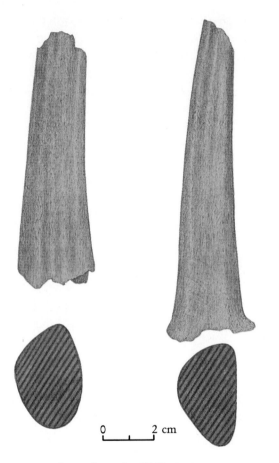

0   2 cm

These two specimens from the Ali Kosh site in Iran illustrate how the horns of wild goats differ in cross section from those of domesticated animals, providing a morphological marker of domestication for this species. The wild goat horn (left) has a more four-sided cross section, with a peak facing toward the front (top), while the horn of the domesticated goat (right) is more triangular in cross section, flat along the medial side with a peak facing backward (bottom).

of domesticated animals in archaeological bone assemblages. A very distinctive change in the cross sections of the horns of domesticated goats and sheep, for example, distinguishes them from wild individuals. Similarly, a distinctive size reduction in

the teeth of pigs has been used to identify the initial domestication of this Old World species. Whether they result from relaxation of selective pressures in the wild or from deliberate human selection over generations, however, such morphological markers of domestication may not appear for some time after the animals have been domesticated. As a result, zooarchaeologists today build their arguments not simply on the presence or absence of a limited number of isolated morphological markers, but on the patterns of change that can be seen only by examining larger assemblages of bones that represent whole herds or flocks.

In the ideal situation for this kind of "whole herd" analysis, one would begin with a deep archaeological site that revealed a vertical sequence of deposits that spanned the full transition from hunting and gathering to agriculture. If each layer in the sequence of deposits yielded large and well-preserved assemblages of animal bones, zooarchaeologists could then start with all the bones of a particular animal species found in the lowest, earliest layer. Let's locate this long-occupied settlement in the Near East, and let's say the bones belonged to goats. By carefully identifying, measuring, and analyzing all of the goat bones found in the lowest layer of the site, zooarchaeologists could determine the group profile of the wild goats hunted by the earliest human inhabitants of the settlement. Various bones could be measured to establish the range in size of the animals culled from the wild herd by human hunters. Their range in age could be determined by analyzing tooth eruption and wear patterns, annual growth rings in the teeth, and whether or not bones had finished growing. By measuring skulls, horns, pelvises, and other distinctive bones, zooarchaeologists could establish how many animals were female and how many were male. They could document the growth patterns and pathology of bones to show the general health of the animals. Tooth eruption patterns, seasonal growth rings in teeth, and the presence of very young animals could indicate the seasons of the year in which the animals were killed. By comparing the numbers of these animals with the representation of other animal species found at the settlement, researchers could determine how important they were as a source of food.

Moving up through time through the layers of the site, the investigators could similarly scrutinize each succeeding deposit of goat bones and produce a profile of each goat herd. Once all the layers of the site had been analyzed in this way, the search would begin for any patterns of change in the herd profiles that might mark increasing human control. A change in one aspect of the herd profile that could be linked to captivity and reproductive control, such as age composition or male-female ratio, would certainly provide some evidence that domestication had begun. A much stronger and more convincing case could be made should related changes be observed in several characteristics of the goat herd, all of which could be linked to captivity and human control of breeding.

To extend this ideal situation to a more regional scale, let's suppose that a good number of such deep-layered settlements scattered across the Near East were all carefully excavated and their goat herd profiles tracked through time. If a characteristic set of changes in goat herd profiles linked to captivity and human control were documented at all of the excavated settlements, then an even stronger case could be made that the observed changes constitute good evidence of the initial appearance of domesticated goat herds at particular times in particular places.

Unfortunately, such an ideal research situation does not exist today. Few settlements have been excavated that provide opportunities to track changes in the profiles of any species through the full transition from wild to domesticated. Lacking a comprehensive set of sites to work with, zooarchaeologists working in different regions of the world have to settle for an incomplete, fragmented mosaic of evidence. Excavated settlements were often occupied for only short spans of time, so each settlement provides information about only one part of the transition. While some sites produce large, well-preserved assemblages of bones, others yield less useful collections. Perhaps the excavation is smaller and less effort is made to recover bones, or perhaps the bones are not as well preserved in the ground. Given the scattered and partial evidence, the small fragments of the domestication puzzle that must be drawn together from many settlements of different times, what are the various changes in herd profiles that zooarchaeologists look for as possible indications that the animals were living in captivity, their reproduction controlled by human herders?

When animals are held in captivity and their movements are constrained, the impact on the captive herd could in some respects be almost immediate. For example, bone pathologies might be brought on by the physical trauma, poor diet, and higher stress and infection rates of confinement. At the agricultural village of Tepe Sarab in western Iran, numerous cases of chronic arthritis and evidence of gum disease in goats have been cited as early evidence of confinement and domestication. A high frequency of bone pathology in goats from a farming settlement at the 'Ain Ghazal site in Jordan has also been proposed as marking the early domestication of this species.

Halfway around the world, on the high puna grasslands of Peru, the Telarmachay rock shelter has yielded another possible indicator of animal domestication. Here, in deposits dating to about 5500 to 5000 years ago, a large number of bones of fetal and newborn llamas have been recovered, perhaps evidence of the earliest corralling of this species by human herders. Jane Wheeler argues that newborn mortality rates, which are low among wild llamas (guanacos) today, are as high as 50 percent in domestic herds that are corralled at night. In present-day domesticated herds, high newborn mortality is the result of infections caused by two *Clostridium* bacteria that thrive in dirty, muddy corrals but are not known to infect wild populations of guanacos.

Another potential early indication of captivity, one that can appear as early as the first or second generation, is a decrease in the size of animals. The cause, it has been proposed, is a marked reduction in the nutritional status of pregnant females. Malnutrition, higher levels of disease and parasites, and in some species the drawing of milk for human consumption could all reduce fetal growth and result in smaller infants that grow up to be small adults.

Toe bones are smaller in domesticated cattle, reflecting an overall reduction in the size of these animals. The 7000-year-old first phalanx of an aurochs (right) is from the site of Umm Qseir in northeastern Syria. The much smaller 7000-to-6000-year-old toe bone of a domesticated animal (left) is from the site of Mashnaqa, also in northeastern Syria.

Earlier weaning and the leaner diets would also result in smaller animals. Individuals with less bulk to sustain would be more likely to survive to adulthood and reproduce successfully. Smaller body size, then, can also be considered one aspect of the adaptive syndrome of domestication in animal species subjected to confinement and crowding.

It is also possible, of course, that human herders could have deliberately selected for smaller, more docile animals, which would then be more likely to survive to reproductive age. Such direct efforts to diminish the size of captive animals would fall into a second general category of changes brought on by initial animal domestication—those resulting from humans managing the reproduction of captive herds.

When herds are kept in isolation from wild populations and cared for by human herders, they are relieved of the selective pressures that shape wild populations. By imposing their own selection of animals for breeding, herders would be free to modify the size and appearance of the animals, the size of the herd, the relative balance of males and females, and the age profile of the herd in any manner that worked to improve the dependability of the herd as a food source, or walking larder. Managers could, for example, decide to remove large and aggressive males in order to reduce disruption in the herd while facilitating their own control of the important lead male position. But because by doing so they would be clearing the way for the reproductive success of the wimps in the group, they would in the process be reducing the size of the animals in the herd.

In a similar fashion, herders could easily produce and maintain the basic structure of a managed population of domesticated animals through selective harvesting. A breeding herd consisting of numerous females of reproductive age would need only

A present-day herder and his assistant in the Alps. Pastoral economies have evolved in many parts of Europe over a period of more than 7000 years.

a few males to impregnate them. The vast majority of the young born every year would be slated for slaughter, to be harvested as the need arose, once they approached adult size. Young animals that exhibited desirable traits could be spared for breeding to fill vacancies resulting from old age or death. Just as the seed stock of a domesticated plant is set aside each year to ensure next year's crop while the rest of the harvest is available for consumption, so the breeding herd is the seed stock of the next generation, and the food-stock animals are stored standing up and ready for slaughter. The restructuring of captive herds can take a variety of forms, depending on the species' primary uses (as sources of meat, milk, or skins, or as pack or draft animals).

All of the herd profiles that human societies in different regions of the world could create, manipulating different captive species for different ends, would be similar in one important respect: they would all leave archaeological bone assemblages that were different from those left by the hunting of wild populations. In sum, it would seem a rather straightforward task to identify in the archaeological record when animal domestication began, and in general it is. The decrease in the size of captive animals provides the best morphological marker of domestication now available. Other clues, such as indications of poor nutrition, disease, and parasites, are also occasionally observed. In addition, herd profiles depart from those of wild populations in age and sex composition. Together, these changes in the individual animals, and the composition of the herd itself, provide a good set of interrelated markers of initial domestication that can be recognized in archaeological bone assemblages. As we shall see, however, recent innovations have enabled researchers to take into consideration a much wider variety of information in their efforts to identify the initial domestication of plants and animals.

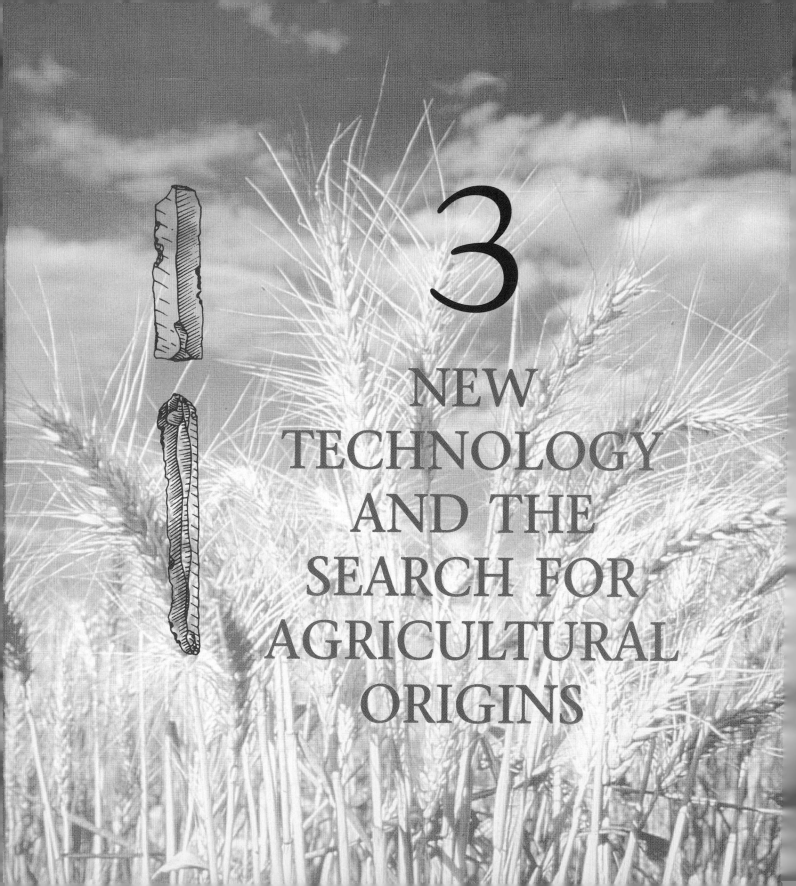

3

NEW TECHNOLOGY AND THE SEARCH FOR AGRICULTURAL ORIGINS

In search of the past. Workers using hand picks, trowels, and brooms excavate the early farming settlement of Gritille in southeast Turkey. In spite of the many sophisticated technologies now used by archaeologists, excavation to recover artifacts such as the sickle blades on the facing page, as well as plant and animal remains, is still hard and demanding work.

Biological and archaeological research on the origins of agriculture has expanded and intensified considerably since the pioneering efforts of Vavilov and Braidwood. Scientific technology in the last quarter of the twentieth century has given us a much more sophisticated understanding of the evidence to be found in the archaeological record. New methods and machines have improved the recovery of small fragments of bones, seeds, and other organic materials scattered through archaeological sites; a new dating method allows us to determine the age of these small seeds and bone fragments with precision; and scanning electron microscopy reveals micromorphological indicators of domestication that early investigators couldn't see. At the same time, biological research on present-day plant and animal species has also made advances: Scientists are able to chart the geographical distribution of domesticates and their potential wild progenitors in more detail, and they can now perform extremely fine-grain molecular analysis of the genetic pathways of evolution.

The Recovery Revolution

As interdisciplinary approaches to the past developed after World War II, archaeologists came to recognize the need for better ways to recover plant and animal remains during their excavations. The often small, fragile, and fragmented animal bones, seeds, and other plant parts scattered through archaeological sites could provide essential information about ancient diets and agricultural origins. The soil removed from ancient settlements was sometimes passed through screens in order to recover objects that were too small to be spotted during excavation, but screening of soil was far from universal in the

1950s, and very small and fragile objects, like seeds, were passing right through the screens. A more fine-grain method was needed, and if it were to become widely adopted, it would have to be relatively simple and inexpensive.

A simple and easy method to recover small seeds and other organic materials had actually been worked out and successfully used by an Austrian botanist, H. Unger, as early as 1860. Unger was interested in studying cereal grains and seeds embedded in ancient Egyptian mud bricks. Recognizing the differences in density of the organic material and

Volney Jones of the University of Michigan, shown here at Awatovi Pueblo in the 1930s, was a pioneer in the analysis of plant remains from archaeological sites.

the clay matrix, he separated the two by simply placing the brick fragments in water and then skimming off the seeds and cereals as they floated to the surface. Volney Jones, who was director of the Ethnobotanical Laboratory at the University of Michigan and one of the founding fathers of archaeobotany in North America, used a similar "flotation" method in the 1930s to recover ancient plant remains from the adobe bricks of the Awatovi pueblo in Arizona.

This simple principle of pouring archaeological soil into water so that organic materials would float out was also applied on a small scale in European laboratories in the first half of this century, but it was not until the late 1960s that flotation recovery was transferred from the laboratory to excavation sites and its scale of application dramatically expanded. In the early 1950s the botanist Hugh Cutler had employed flotation recovery at excavations in the Southwest, and he introduced the idea to the archaeologist Stuart Struever in the early 1960s. Struever in turn tried out the "new" recovery method in eastern North America and urged its wide-scale application. Hans Helbeck, a German archaeobotanist, similarly reported on his successful use of flotation at several sites of the Deh Luran plain in southwest Iran.

From these various beginnings in both the Old and New Worlds, the use of flotation techniques rapidly expanded during the 1970s, producing a revolution in the recovery of information relevant to ancient agricultural origins. A wide variety of water-separation devices were soon perfected and put into service at excavations on both sides of the Atlantic. As a result of this explosion in the deployment of flotation procedures, along with the development of other recovery methods and the deliberate targeting of sites that promised good preservation of organic materials, seeds and other plant parts be-

Flotation recovery of seeds and other plant remains at the Gritille site in southeast Turkey. Water sluicing out of the top of a flotation device carries buoyant carbonized seeds, charcoal, and other small plant parts, to be caught in a cloth filter.

gan to be routinely recovered in far greater abundance from archaeological deposits.

Direct Dating

Flotation devices provided an excellent low-technology method to separate small organic remains from their soil matrix. A high-technology solution was also developed in the 1970s for an equally difficult problem that had long plagued research on agricultural origins—establishing an accurate age for these small bits of evidence. Conventional radiocarbon dating, developed in the late 1940s and early 1950s, is a reliable means of establishing the age of sizable organic materials recovered from archaeological sites, and it has produced more than 100,000 such dates. The limitations of this method, however, have restricted its usefulness to researchers seeking to establish the beginnings of plant and animal domestication.

The most serious limitation has been the amount of material needed to determine age. To appreciate this problem, it is necessary first to understand how conventional radiocarbon dating works. All living organisms contain carbon. The radioactive isotope carbon-14 (^{14}C) constitutes a tiny proportion of this carbon. In fact, there are a million million (10^{12}) carbon-12 atoms for each ^{14}C atom in a modern sample. After an organism dies, this ratio becomes even more lopsided with time, as ^{14}C atoms are lost to radioactive decay. The decay proceeds at a known rate: after an organism has been dead for 5730 years, the number of remaining ^{14}C atoms in relation to ^{12}C atoms will have been reduced by half (hence the "half-life" of ^{14}C is 5730 years). In principle, then, it is possible to establish how long ago an organism lived by measuring the ratio of ^{14}C to ^{12}C in its remains.

Scientists using conventional radiocarbon dating establish this ^{14}C/^{12}C ratio by detecting and counting individual ^{14}C decay events, which are signaled by emitted beta particles. Over a period of several hours or more, the rate of radioactive breakdown indicated by the emission of beta particles in turn allows them to estimate the number of ^{14}C atoms remaining in their sample, and hence its age. Since only a small proportion of the ^{14}C atoms break down in the measuring period, however, the sample must be large enough to provide an adequate number of decay events to be counted. Samples containing 1 to 5 grams of carbon, and often more, are usually required.

The need for such a large sample presents particular problems when the materials to be dated are as small as seeds or have such a low carbon content as bone, particularly when they are poorly preserved. Often the amount of carbon available is far less than the minimum required, or if a specimen does contain enough carbon, it would have to be completely destroyed in the dating process.

Until the early 1980s, this sample-size barrier meant that scientists could establish the age of these small materials only indirectly, by dating larger samples of organic material, usually charcoal, thought to be contemporary with the smaller samples. Such charcoal samples certainly yield reliable age determinations through conventional radiocarbon dating, but how confident can we be that the charcoal sample is the same age as the small seeds or animal bones found in "association" with it? Seeds and other small objects are particularly difficult to date reliably in this way because they may have been displaced up or downward by a variety of agents known to operate in archaeological sediments, including burrowing organisms of various kinds. J. A. J. Gowlett of the Oxford Radiocarbon Laboratory has estimated, for example, that one of every five small pieces of organic material considered for dating has moved upward or downward in its ar-

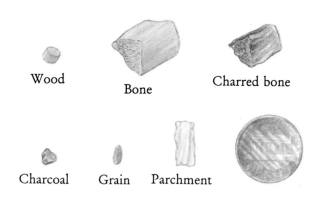

The average amount of material of various kinds needed for AMS dating, compared in size to a U.S. penny.

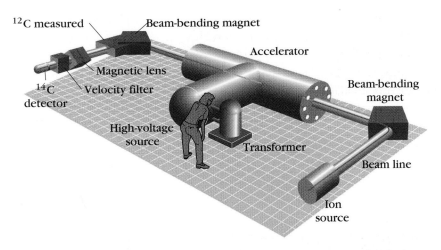

^{12}C measured

Beam-bending magnet

Accelerator

Magnetic lens

^{14}C detector

Velocity filter

Beam-bending magnet

High-voltage source

Transformer

Beam line

Ion source

The accelerator mass spectrometer can determine the age of a sample material by counting the number of ^{14}C atoms present. Starting from the ion source, ionized carbon atoms from the sample are first pulled as a beam toward the accelerator. As the beam passes through the first beam-bending magnet, lighter atoms turn more sharply than heavier ones, and move to the inside of the diverging beam, where a filter blocks the further progress of all charged particles except those of atomic mass 14. When the beam enters the accelerator, it is stripped of the many molecules of mass 14 that might be indistinguishable from single ^{14}C atoms. The accelerator then pushes the remaining ions through a second beam-bending magnet, filtering out more non-^{14}C particles. The beam is focused before arriving at an extremely sensitive detector that counts the number of ions left.

chaeological deposit, into a layer that is either younger or older than it is.

Fortunately, following closely on the recovery revolution, the late 1970s and early 1980s witnessed the development of a radiocarbon dating method for small samples. This accelerator mass spectrometry (AMS) technique was first tested in principle in 1977 and first tried on archaeological samples in 1983. It has gained acceptance rapidly, so that more than 2000 samples a year are now being dated by the AMS technique. The technique differs from the conventional method in the way it assesses the amount of ^{14}C remaining in a sample. Rather than counting decay events (beta counts), investigators estimate the remaining ^{14}C by directly counting ^{14}C atoms. The technique thus enables them to determine the ages of samples up to 1000 times smaller than those required by the conventional method.

Mass spectrometers have been used for a number of years to measure the relative abundance of various isotopes in samples on the basis of the differences in their masses. Conventional mass spectrometers could not accurately measure the amount of ^{14}C in a sample, however, both because the ^{14}C was present in such small amounts and because the overwhelming quantity of ions or molecules of similar mass (^{14}N, ^{13}CH, and so forth) would mask its presence. The development of small accelerators as high-energy mass spectrometers solved the problem of background noise. These instruments filter out mass-14 competitors of ^{14}C at various points, as a portion of a sample's constituent atoms are propelled through an accelerator system toward a detector.

With the development of this new instrument, small seeds or portions of bone exhibiting morphology indicative of early domestication can now be dated fairly routinely. In 1987, for example, Wesley Cowan of the Cincinnati Museum of Natural History and I extracted small seeds of the plant *Chenopodium berlandieri* from human paleofecal samples that had been recovered from the Newt Kash and Cloudsplitter shelters in eastern Kentucky. When we examined the seeds under an ordinary light microscope, we saw the distinctive thin seed coats that indicate low germination dormancy, so we knew the seeds came from domesticated plants. We submitted two seeds, each weighing less than 0.03 gram, for AMS age determination, and the resultant 3500 B.P. dates provide the earliest evidence currently available for the domestication of this eastern North American plant species.

Our work on *Chenopodium* is also an example of the importance of microscopes in research on agricultural origins. Like other researchers, for closer views we turned from light microscopes to scanning electron microscopy (SEM).

Scanning Electron Microscopy

Like other scanning electron microscopy facilities around the world, the SEM laboratory of the National Museum of Natural History (NMNH), Smithsonian Institution, in Washington, D.C., allows scientists from a variety of disciplines to study the micromorphology of both present-day and fossil organisms. NMNH researchers seek out Walter Brown, director of the museum's SEM laboratory, for the same basic reason I did in 1982—they need to analyze something too small to be seen clearly with standard optical microscopes that employ lenses and light.

I wanted to measure precisely the thickness of the outer wall or testa of some 2000-year-old seeds of *Chenopodium berlandieri* that had been excavated in the 1950s from a grass-lined storage pit in Russell Cave, Alabama. When I viewed them under a light microscope, they seemed to have much thinner seed coats than the seeds of modern wild *Chenopodium berlandieri* plants, and thus held the promise of providing the first good evidence that this plant was domesticated long ago in eastern North America. But I needed more accurate measurements of these seed coats.

SEM technology gave me the closer look I required. I glued cross-sectioned chenopod seeds from Russell cave, along with comparable seed specimens from present-day wild and domesticated plants, onto small mounts, and then took them to the SEM lab. There they were given a very thin coating of palladium, and were ready to be viewed in the SEM. Once I placed them in the vacuum chamber of the microscope, the seeds were scanned by an electron beam. When that beam is deflected to a detector, it is then transformed into an image on a viewing screen. By rotating a few dials I could observe selected portions of the seeds at progressively higher magnifications, and the SEM's built-in measurement capabilities enabled me to determine the precise thickness of the seed coats.

With this improved technology, establishing that the *Chenopodium berlandieri* seeds from Russell Cave (and other prehistoric sites in the eastern United States) represented a domesticated crop was

A view looking outward from Russell Cave National Monument in northeast Alabama.
Like other dry caves and rock shelters throughout the Americas, Russell Cave has
yielded remarkably preserved plant remains suitable for SEM analysis in search of
micromorphological markers of domestication.

a relatively straightforward proposition. Not only were their seed coats comparable in thickness to those of modern domesticated chenopod varieties and far thinner than those of modern wild populations, but when I viewed them under the SEM, I could also see other distinctive micromorphological characteristics that distinguished them as domesticated. More recently, Carol Nordstrom and Christine Hastorf, of the University of Minnesota and University of California, Berkeley, have extended SEM analysis of seed-coat thickness to document the

domestication of another chenopod species, *C. quinoa,* in the Peruvian Andes by 5000 to 4000 years ago. Donald Ungent of Southern Illinois University at Carbondale also employed a scanning electron microscope in the early 1980s to examine the micromorphology of early domesticated potatoes from the desert coast of Peru.

In Great Britain and in Europe too, scanning electron microscopy has been increasingly employed since the 1980s in the analysis of prehistoric plant remains, with interesting results. In Germany, for

An SEM photomicrograph of a 3500-year-old *Chenopodium berlandieri* seed from Newt Kash rock shelter in eastern Kentucky. With a seed coat only 15 microns (millionths of a meter) thick, this remarkably preserved seed provides the earliest evidence for the domestication of this species in eastern North America.

Pollen Sequences

As anyone with pollen allergies knows only too well, a rich variety of flowering plants produce pollen each growing season. Pollen is formed in the male portion of a flower and released for transfer to the female portion of another flower. Some flowering plants rely on insects, birds, animals, or water to carry their pollen. Many species of plants rely on the wind to disperse their pollen, and it is these wind-transported pollen grains that fill the air and torment allergy sufferers. A single flower of a wind-pollinated plant generally produces from 10,000 to 70,000 pollen grains. Wind-dispersed pollen grains have aerodynamic designs, and are sometimes transported over considerable distances by air current before they are deposited over the land surface as "pollen rain."

Some, but not many, of the millions of grains in each year's pollen rain actually fulfill their mission by landing on flowers. Some pollen grains that miss their targets come to rest on the calm surface of a small lake or pond. They soon sink to the bottom, and there become incorporated in the annual sediment layer being formed that year. Decay processes are often inhibited in the sediments that slowly build up over the centuries on the bottoms of such bodies of water, allowing each year's pollen rain to be preserved. Throughout their span of existence, small lakes and ponds (5000 square meters is about the optimal size) thus serve as excellent collection and storage devices. Because the often distinct shapes of the pollen grains indicate their parent species, the pollen sequences preserved in lakes and ponds record the history of vegetational development and change in the surrounding area.

The scientists who study pollen, called palynologists, gain access to these sequences by sending long tubelike devices called corers down through

example, SEM has enabled Udelgard Korber-Grohne of the University of Hohenheim to distinguish between different species of cereals grown in the ancient Near East on the basis of microstructural surface patterns of grains recovered from archaeological sites. In Israel, investigators have employed SEM to identify micromorphological changes in barley associated with its initial domestication in the Jordan Valley 10,000 years ago.

Although scanning electron microscopy has now become a fairly standard tool in the analysis of archaeobotanical specimens, its application to questions of early plant domestication is just beginning. The opening of new microscale research frontiers in the study of agricultural origins has not, however, been limited to the development of such technology as AMS and SEM. Reasearchers using standard light microscopes are finding important evidence in grains of pollen of climatic change, land clearing, and cultivation.

these sediments and extracting the cylinders, or "cores," of sediment retrieved in the tubes. By analyzing the assemblages of pollen grains in different layers, palynologists can reconstruct the composition of past forests and patterns in their change over time. Using pollen sequence information recovered from hundreds of pond bottoms across eastern North America, Hazel and Paul Delcourt of the University of Tennessee have reconstructed the broad and complex patterns in how the region's vegetation has changed over the past 18,000 years. The Delcourts have also used these pollen cores to study quite small changes brought about by Native Americans' land-clearance practices and farming economies before the arrival of Europeans.

The pollen profiles of two ponds located close to the Little Tennessee River in eastern Tennessee provided the Delcourts with evidence that over more than a thousand years Native American societies steadily increased their clearing of forests along the bottomland and terraces of the valley. Tuskegee Pond, on an intermediate-level terrace of the Little Tennessee Valley, contained 6 feet of bottom sediments that had accumulated from about A.D. 400 up to the present day. Working from a small raft, the Delcourts thrust a 2-inch-diameter stainless steel corer down through the bottom sediments. From its earliest strata right up to the twentieth century, the Tuskegee Pond pollen core contained maize pollen in small but consistent percentages.

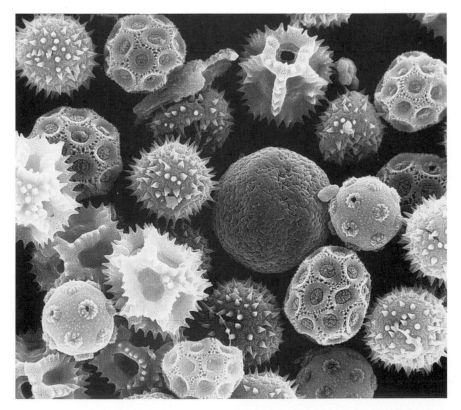

This scanning electron micrograph shows pollen grains from five different species. Because pollen grains have such distinctive shapes, the plant species that produced them can often be identified.

Since maize pollen is heavy compared to other wind-borne pollens, and on the average travels only about 60 meters, its continual presence along with that of such crops as *Chenopodium* and marsh elder showed the lake to have been adjacent to permanent Indian fields from A.D. 400 onward. While maize and other crops were small but steady contributors to the Tuskegee Pond pollen rain, ragweed, a key indicator of land clearance, accounted for anywhere from 30 to 50 percent of the earliest strata of the pond's pollen record. Reflecting considerable deforestation, this remarkably high ragweed pollen count shows that Native American agricultural activities had substantially modified the landscape of the Little Tennessee Valley by A.D. 400.

Judging from plant remains recovered from earlier archaeological sites in the valley, humans had begun to clear the forest and cultivate the land long before the earliest sediments were deposited at the bottom of Tuskegee Pond. Crop species such as squash, sunflower, marsh elder, and chenopod, along with pine, cane, and other wild species that invade disturbed ground, first appear in the archaeobotanical record about 3500 B.P., marking the first and quite limited farming efforts, which were confined to the bottomlands and lowest terraces.

From this modest beginning the amount of land cleared and planted expanded over the centuries across much of the bottomland and up onto the lower and intermediate terraces. By A.D. 400, when the Tuskegee Pond pollen record picks up the story, large portions of the first, second, and third terraces of the Little Tennessee Valley had been cleared for farming.

The pollen core the Delcourts extracted from Black Pond, in the uplands 4 kilometers to the north of the Little Tennessee River, suggests that the expansion of the agricultural landscape at the expense of valley forest then slowed and stabilized until the Europeans arrived. Extending back over 3000 years, the Black Pond pollen record showed a stable upland forest of pines and deciduous trees until about 400 years ago, when an increase in ragweed pollen signals the arrival of European settlements and the use of metal tools to clear higher terraces and upland forests growing over bedrock.

The Delcourts' analysis of the pollen cores from Tuskegee and Black ponds, in concert with the analysis of plant remains from archaeological sites, thus offers a detailed view of a long process of expanding human impact on the landscape of the Little Tennessee Valley. The insights gained through pollen analyses of the kind carried out by Hazel and Paul Delcourt are based on individually identifying thousands upon thousands of individual pollen grains extracted from layers of sediment. It is from this painstaking process that general patterns of change in the pollen rain and evidence of early agriculture emerge.

Searching for Wild Ancestors at the Molecular Level

Investigators have been intensifing their efforts to identify the wild ancestors of present-day domesticates since the 1970s, when new biochemical methods were developed for working out the taxonomic and evolutionary relationships between domesticates and their potential wild progenitors. The success of John Doebley, a biologist at the University of Minnesota, in identifying the wild ancestor of maize provides a good case study of this new molecular research. The origin and evolution of maize has been a topic of great interest among botanists since the mid-nineteenth century, and opinion has long been divided on the identity of its wild ancestor. Teosinte is the common name given to a diverse and widely distributed group of wild grasses long suspected to include the wild ancestor of maize. Interest has focused on teosinte since the turn of the century, when it was discovered that maize and some forms of teosinte formed fully fertile hybrids, and enough information had accumulated by the late 1930s for George Beadle to present a strong argument that teosinte was the direct ancestor of maize. Not everyone agreed. Some researchers, principally Paul Mangelsdorf of Harvard University, were convinced that maize was derived not from teosinte but from a hypothetical "wild maize." Both the teosinte and the hypothetical-wild-maize theories have had

their supporters over the years, and it is only recently that molecular evidence has convincingly resolved the debate.

John Doebley's landmark molecular work began with wide-ranging field research on teosinte. Throughout this century botanists have been seeking out new populations of teosinte across rural and often remote areas of Mexico and Central America. By 1980 three perennial and three annual teosintes had been identified and their geographical distribution had been plotted. Two of the annuals (*Zea mays mexicana* and *Zea mays parviglumis*) were found to be most similar to maize, and became the focus of Doebley's research. The *mexicana* subspecies grows today at altitudes of 1800 to 2500 meters on the

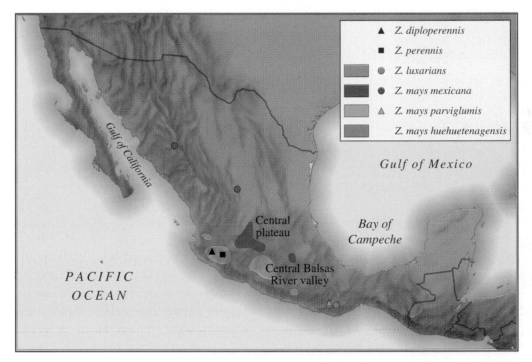

The modern geographical distribution of different teosintes in Mexico and Central America.

A seed spike of the wild grass teosinte (left), consisting of a single row of kernels, with each kernel enclosed in a hard shell-like case. On ripening, the spike shatters, scattering the seeds. When teosinte was domesticated, human selection transformed this seed spike into the much larger maize ear (right), which has many more rows of kernels that are not protected by fruit cases and that adhere to the cob rather than dispersing when ripened.

plains and valleys of central and northern Mexico. Adapted to wetter, warmer zones, the subspecies *parviglumis* is found at altitudes of about 400 to 1700 meters on the upper slopes of the river valleys of more southern and western Mexico. Each of the two subspecies has each been further broken down into three subdivisions found naturally at distinct latitudes.

Doebley included samples from all six of these natural geographic divisions of subspecies *mexicana* and *parviglumis* in his genetic research, along with samples from the other annual and perennial teosintes, representing the entire geographic range of the wild taxa of the genus *Zea*. Once Doebley had assembled all the known forms of teosinte, he was ready to examine their genetic profiles and to compare them, each in turn, with domestic maize. If teosinte is the ancestor of maize, then the particular type of teosinte ancestral to maize should be very similar to maize in its molecular features, while other types of teosinte should show varying degrees of dissimilarity. In comparing specific proteins in the various wild teosintes with those in maize, Doebley found that the proteins of maize and the teosinte subspecies *parviglumis* could not be distinguished, and that *parviglumis* is much more similar to maize than to any of the other teosintes.

Once *parviglumis* was identified as the ancestral source of maize, Doebley looked more closely at its three geographical subdivisions, and found the populations of *parviglumis* growing in the central portion of the Balsas River drainage to be biochemically most similar to maize. Through molecular

research he was thus able to resolve a long debate by convincingly demonstrating that it was teosinte and not an elusive "wild maize" that gave rise to the maize we know today. Even more remarkably, Doebley further proposed that the source of maize could be narrowed to a particular set of teosinte populations in the Balsas River valley, southwest of Mexico City.

Over the past quarter century scientists have employed all of the scientific advances briefly discussed above, and a variety of others, in their efforts to obtain a better understanding of the origins of agriculture. Now let us see how these new approaches and technologies have illuminated this landmark transition in the area where human societies first developed agriculture, the Fertile Crescent of the Near East.

4

THE FERTILE
CRESCENT

 A Babylonian bull. By the time this enameled tile and ceramic brick bull had been placed on the Ishtar Gate of the city of Babylon, Mesopotamia, around 600 B.C., domesticated cattle had been an important draft animal and source of meat in the Near East for more than 5000 years.

At the eastern end of the Mediterranean, across a broad arching zone of grasslands and open oak-pistachio woodlands called the Fertile Crescent, the world's first agricultural economies emerged between 10,000 and 8000 years ago. Bounded on the north and east by higher-elevation forests and rugged landscapes, on the west by the Mediterranean, and on the south by arid deserts and dry grasslands, the Fertile Crescent curves some 2000 kilometers from the Mediterranean coast and the Negev Desert in the west to the Zagros Mountains in the east.

With the end of the Pleistocene ice age and the onset of warmer, wetter weather about 13,000 years B.P., growing conditions improved for the wild grasses, including wild barley and wild emmer and einkorn wheat, whose seeds were important food sources for the people who lived in the Fertile Crescent. Open forests and grasslands expanded in area, and this expansion encouraged increases in the

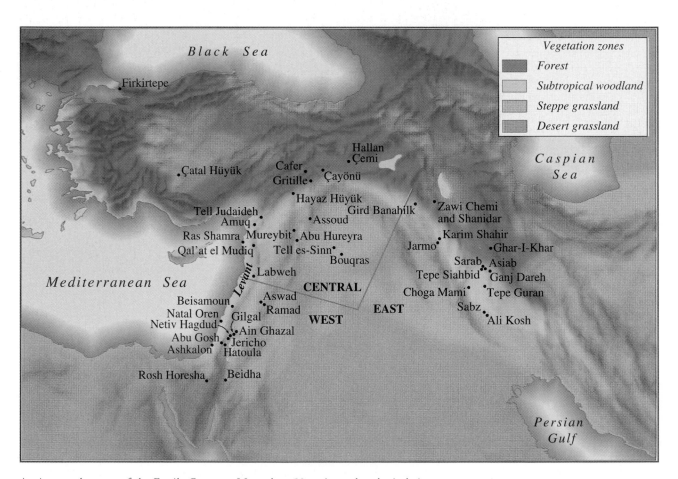

Ancient settlements of the Fertile Crescent. More than 50 major archaeological sites have provided evidence of the emergence of agriculture in the Fertile Crescent between 10,000 and 8000 years ago.

populations of the most important animal species these people hunted—primarily grazers such as sheep, two species of gazelles, onagers (wild asses and half-asses), wild goats, and aurochs (wild cattle). Wild pigs foraged in the stream valleys that cut through the grasslands and woodlands. Browsing animals—red, roe, and fallow deer, along with wide-ranging wild goats—frequented the habitats at the edges of open woodlands.

By 10,000 years ago, at the beginning of the two-millenia-long period that would witness the development of agriculture, human societies had taken advantage of this post-Pleistocene proliferation of plant and animal resources, and the Fertile Crescent was inhabited by a diverse array of hunter-gatherer societies. All of these small hunter-gatherer groups relied for food on some combination of the wild plants and animals that thrived in the Fertile Crescent, but the species that were most important in their diets varied considerably from place to place. Each group developed its own strategy for survival. They structured their way of life in accordance with the surrounding landscape and relied on food sources that were available locally. In the Levant, for example, which forms the western third of the Fertile Crescent, societies on the verge of the transition to agriculture lived in permanent year-round settlements and relied on more than forty species of wild plants. They hunted and trapped a rich variety of waterfowl, small mammals, and grazing animals, particularly gazelles. In the eastern third of the Fertile Crescent, in contrast, hunter-gatherers at the edge of the Zagros Mountains practiced what is called vertical transhumance: they moved each spring from winter campsites at lower elevations to settlements in the highlands where they could harvest ripening wild grasses. There they hunted the herds of wild goats and sheep that also had moved to higher elevations, following the ripening grasses.

If we jump forward two millennia, to 8000 years ago, leaving behind this mosaic of local hunting-and-gathering strategies, we find that the organization and economic basis of human society have undergone profound changes in many parts of the Fertile Crescent. Permanent agricultural villages now dominate the landscape and sophisticated food-production economies are in place, based on the cultivation of prolific field crops—wheats, barleys, and legumes—and the management of domesticated goats, sheep, pigs, and cattle. What happened in the Fertile Crescent during those 2000 years to transform hunter-gatherers into village-based agricultural farmers? We can best understand the events of this period by first focusing on the developmental history of the individual species of plants and animals that were brought under domestication, and then combining those individual histories into the more complex overall story of the emergence of agriculture in the region. By taking a close look at the evidence, we can appreciate the various approaches that researchers use and the problems they encounter as they attempt to interpret indications of early farming and herding activities.

To trace the individual histories of the seven primary domesticates of the Fertile Crescent (sheep, goats, cattle, pigs, barley, emmer wheat, einkorn wheat), I have divided the region into three sections: an eastern section, which comprises the foothills and margins of the Zagros Mountains; a central section, made up mostly of broad rolling grasslands; and a western section, the Levant, whose central axis is the important Levantine corridor and Jordan Valley. As we follow the individual history of each domesticate up through time from 10,000 to 8000 years ago, we will see that each of the three sections of the Fertile Crescent played different roles at different times in the emergence of farming economies.

The transition to agriculture was not a single

A Kurdish sheep herd in Iraq near the border with Turkey. Herds of domesticated sheep have been an important part of the agricultural landscape in this part of the Fertile Crescent for 8000 years.

event in one specific place. Different parts of the story involving different domesticates and different human societies unfolded in the eastern, central, and western sections at different times. Out of the varied local experiments in manipulating certain plant and animal species came a variety of new solutions to survival. These societies, developing various domesticates in different ways at different times in different areas, eventually combined them into a remarkably powerful and revolutionary new way of life.

None of the individual histories of the seven core domesticates of the Fertile Crescent can yet be written in great detail, and much is still to be learned. As always, what we can say is limited by the archaeological sites that have and have not yet been excavated, by the quality and quantity of plant and animal evidence that has been recovered and analyzed, by the accuracy of the dating of the evidence, and by the various analytical approaches that have been taken. Although it is neither the earliest nor the best documented of the domesticates, the sheep (*Ovis aries*) is a good species to start with, because attempts to outline the history of its transition to domesticated status demonstrate the variety of approaches that can be taken and the kinds of difficulties that one often encounters in this kind of research.

Sheep

Nikolai Vavilov and Robert Braidwood both recognized how much it helped to know the extent of the geographical range of the wild progenitor of a domesticated plant or animal, since the distribution of the wild ancestor should define the area where the species was first domesticated. We are assuming, of course, that the range of the wild ancestor is not too large, and that it has not changed that much since the plant or animal in question was domesticated.

Knowing the extent of the geographical range of wild cattle and wild pig, for example, does not help much in determining where these two species were first domesticated, since both were broadly distributed throughout Eurasia and north Africa. The wild ancestors of domesticated goats and sheep, though, had restricted geographical ranges that provide a clear starting point.

Genetic studies identify the Armenian variety of the West Asiatic mouflon, or red sheep (*Ovis orientalis*), as the wild ancestor of the domestic sheep (*Ovis aries*). By identifying the bones of *Ovis orien-*

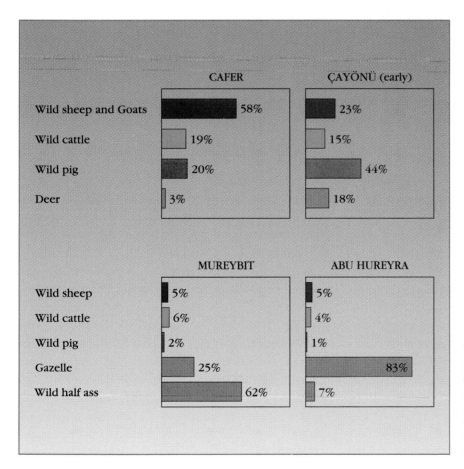

Wild sheep played a consistent supporting role in otherwise very different hunting economies. The bar graphs show the relative importance of sheep compared to other animal species in the diets of four 9000-year-old settlements in the central section of the Fertile Crescent.

talis in archaeological sites on the one hand and mapping its present-day distribution on the other, it is possible to draw a line around the area where it was probably first domesticated. Many of the skeletal elements of a sheep, however, are so similar to the corresponding bones in a goat that the two species are sometimes hard to tell apart, particularly when the bones are fragmentary, as those recovered from archaeological sites often are. As a result, archaeologists have no choice but to lump together many of the sheep and goat bones they recover into a combined sheep/goat or "caprine" category.

Those bones that can be positively identified as wild sheep, however, enable us to establish the relative abundance of this animal in archaeological sites across the Fertile Crescent, and to chart both the distribution of *Ovis orientalis* and its relative popularity as a hunted species before it became domesticated. Interestingly, evidence for wild sheep is almost entirely absent from the western third of the Fertile Crescent (the Levant); only two bones have been identified from deposits of 10,000 to 9500 B.P. at the site of Jericho, and perhaps another ten bones from pre-9500 B.P. deposits at Hatoula. So wild sheep were not an important prey species in the Levant before they were domesticated, and they were likely not very abundant in the area. While wild sheep do not appear ever to have been the most important prey species of hunters in the central third of the Fertile Crescent either, their remains account for from 5 to 15 percent or more of the bones recovered from two pairs of sites, all dating to about 9000 B.P. or earlier—Cafer and Çayönü, only 100 kilometers apart, and Mureybit and Abu Hureyra, 35 kilometers apart. The consistent presence of wild sheep in a supporting role is all the more interesting in view of the fact that these two pairs of settlements appear to have been home to hunter-gatherer groups that otherwise had very different

patterns of prey selection. Turning to the eastern third of the Fertile Crescent and the foothills of the Zagros, we find that wild sheep were clearly an important hunted species, judging from four sites that date to around 10,000 years ago or earlier. Wild sheep represent 11 percent of the animal bones recovered from Asiab, and from 40 to 60 percent of those recovered from Shanidar Cave, Zawi Chemi, and Karim Shahir.

The extent to which the hunter-gatherer societies in different parts of the Fertile Crescent relied on wild sheep for food probably reflects the animal's abundance in their local environments 10,000 to 8000 years ago. That abundance seems to have varied considerably. *Ovis orientalis* probably was not very abundant in the far northern portion of its range 10,000 years ago, since the higher elevations there were probably thickly forested. Sheep are grazers, and they prefer open hilly grasslands with good-quality pasturage. They do not have a goat's ability to survive in a wide range of habitats: they do not easily penetrate forested or arid regions and are much less suited than goats to rugged mountain terrain. In view of the geographical range of wild sheep, their preference in habitats, and their increased abundance and greater role as a prey species as we move from the Levant in the west to the Zagros in the east, we can reasonably look to the rolling grasslands of the central and eastern sections of the Fertile Crescent as the likely areas where hunter-gatherers domesticated them.

Turning to the archaeological record, we find that the clearest evidence for the initial domestication of sheep is limited to the central section of the Fertile Crescent. It is true that the abundance of caprines (sheep and goats combined) increased dramatically in sites of both the Levant and the central section of the Fertile Crescent that date from 9000 to 8000 years ago. Even in the absence of any other

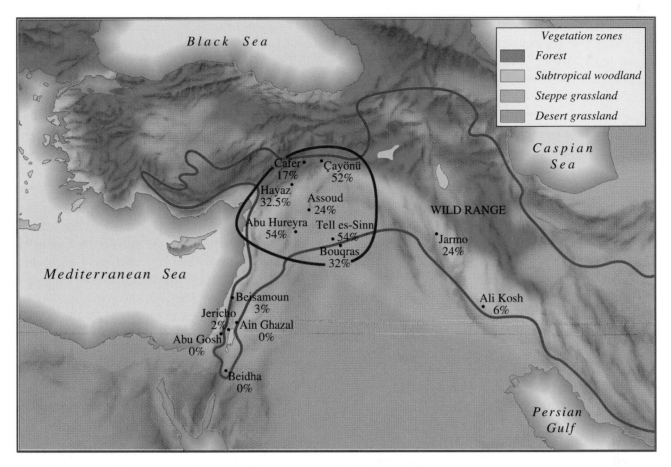

The wild ancestor of domesticated sheep ranged throughout much of the Fertile Crescent (mauve), but sheep were first domesticated in the much smaller region outlined in (maroon). There sheep herding first became an important component of agricultural economies. Each site is labeled with the percentage of sheep bones found in animal bone assemblages dating between 9000 and 8200 B.P.

indications of domestication, such a large-scale shift toward animals that earlier played only a secondary role in the diet can often be taken as good evidence that the societies in question had begun to rely on domesticated herds. But in the western section of the Fertile Crescent—the Levant—goats, not sheep, dominate early herding economies. Continuing the earlier absence of wild sheep in the Levant, *Ovis* accounts for only 2 percent of the bones recovered from deposits dated at 9500 to 8500 B.P. at Jericho, 3 percent of the bones excavated at Beisamoun, and sheep are absent entirely at other sites (Beidha, Abu Gosh, and 'Ain Ghazal). This overwhelming absence of sheep, both wild and domesticated, in the Levant probably reflects the scarcity of good habitats for this species.

In the central section of the Fertile Crescent, where more of the land is suited to *Ovis* and where wild sheep were a common target of hunters in earlier periods, domestic sheep account for much of the caprine shift of 9000 to 8000 years ago. At Çayönü and Abu Hureyra sheep bones increase from less than 10 percent to more than 50 percent of the animal bones recovered from deposits of 8700 to 8500 B.P., and they account for anywhere from a quarter to more than half of those recovered from sites dating to about 8500 to 8000 B.P. (Assoud, Bouqras, Hayaz, and Tell es-Sinn).

Along with this increase in the importance of sheep, another change occurred that provides an even better indication that humans were now managing herds of these animals—the sheep became smaller in size. A variety of strong selective pressures for smaller body size would have been imposed on captive herds, from deliberate efforts to cull large aggressive males to the unintentional effects of earlier weaning and having to live on less food under human management than would have been the case in the wild. Adult animals would also be smaller, on average, than in wild populations because of the sex ratio of managed herds. While a rough parity should be expected between adult males and adult females in wild populations, such would not be true for herds of domesticated animals. Under human management, herds were structured to produce a maximum number of young for slaughter, and would have had many more females than males in the adult breeding population. Since adult females are smaller than adult males, a shift toward females in the adult portion of the population might also contribute to an overall reduction in the average size of the adults in the herd.

Hans-Peter Uerpmann of the University of Tübingen in Germany was able to establish that the sheep at the sites of Bouqras and Çayönü were smaller than an earlier population of hunted wild sheep. Daniel Helmer of the Center of Archaeological Research in Valbonne, France, charted a similar reduction in the size of sheep at several sites dating to 8500–8000 B.P. (Bouqras, Tell es-Sinn, Assoud, Ras Shamra), when compared to an earlier (9000 B.P.) population of hunted wild sheep from the site of Mureybit. Taken together, these two markers of domestication—a dramatic increase in the proportion of sheep bones among animal remains, and an associated reduction in size—suggest that *Ovis aries* was first domesticated in the central section of the Fertile Crescent in the five centuries between 8700 and 8200 B.P. The three sites that predate 8500 B.P. (Cafer, Çayönü, and Abu Hureyra) provide the earliest evidence of sheep domestication.

In the eastern section of the Fertile Crescent, where our information on sheep domestication is more limited, a reduction in size again provides one of the clearest markers of the shift to managed herds. When Uerpmann measured sheep bones from the famous site of Jarmo, dating in the range of 8700 to 8000 B.P., he found that the size of sheep had diminished substantially from wild population baselines. In fact, the sheep of Jarmo had become very similar in size to the sheep of Çayönü.

Several hundred kilometers south of Jarmo, the Ali Kosh site has yielded a different kind of evidence of sheep domestication. In the lowest level of the site, resting on a house floor dating from 8500 to 8000 B.P., was found the top portion of a hornless sheep skull. Hornless females are quite rare among wild sheep populations, while female domesticated sheep almost never have horns. Although domesticated sheep were clearly present in the eastern third of the Fertile Crescent, after domestication *Ovis* appears to have actually declined in importance in comparison to its wild ancestors earlier in time. At Jarmo, for example, domesticated sheep contributed only

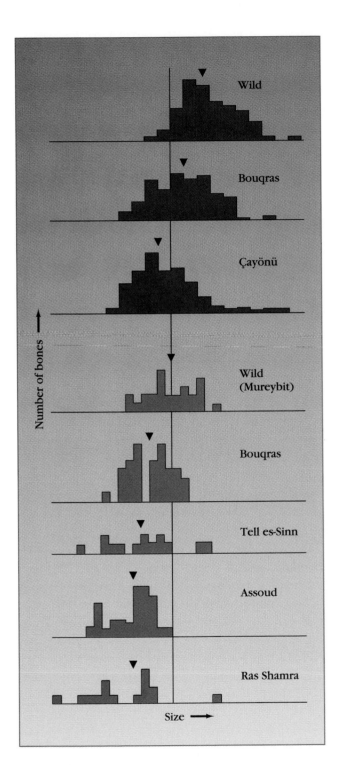

Domesticated sheep are smaller than wild sheep. Thus the average size of sheep bones (vertical arrows) measured by Hans-Peter Uerpmann (blue) and Daniel Helmer (brown) chart the presence of domesticated sheep at five settlements between 8700 and 8200 B.P.

24 percent of the bones analyzed, while goats made up 61 percent of the collection. Clearly, in the eastern third of the Fertile Crescent, the early herding of caprines centered not on sheep but on goats.

In sum, the earliest clear pattern of evidence for the domestication of sheep dates to the 500-year period from 8700 to 8200 B.P. The greatest concentration of evidence from those five centuries is found at a number of sites in the apex of the Fertile Crescent (Cafer, Çayönü, Hayaz, Assoud, Abu Hureyra, Tell es Sinn, Bouqras, and Ras Shamra). It is within this region, too, that domesticated sheep reached an early peak of economic importance, contributing an estimated one-third to one-half of the animal remains at five of the eight sites mentioned above.

Goats

The Persian wild goat, or bezoar (*Capra aegagrus*), has been identified as the wild ancestor of the domestic goat (*Capra hircus*). While wild sheep and wild goats show considerable overlap in their ranges of distribution across the Fertile Crescent, goats are found in more rugged terrain since they are much less selective in what they eat and can thrive in lands not suited to sheep. At the same time, goats do not fare so well in the flat grassland habitats dominated by gazelles, or in the rolling hill country that sheep prefer.

The bezoar goat is the wild ancestor of domesticated goats. A small-horned female stands in front, and a larger male with scimitar-shaped horns in the rear.

As was the case with wild sheep, it is not yet clear how far the range of the wild goat extended south into the Levant. The southern, more arid portion of this region was inhabited by the wild ibex (*Capra ibex*). Unfortunately, it is very difficult to distinguish between the bones of the ibex, which was never domesticated, and the bezoar goat, which was. In this area of the southern Levant, where ibexes and goats might have overlapped in their geographical range, caprines (either goat or ibex) were heavily hunted more than 9000 years ago, accounting for 50 to 70 percent of the animal bones found at Beidha and Rosh Horesha. The hunters of this area may

well have been killing ibex rather than goats, however, since the representation of any caprines, whether ibex, sheep, or goats, drops markedly once we move north beyond the ibex's likely habitat.

As we look north of the range of ibexes, the evidence disappears for either wild goats or northern ibex outliers before 9500 B.P., and this empty zone extends across into the central section of the Fertile Crescent. Goats are absent from the pre-9000 B.P. settlements of Abu Hureyra and Mureybit, which appear to lie south of the range of the wild bezoar goat. Two hundred and fifty kilometers to the north, however, back within its projected geographical distribution, the proportion of bezoar bones jumps to 15 and 45 percent at the sites of Çayönü and Cafer. In the eastern section of the Fertile Crescent, wild goats become even more prominent among the animals people hunted before 9000 B.P. While wild goats contribute less than 10 percent of the animal bones at the Zagros site of Karim Shahir, they account for from 25 to 55 percent of those at Asiab, Ghar-I-Khar, and Shanidar, and a full 80 percent of the bones from the lowest level at the key site of Ganj Dareh. The increasing importance of wild goats to human hunters as we move from west to east, from the Levant to the Zagros, is easy enough to understand in view of the geographical distribution and habitat of *Capra aegagrus*: the eastern section of the Fertile Crescent has large tracts of the rugged terrain preferred by goats.

Ganj Dareh is a small mound at the southern edge of the Kermanshah Valley of west-central Iran, measuring 40 meters in diameter and 8 meters high. Philip Smith of the University of Montreal has excavated about 20 percent of the site, exposing a sequence of five layers of human occupation (labeled A–E, from top to bottom). The lowest level at Ganj Dareh (E), dating perhaps as early as 9000 B.P., contained a large number of round pits; the overlying four layers (A–D), dating from about 9000 to 8800 B.P., each contained evidence of rectangular mud-brick houses.

Because Ganj Dareh was occupied so early and yielded almost 5000 identifiable goat bones, the site provided Brian Hesse of the University of Alabama at Birmingham with a rare opportunity to use several new analytical techniques in the search for ev-

idence of the domestication of the goat. Hesse was particularly interested in looking for evidence of the distinctive population structure of a goat herd managed for meat production. In theory, such a managed herd should have two clear distinguishing characteristics: (1) a large percentage of animals slaughtered for meat late in their immaturity, when they had attained much of their adult size; (2) an

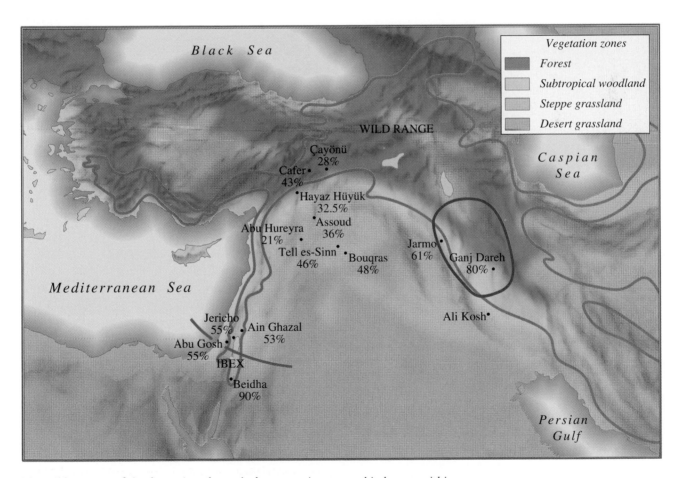

The wild ancestor of the domesticated goat had an extensive geographical range within the Fertile Crescent (mauve). They were likely first domesticated in the Zagros Mountains, in the area outlined in (maroon). Each site is labeled with the percentage of goat bones found in animal bone assemblages dating between 9000 and 8000 years ago.

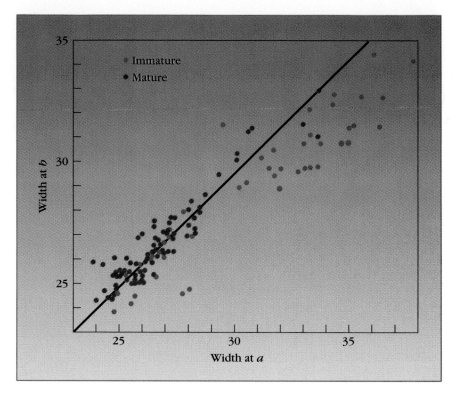

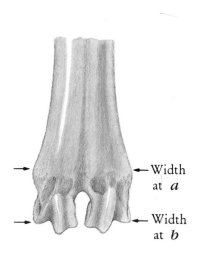

Left: To determine the relative size of goats at Ganj Dareh, Brian Hesse measured the width of the distal metatarsal bone (the lower end of the lower rear leg bone) in two places. Since male goats are larger than female goats, these two measurements separate males from females of the same age. Right: Most of the small (female) goats have fully fused metatarsals (blue dots), indicating they survived to more than two years of age, while those of most large (male) goats were unfused (brown dots), showing that they were killed before they reached the age of two years. The Ganj Dareh goats thus fit the age and sex profile of a domesticated herd managed for meat production, with females far outnumbering males in the adult breeding population.

adult breeding population in which females far outnumbered males.

Hesse expected that some degree of sexual dimorphism existed (male goats are larger than females), and that he could distinguish immature from adult animals by the closure of growth zones in bone (epiphyseal fusion). He measured a large sample of lower leg bones (metatarsals) from Ganj Dareh and found a very clear and interesting pattern. The vast majority of the adult goats were small (female), whereas most of the goats killed before they reached adulthood (their metatarsals had not yet fused) were large (males). In the overwhelming representation of adult females and large percentage of immature animals, the Ganj Dareh goats differed in age and sex from typical hunted populations, which have fewer young and a balance of adult males and females. The Ganj Dareh goat bones indicated

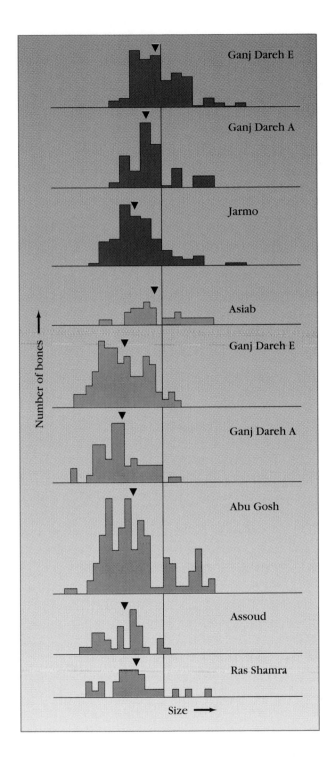

Number of bones

Ganj Dareh E

Ganj Dareh A

Jarmo

Asiab

Ganj Dareh E

Ganj Dareh A

Abu Gosh

Assoud

Ras Shamra

Size ➞

an age and sex profile that closely agreed with that of a herd of domestic goats managed to provide meat.

Hesse noted that bones of very young animals were more abundant in the lowest level of the site (level E), dated to 9000 B.P., suggesting that the first inhabitants may have seasonally hunted "nursery herds" of wild goats comprising adult females and animals less than a year old, rather than managing domestic herds. In the next level up (level D), which dates to about 8900 B.P. and contains the first evidence of mud-brick architecture, Hesse documented a shift to animals killed late in their immaturity, which he identified as marking the shift to management of domestic herds of goats. Noting that the goats from the lowest level at Ganj Dareh were smaller than earlier wild goats, however, Hans-Peter Uerpmann concluded that these level E animals were also domesticated and part of a managed herd. Daniel Helmer found the same pattern of size diminution when he compared these level E goats with earlier populations of wild goats. Clear demographic evidence thus appears to indicate that goats were domesticated at Ganj Dareh somewhere around 9000 B.P. The site of Jarmo provides further evidence of goat domestication in the eastern third of the Fertile Crescent. Dating to somewhere in the period from 8700 to 8000 B.P., Jarmo shows a continuation of the trend of size diminution in goats demonstrated at the earlier site of Ganj Dareh.

In the central third of the Fertile Crescent, the shift to herding of domesticated goats for meat production occurs about 8700 to 8200 B.P., 300 to 800

A reduction in size provides evidence of the domestication of goats. The average size of goat bones (vertical arrows) measured by Hans-Peter Uerpmann (brown) and Daniel Helmer (blue) chart the presence of domesticated goats at Ganj Dareh at 9000 B.P., at Jarmo by perhaps 8700 B.P., and at Abu Gosh, Assoud, and Ras Shamra between 8700 and 8200 B.P.

years after Ganj Dareh, at the same time that sheep herding emerged as a major economic undertaking. As in the case of sheep, the shift to goat herding is signaled by an increase in the proportion of goat bones among the animal remains, and evidence that the goats had become progressively smaller at a number of sites, including Assoud and Ras Shamra.

A parallel dramatic increase in the abundance of goats at sites in the western section of the Fertile Crescent marks the shift from hunting economies centered on gazelles (with few or no goats) to a core reliance on goat herding. Goats account for just over half of the animal bones at Jericho, 'Ain Ghazal, and Abu Gosh during this time period. The age and sex profile characteristic of a domestic goat herd structured for meat production has also been identified at 'Ain Ghazal, where the majority of goats were killed before they reached maturity, and two-thirds of the adult animals were females. Although some researchers have suggested that goats were herded as early in the Levant as in the eastern third of the Fertile Crescent, I think that the practice was part of a broader shift that swept across the central and western two-thirds of the Fertile Crescent between 8700 and 8200 B.P., a full three to eight centuries or more after goats were first domesticated in the Zagros.

Pigs

The wild ancestor of the domestic pig (*Sus scrofa*) has a broad geographical range that extends far beyond the Fertile Crescent to encompass large areas of Europe and Asia. It is quite possible that the wild pig, rather than being domesticated only once in a single location, was independently domesticated twice—in the Fertile Crescent and in China.

Wild pigs are omnivorous browsers and prefer habitats with rich vegetation, particularly river valleys and marshy areas. In several respects wild pigs also matched the behavioral profile of animals preadapted to domestication, though not so closely as goats, sheep, and cattle, the other three animal species domesticated in the region. Rather than forming large herds, pigs form smaller family groups, but within these small groups one animal is dominant and it is easy for humans to usurp control. Pigs have other advantages, particularly for people who live in permanent settlements. Young animals would have been easy to tame, and the ability of pigs to subsist on just about anything edible preadapted them to survive on the garbage of permanent settlements. Their ability to grow quickly and produce large litters also makes pigs excellent animals to raise in captivity for meat.

Like other animals, pigs become smaller under human management, and it is in their teeth that this size diminution is most easily seen. The reduction in the length of the snout of pigs when they become domesticated apparently reflects an early onset of sexual maturity, so that they stop growing while they are still young and a juvenile developmental stage persists into adulthood. Pig's teeth fortunately are easily identified and have a good chance of being preserved in archaeological sites. A landmark study by Kent Flannery of the University of Michigan has led to the adoption of the third molar as one of the standard benchmarks for identifying smaller-toothed domesticated pigs: the approximate boundary between domesticated and wild forms is 30 millimeters for upper third molars and 36 millimeters for lower third molars.

A reduction in snout length is not the only kind of evidence, however, that will lead us to the time and place at which pigs were first domesticated. Archaeologists can also look at how abundant wild pigs

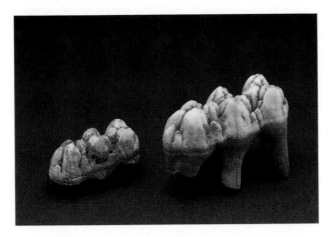

As domesticated pigs became smaller, so naturally did their teeth. Domesticated pigs have shorter snouts and smaller teeth than wild pigs, as demonstrated by these lower left third molars. The large molar is from a wild pig and was found at Tell Halif in southern Israel; the small molar is from a domesticated pig that lived 7600 years ago at the Umm Qseir site in northeast Syria.

were in each section of the Fertile Crescent and to what degree they were hunted before domestication and herded after.

Although wild pigs ranged throughout much of Asia and Europe, they were not equally prevalent everywhere. Wild pigs do not appear to have been very plentiful in the eastern section of the Fertile Crescent, for example, perhaps because the area was not rich in the well-watered habitats pigs prefer. A scarcity of pigs would explain why they were so little hunted in the region. Before 8000 B.P., wild pigs do not appear at all in some sites of the eastern Fertile Crescent, while in others (Asiab, Tepe Guran, Ganj Dareh, Ali Kosh, Shanidar) long-snouted wild pigs account for only 2 to 10 percent of the animal bones found.

Pigs did not become domesticated in the eastern Fertile Crescent—they arrived already domesticated. When did domesticated pigs first appear in the eastern section of the Fertile Crescent? The famous site of Jarmo, excavated by Robert Braidwood, provides part of the answer. Kent Flannery has analyzed the pig teeth recovered from the various levels of occupation in the more than 5 meters of deposits at Jarmo, and his work provides a clear picture of the transition from hunting to herding of pigs. In the lower levels at Jarmo, in the range of 8700 to 8000 B.P., pig bones contributed only about 2 percent of the 1400 bones recovered, and all five of the measured third molars from these lower levels were from long-snouted wild pigs. The pig's teeth recovered from the upper 2.25 meters of deposit, which date after 8000 B.P., are smaller, and almost all fall outside the size range of wild pig's teeth. As Flannery moved through the upper occupation layers at Jarmo, pigs also became progressively smaller, a trend that continued in the region, for even smaller pigs are recorded at several sites dating to 7800 B.P. (Gird Banahilk and Tepe Siahbid).

Once domesticated pigs had made their appearance in the eastern section of the Fertile Crescent by about 8000 B.P., they seem not to have been wholeheartedly adopted at first. Pigs apparently were not raised in every settlement before 7000 B.P. (Ali Kosh, Tepe Guran, Sarab, and Sabz are examples), and in those sites that have yielded pig bones, such as Jarmo and Choga Mami, they contributed only 7 to 8 percent of the animal remains. Since wild pigs do not appear to have been abundant in the eastern third of the Fertile Crescent, and *Sus scrofa* was not hunted or herded much in this area, it seems likely that pigs were first domesticated elsewhere. In our consideration of sheep and goats, the heartlands of domestication were found to be those areas where the species was important both before and after domestication.

Will the same pattern hold for pigs? If so, then

the western section of the Fertile Crescent seems even less likely to be the source of the first domesticated pigs. There as well, pigs were neither much hunted nor herded before 7000 B.P. In the 2000 years from 10,500 to 8500 B.P., Jericho, with its powerful spring and lake-edge habitat favorable to wild pigs, is the only site where wild pigs make up more than 10 percent of the animal bones. Between about 8500 and 8000 B.P. wild pigs contribute more than 10 percent of the animal bones at two additional sites in the Levant (Abu Gosh, with 12 percent and Beisamoun, with 18 percent), while the residents of other settlements still did little hunting of this animal. Even at Abu Gosh and Beisamoun, there is not yet any convincing morphological evidence of domestication. With the possible exception of a small sample of pig bones from Abu Gosh, on the coastal plain of the Levant, which appear to be smaller than we would expect those of wild animals to be, we still have no evidence that people raised domestic pigs in the western section of the Fertile Crescent much before 7000 B.P.

When we turn to the central section of the Fertile Crescent, however, a distinctly different pattern can be seen. Up until 8000 B.P. the people who lived in settlements in the southern and eastern parts of this area (Abu Hureyra, Mureybit, Bouqras, Tell es-Sinn) had little or nothing to do with wild pigs. In the northern part of this range, in contrast, hunters were killing wild pigs in significant numbers by about 9000 B.P. Wild pigs account for 45 percent and 20 percent of the animal remains at Çayönü and Cafer respectively. Even more interesting, pigs continued to be important to the people of this northern area even after they shifted to sheep and goat herding at 8700 to 8200 B.P. Pigs account for from 10 to 25 percent of the animal bones at five sites dating to 8500 to 8000 B.P. (Assoud, Çayönü, Gritille, Hayaz, and Cafer). From studies of

third molars and bones, we know that management of domesticated pigs had begun at three of these northern sites (Gritille, Çayönü, and Assoud). Of these three, Çayönü, at 8500 B.P., appears to have the earliest evidence of domesticated pigs in the Fertile Crescent. To the west, along the Mediterranean coastal plain, three other sites in the central third of the Fertile Crescent have yielded early evidence for pig domestication in the form of short snouts and size reduction (Ras Shamra, which dates to before 8000 B.P., and Labweh and Tell Judaideh, which date to just after 8000 B.P.).

For a number of reasons, then, this northern portion of the central Fertile Crescent, extending over to the Mediterranean coast, stands out both as the area where pigs were probably first domesticated and as the only area of the Fertile Crescent where domesticated pigs played a substantial role in local economies before 7000 B.P. Of the seven Fertile Crescent sites providing evidence of domesticated pigs that predate 7750 B.P., six fall within this north and coastal portion of the central third of the Fertile Crescent; only Jarmo, east in the Zagros, gives evidence of domesticated pigs outside of the north-central heartland before 7500 B.P.

Is it possible that pigs might have been domesticated in this central section of the Fertile Crescent even earlier than we now think? After making a preliminary analysis of 334 pig bones recovered from the site of Hallan Çemi, Richard Redding of the University of Michigan suggested that *Sus scrofa* might have been domesticated in this central section before 10,000 B.P. His evidence for domestication, however, is still tentative. The age profile of the pigs at Hallan Çemi is similar to what one might expect from a managed herd of domesticated animals: only 35 percent of the animals lived to be more than 3.5 years of age, and 29 percent died at less than a year old. But since we know lit-

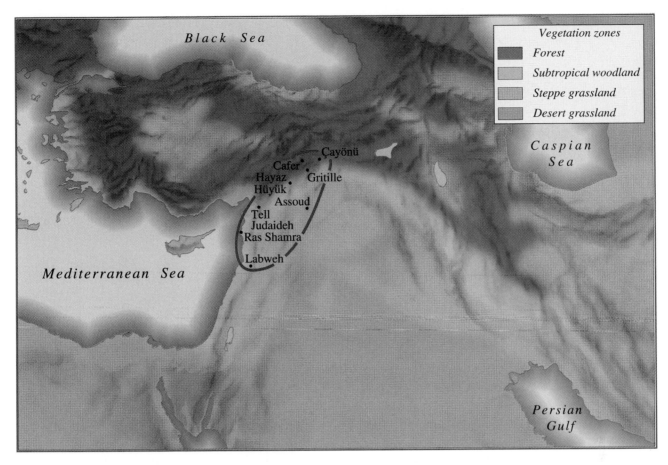

The outlined area shows the heartland of pig domestication, where pigs first became
an important component of agricultural economies.

tle about the age profile of wild pigs killed by
hunters, it is not possible to confidently identify the
Hallan Çemi pigs as domesticated based on their
age profile alone. Similarly, the two lower third molars measured so far (38.4 and 40.0 millimeters)
could come from either domesticated or wild animals. For now, it remains an unconfirmed but tantalizing possibility that pigs were domesticated
much earlier than the evidence now shows. As Redding works his way through the remaining ton of

animal bones from this site, perhaps he will find
stronger evidence for domesticated pigs.

Cattle

Cattle, so dominant in the world today, played a distant second to sheep and goats in the ancient Fertile Crescent. Perhaps their large size intimidated

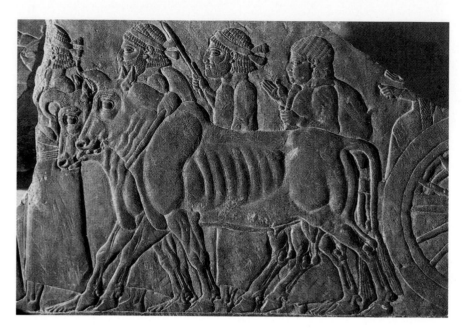

Cattle were important not only as a source of food, but also as draft animals that pulled plows and later carts, as shown in this 600 B.C. alabaster bas-relief from Niniveh, Mesopotamia. It depicts an ox-cart flanked by Assyrian soldiers.

the hunter-gatherers of the region. The aurochs (*Bos primigenius*), the long-horned ancestor of domestic cattle (*Bos taurus*), stood as high as 2 meters at the shoulder. It was both a dangerous prey species for early hunters of the Fertile Crescent and an attractively large package of meat. Wild cattle were clearly hunted throughout the Fertile Crescent before 8000 years ago, but only rarely do they represent more than 10 percent of the animal remains recovered from settlements. Four sites along the Jordan Valley in the Levant dating between 9000 and 8000 B.P. have yielded some of the highest frequencies of aurochs bones (Abu Gosh, 18 percent; Jericho, 13 percent; 'Ain Ghazal, 14 percent; and Beisamoun, 50 percent).

Like wild pigs, aurochs once had a broad geographical range that extended far beyond the Fertile Crescent, and recent initial mitochondrial DNA research by Ronan Loftus and his colleagues at Trinity College, Dublin, suggests that today's large-humped Zebu cattle of South Asia were domesticated independently from the humpless taurine types of Europe and northern Asia. While the proposed independent domestication of Zebu cattle has yet to be archaeologically documented in South Asia, taurine cattle appear to have arisen from aurochs in the western half of the Fertile Crescent and the adjacent Anatolian peninsula.

Caroline Grigson of the Royal College of Surgeons, London, has carefully documented a clear regional pattern of size reduction between 8000 and 7000 B.P. Searching through animal remains from numerous Fertile Crescent sites that predate 8000 B.P. for those few cattle bones still intact enough to yield key measurements, Grigson was able to construct a composite size-range profile for wild cattle.

When sites dated at 8000 to 7000 B.P. in the western half of the Fertile Crescent and Anatolia (Firkirtepe, Jericho, Ashkalon, Qaint el Mudiq,

Amuq) were compared with Grigson's baseline profile for wild cattle, they showed a dramatic reduction in size, whereas in the eastern half of the Fertile Crescent, aurochs remains are within the range of wild cattle until after 7000 B.P. In parallel studies, a reduction in the size of cattle bones has been documented at the coastal Mediterranean site of Ras Shamra, at Gritille in the Taurus Piedmont, and at Çatal Hüyük, in south-central Anatolia, where wild cattle documented at 8400 B.P. were followed by smaller domesticated stock by 7800 B.P.

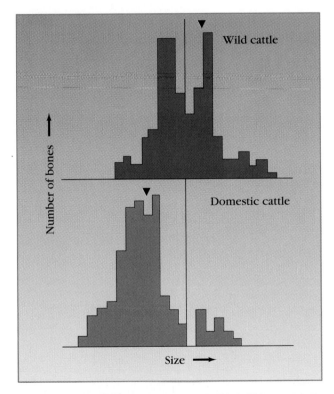

Caroline Grigson measured cattle bones from 8000- to 7000-year-old settlements in the western half of the Fertile Crescent (bottom). Her measurements showed the bones to be much smaller than bones from wild cattle of earlier time periods (top), providing clear evidence that cattle had been domesticated.

Grigson's study is an excellent beginning, but clearly more research is needed to refine the timing, location, and causes of domestication of cattle. Cattle were the last of the four core animal species to be domesticated in the region, and while they would be very important later, they had a minimal part in the emergence of agriculture between 10,000 and 8000 B.P.

Now that we have surveyed the individual developmental histories of four of the seven core domesticates of the Fertile Crescent, several patterns are beginning to emerge. Four main lines of evidence (geographical range, increase in abundance, reduction in size, change in age/sex profiles) indicate that these histories were distinct for each species. It appears that goats were the first animals domesticated, and that people had brought them under control in the eastern section of the Fertile Crescent by about 9000 years ago. Between about 8700 and 8000 years ago sheep, pigs, and cattle were then domesticated in overlapping parts of the central section of the Fertile Crescent.

How do the other domesticates—the plants—fit into this increasingly complex developmental puzzle? At least eight species were domesticated in the region between 10,000 and 8000 years ago. We have relatively little information on the early history of five of these plants: lentils (*Lens culinaris*), peas (*Pisum sativum*), chickpea (*Cier arietium*), bitter vetch (*Viciaervilia*), and flax (*Linum usitatiss*). The other three species, which would develop into crops of overwhelming importance, are all cereals of similar appearance: emmer wheat, einkorn wheat, and barley. Let us now turn to barley and wheat, and to the western section of the Fertile Crescent. The Levant did not play much of a role in the initial domestication of animals in the Fertile Crescent, but as we shall see it was very important in the first cultivation of plants.

Emmer Wheat

Using genetic analysis, biologists have now picked out the wild ancestors of the three cereals from larger pools of look-alike candidates. Physical appearances alone, it turns out, can be deceiving. Timopheev's wheat (*Triticum araraticum*), for example, is morphologically indistinguishable from emmer wheat and seemed a likely candidate for emmer's wild ancestor. Yet efforts to crossbreed it with emmer failed, proving that it played no part in that crop's origin. The true ancestor could successfully interbreed with emmer and was shown to have identical chromosomes.

Now that the wild ancestors of the three core domesticates have been solidly identified, botanical nomenclature has been revised to indicate the close genetic relationship between the wild types and their cultivated derivatives. No longer are the wild progenitors classified as separate species, but rather they are ranked as the *wild race* (subspecies) of the crop. For example, the scientific name of emmer wheat is *Triticum turgidum* subsp. *dicoccum,* and the wild ancestor, until recently called *Triticum dicoccoides,* is now classified as *Triticum turgidum* subsp. *dicoccoides,* within the same species as the domesticated crop.

Wild emmer wheat is closely confined to the Fertile Crescent, and it was widely harvested within this range as a wild plant before it was domesticated, from Netiv Hagdud and Jericho in the Levant north to Çayönü and Gritille and across to Jarmo in the east. As emmer was domesticated, the shape

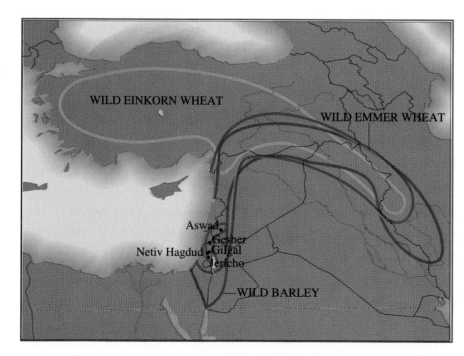

The geographical ranges of the wild ancestors of emmer wheat, einkorn wheat, and barley. The small area outlined in dark brown is the Levantine corridor, where all three were domesticated 10,000 to 9600 years ago.

and size of the grain changed, as did the structure of the rachis, the miniature stem that attaches the grain to the plant. The grains became larger and plumper, and the rachises tougher and less brittle, so that grains were less easily lost before harvesting. These changes provide clear morphological indications of when emmer, as well as einkorn and barley, was domesticated.

These larger, plumper grains and tough rachis fragments first appear at two sites in the Levant. Although not recovered in large amounts or described in any detail, domesticated emmer is reported as being present at the site of Jericho in the southern Jordan Valley by 9800 to 9500 B.P. and perhaps a few centuries earlier. Larger grains and nonbrittle rachises from about the same time also appear in the lowest levels at the site of Aswad, near Damascus. These two sites provide the earliest evidence of domesticated emmer wheat.

Three hundred kilometers north of Aswad, and several centuries later, the site of Abu Hureyra has also yielded early evidence of cultivated emmer wheat dating to about 9500 to 9000 years ago. The use of flotation made the recovery of plant remains more successful at these two sites than at Jericho, which was excavated in the 1950s, before flotation recovery was widely employed. As a result, we know that emmer was the most important early cultigen at both Abu Hureyra and Aswad, and that it continued to be important up through the centuries. By 9000 B.P. it shows up at two more Levant sites, 'Ain Ghazal and Natal Oren, as well as at Çayönü, in the central section of the Fertile Crescent, which yielded a cache of 1500 seeds. After 9000 B.P. it must have been widely adopted, since it has been found at a number of other sites across the region that date to 8500 to 8000 B.P. (Ali Kosh, Bouqras, Hayaz, Tell es-Sinn, Ramad, Ras Shamra, Jarmo).

Einkorn Wheat

The wild ancestor of einkorn wheat grows naturally in massive stands across the northern portion of the Fertile Crescent and on west through much of the Anatolian Peninsula, but it does not extend down into the western section of the Fertile Crescent. While wild einkorn (*Triticum monococcum* subsp. *boeoticum*) is absent from sites in the Levant, it occurs in the eastern section of the Fertile Crescent at sites such as Jarmo and Ali Kosh. Evidence of it being harvested by hunter-gatherers before it was domesticated is most evident, however, in the central section of the Fertile Crescent, at Çayönü and Bouqras and the important sites of Mureybit and Abu Hureyra.

When Abu Hureyra, on the Euphrates, was excavated in the early 1970s, Gordon Hillman and his colleagues at the Institute of Archaeology of University College, London, conducted a large-scale flotation recovery program that provided them with an exceptionally large and diverse assemblage of charred plant remains. Painstakingly analyzing all 712 samples recovered, each of which contained on average 500 seeds representing 70 species or genera, Hillman and his co-workers were able to reconstruct the plant-food diet of both the farming community that existed at Abu Hureyra from about 9500 to 8000 B.P. and the earlier hunter-gatherer group that lived there in a permanent year-round settlement from 11,000 to 10,000 years ago. Of the 157 seed-bearing species harvested by the hunter-gatherers, wild einkorn was among those most frequently found; its seeds showed up in almost all of the flotation samples from these early levels.

At the nearby site of Mureybit, also at the edge of the Euphrates Valley, meticulous analysis of plant remains by Willem van Zeist and Johanna Bakker-

Heeres of the Biologisch-Archaeologisch Instituut in Groningen, the Netherlands, produced even stronger evidence that hunter-gatherers relied heavily on wild einkorn. The abundance of grains and rachis fragments of the wild cereal in the samples indicated a pattern of intensive harvesting. Few other preagricultural settlements in the Fertile Crescent have yet produced plant assemblages so impressive and so carefully analyzed as those at Abu Hureyra and Mureybit, and few contain such clear and compelling evidence of the importance of wild cereals to sedentary hunter-gatherers before they brought these wild grasses under cultivation.

Even though this evidence of a strong reliance on wild cereals so far comes only from a few sites, researchers have convincingly documented the remarkable potential of these grasses to provide large harvests. Twenty-five years ago Jack Harlan of the University of Illinois undertook a now classic study of wild wheat yields. Harvesting stands of wild einkorn by hand in southeastern Turkey, Harlan was able to show that in only three weeks a small family group could have gathered enough grain to sustain them for a full year. Follow-up studies have confirmed Harlan's conclusions—that these wild grasses grew in rich abundance, were easily harvested, and almost certainly played a major role in the economy of hunter-gatherers.

Emmer, einkorn, and barley are edge, or ecotone, species in the wild. They grow naturally not in the well-watered alluvial soils near rivers or on the open steppe, but rather in the fine-grained soils that form on basalt and other rocks of low acidity at higher elevations. Here, massive stands of these wild grasses thrive on open slopes at the margins of scrub oak woodlands as they fade into the grasslands.

How easy or how difficult would it have been to relocate these high-yield wild plants from their natural habitats to the vicinity of hunter-gatherer settlements? This is an important question, for several of the farming settlements that have yielded the very earliest evidence of domesticated einkorn (Aswad and Jericho for instance) seem to fall outside its wild ancestor's geographical range.

Israeli field studies in the 1980s have shed light on this question. They were designed simply to look for resistance to disease in wild populations of barley and emmer wheat in the hope of benefiting modern crops, but they also convincingly demonstrated the ease with which the wild grasses can be cultivated outside their natural habitat. Wild emmer and wild barley were easily grown in new settings, both in areas that received enough rain for cultivation and in drier areas with supporting irrigation. Their large seeds tolerated being covered by variable amounts of soil, and germinated quickly, producing vigorous seedlings. Stands of both these wild cereals, and their yields, were very similar to those of local domesticated varieties grown under the same conditions. Daniel Zohary of the Department of Genetics at Hebrew University in Jerusalem, an authority on the wild cereals of the Near East, concludes that it would have been easy to start wild emmer or wild barley cultivation both in areas of sufficient rainfall or, with the help of irrigation, in drier and warmer places. In the latter, an initial irrigation (in September or October) and one or two subsequent ones produced remarkable stands. Although einkorn was not included in this ten-year study, it would almost certainly have shown the same preadaptation to cultivation outside of its natural habitat—an important point, since the earliest domesticated einkorn was found outside its natural range.

The early record of domesticated einkorn wheat parallels that of emmer very closely. Domesticated einkorn accompanies emmer both at the earliest level at Aswad (9800 to 9600 B.P.), near Damascus, and in deposits dated at 9500 to 9000 B.P. at Abu Hureyra, 300 kilometers to the north along the Euphrates. Domesticated einkorn also accompanies emmer at Jericho at about 9800 to 9500 B.P. and at later settlements, including Çayönü, by 9000 B.P. and at Bouqras, Ramad, Ali Kosh, and Jarmo by 8500 to 8000 B.P. This early pattern of emmer and einkorn being cultivated together is not universal, however; einkorn but not emmer is found at Gritille, and emmer but not einkorn is found at numerous sites ('Ain Ghazal, Beidha, Huyuk, Tell es-Sinn and Ramad).

Barley

The geographical range of barley's wild ancestor (*Hordeum vulgare* subsp. *spontaneum*) stretches the full length of the Fertile Crescent, and hunter-gatherers and early farmers harvested wild barley throughout the extent of its range, from Ali Kosh, Jarmo, and Ganj Dareh in the east across to Mureybit and Abu Hureyra in the center and south to Gilgal, Netiv Hagdud, Jericho, and Beidha in the Levant.

While the record of early domesticated barley overlaps to some extent with the records of emmer and einkorn wheat, it also exhibits several interesting differences. Two types of domesticated barley have been recovered from early farming settlements in the Fertile Crescent. One, like its wild progenitor, had two vertical rows of grains, with each grain protected by an outer hull or glume (two-rowed hulled barley—*Hordeum vulgare* subsp. *distichum*), and the other had six vertical rows of grains (six-rowed hulled barley—*Hordeum vulgare* subsp. *hexastichum*). Domesticated six-rowed hulled barley was developed after the domesticated two-rowed hulled barley, in response to harvesting selection pressure: by increasing the number of grains packaged at the end

Spikes of two-rowed and six-rowed barley. With six vertical rows of grain rather than two, a spike of six-rowed barley provides a larger, denser package of seed for human harvesters.

of stalks, individual plants increased their chances of contributing grain to next year's planting. Six-rowed barley appears in the archaeological record soon after the two-rowed domesticate.

At Aswad, outside Damascus, domesticated two-rowed hulled barley accompanies domesticated emmer and einkorn in the earliest level, about 9800 to 9600 B.P. By 9500 to 9000 B.P., six-rowed barley is present, along with einkorn and emmer, but the two-rowed type is absent. Both the two-rowed and six-rowed types are present, along with emmer and einkorn, at Jericho (9800 to 9500 B.P.), as well as in the earliest levels (8500 to 8000 B.P.) at Ali Kosh, far to the east. Yet at other eastern sites, barley was the only cereal grown. Two-rowed barley is the only crop plant present both at the earliest levels at Ganj Dareh in the Zagros, dating to 9000 B.P., and at Netiv Hagdud and Gilgal in the Levant, which date between 9900 and 9700 B.P. By 8500 to 8000 B.P. two-rowed and six-rowed barley are found alone and together at numerous other sites across the Fertile Crescent, in various combinations with other crops, including emmer, einkorn, and lentils.

The absence of any clear patterns of crop combinations is perhaps one of the most interesting observations that can be made regarding the early history of domesticated barley, emmer, and einkorn. Far from constituting a tight crop complex, with all three domesticates consistently being cultivated together in early farming villages, these crops appear to have been adopted in various combinations by societies across the Fertile Crescent. Yet several important developmental patterns can be discerned in the early history of these three "principal founder crops," as Daniel Zohary calls them, particularly when they are viewed in the larger context of the other domesticates and the cultural history of the human societies responsible for their domestication.

The Beginning of Agriculture in the Levantine Corridor

Of the seven core domesticates, the three grasses were the first species that human societies in the Fertile Crescent brought under domestication. All of the evidence available indicates that this may have happened during a span of only two to three centuries, from about 10,000 to 9700 B.P. At well-studied sites such as Abu Hureyra and Mureybit, there is no sign of nonshattering rachises or any other morphological indicators of domestication of these three cereals before 10,000 B.P., even though wild stands were an important source of food. But by 9700 B.P., 300 years later, clear indications that all three cereals had been domesticated show up at Aswad, Netiv Hagdud, Gilgal, and Jericho.

Is it possible for these grasses to have been domesticated in only three centuries? It is certainly conceivable that evidence of domestication may yet be found in settlements that date earlier than 10,000 years ago, but research by Gordon Hillman of the University of London and M. Stuart Davies of the University of Wales indicates that three centuries would have been time enough for human cultivation to have produced the morphological changes in emmer, einkorn, and barley that signal domestication. Hillman and Davies concluded that wild plants with brittle rachises could have been almost completely replaced by domesticated plants with "semi-tough" rachises relatively quickly. The appearance of tough rachises thus provides a clear marker of one of the most revolutionary and significant innovations in human history—the intentional planting of stored seed stock.

The hunter-gatherers who first attempted to cultivate these grasses would have had to get their seeds from wild plants. The vast majority of these plants would have had the fully brittle rachises essential for the successful dispersal of seeds in the wild. These rachises are segmented so that individual spikelets and their grains can be shed in a sequence from the top down as the plants ripen.

In perhaps one wild plant out of every 2 to 4 million, however, a mutation would have produced a semitough rachis that retained the spikelets. Even though plants with semi-tough rachises would have

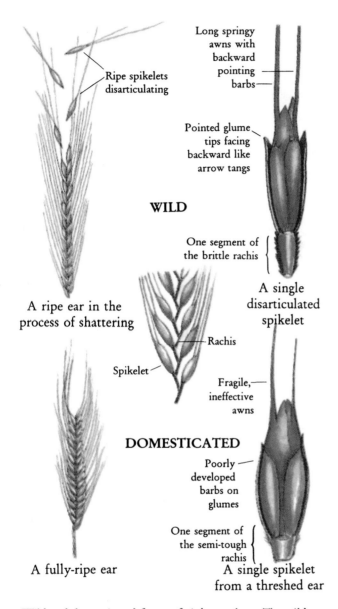

Long springy awns with backward pointing barbs

Pointed glume tips facing backward like arrow tangs

WILD

One segment of the brittle rachis

A single disarticulated spikelet

Ripe spikelets disarticulating

A ripe ear in the process of shattering

Rachis

Spikelet

Fragile, ineffective awns

DOMESTICATED

Poorly developed barbs on glumes

One segment of the semi-tough rachis

A fully-ripe ear

A single spikelet from a threshed ear

Wild and domesticated forms of einkorn wheat. The wild form needs to be able to disperse its seeds effectively and has thus evolved easily shattered ears with brittle rachises and thin, arrow-shaped spikelets designed to penetrate surface litter and imbed themselves in cracks in the ground. In the domesticated form, plumper spikelets have lost some of the key structures necessary for self-implantation, seed dispersal, and success in the wild.

been very rare in early fields planted with wild seed, they could have come to dominate such fields in only 20 to 200 years, once human management met two simple criteria.

First, the cultivators would have had to begin harvesting the plants each year only after the cultivated stands had become partly to nearly ripe, when the brittle-rachis plants had begun to shed spikelets and were ready to shed even more when anyone touched them. Second, cultivators would have had to carry out the harvest in a way that favored the recovery of grain from the few plants with semi-tough, nonshattering rachises, and that worked against the recovery of spikelets from brittle-rachis plants. The harvesters should thus aim to recover spikelets that stayed attached to the plants rather than those ready to shatter off. If they beat the grain heads with paddles and caught the shed spikelets in baskets, for example, they would never produce domesticated plants, since they would be recovering spikelets from brittle-rachis plants, and would not capture those spikelets that stayed attached to the plants. If they harvested the complete plants, however, either by uprooting them or by cutting the stalks with hand-held sickles having sharp flint cutting edges, they would miss many of the spikelets from brittle-rachis plants. Rather than becoming next year's seed stock, the spikelets from brittle-rachis plants would lie exposed on the ground, ready to be consumed by birds and small rodents. Some would survive to sprout the following year, but many would not. Once humans began to harvest by sickle or by uprooting plants, spikelets that stayed attached to plants during harvesting would thus gain a tremendous statistical advantage—a much better likelihood of contributing to next year's fields of cultivated plants.

The seemingly simple step of harvesting with sickles once the grain was ripe could lead in a few centuries or less to the dominance of domesticated plants with semi-tough rachises in cultivated fields. These new domesticated plants, human creations, could not compete on their own in the wild against their cousins with brittle rachises. By harvesting in this manner, early farmers imposed an entirely new set of selection pressures on cultivated stands of grasses; these pressures were far different from those that dictated which seeds would survive in the wild to become the next generation.

Why, then, did people first begin to plant seeds? Part of the answer has to do with where in the Fertile Crescent this new set of selection pressures was established. Where did human societies first create cultivated stands of domesticated cereals with nonbrittle rachises? They appear to have first domesticated emmer, einkorn, and barley in a very small region of the Fertile Crescent termed the "Levantine corridor" by Ofer Bar-Yosef of Harvard University. This 10- to 40-kilometer-wide zone extends from the Damascus Basin (the site of Aswad) down into the lower Jordan Valley in the south (the sites of Jericho, Gilgal, and Netiv Hagdud). It may also extend north to the middle Euphrates Valley (Abu Hureyra).

These sites of the Levantine corridor all have a common characteristic—a dependable source of water for growing crops in the form of a high water table. The hunter-gatherers who first cultivated cereal grasses appear to have done so where springs, lakes, or river floodplains guaranteed a good supply of water, enough to ensure good harvests from species they had moved down from their natural habitats on dry slopes at higher elevations. By planting their seeds in these areas of high water table, farmers could have avoided the risk of drought, in relying exclusively on rainfall.

At Abu Hureyra, for example, high water tables along the valley floor could have provided supplementary water for cultivated fields, while to the south the settlement of Aswad stood on the edge of a large freshwater lake surrounded by marshes.

In the southern Jordan Valley, early farmers obtained water for their fields from the high water tables under alluvial fans, and from springs and spring-fed ponds and lakes. The springs at Gilgal and Netiv Hagdud have long been dry, but the substantial spring at Jericho today still creates an oasis in the arid summer landscape of the valley. The waters of this spring, along with winter runoff from streams flowing from the Judean Hills, would have ensured the harvest of the early farming settlement at Jericho. These waters actually helped to shape the settlement itself. Ofer Bar-Yosef has shown that the famous walls of early Jericho were not defensive but rather were designed, along with systems of ditches, to divert the flow of floodwaters and sediment away from the circular mud-brick houses of the 2.4-hectare village.

The early farming communities at Jericho are buried under many meters of disintegrated mud-brick and other debris that constitute the twenty-five or so building levels of the massive tell, and they have not been uncovered to any great extent. Excavated in the 1950s, the early farming village layers of Jericho were not screened or subjected to flotation recovery, so only limited plant and animal remains were recovered. As a result, Jericho has yielded only tantalizing partial glimpses of the way of life of the world's first agriculturalists.

Netiv Hagdud: A Clear View of the Revolution

In striking contrast to Jericho, the smaller contemporaneous farming settlement at Netiv Hagdud, 13 kilometers north of Jericho, was abandoned around

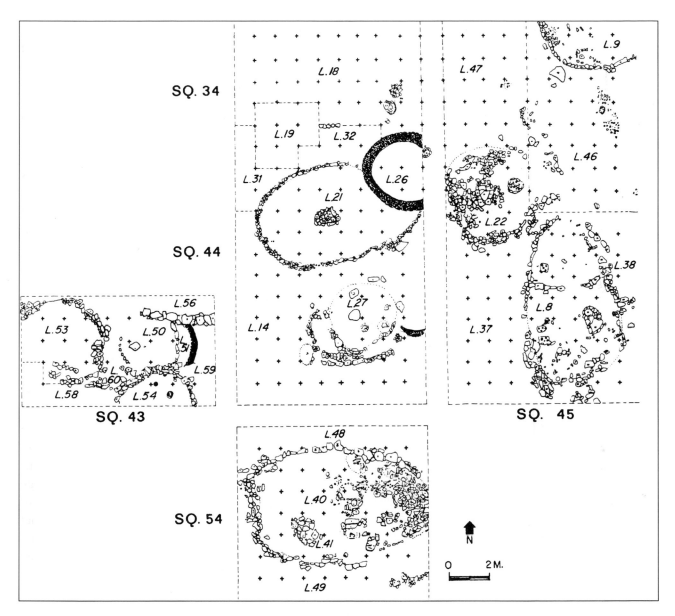

A community plan of part of the small farming settlement of Netiv Hagdud, showing the oval and round limestone slab foundations of houses. Occupied for a few centuries about 10,000 years ago, this small village has yielded some of the earliest evidence of plant cultivation in the world.

9500 B.P., after only about 300 years of occupation, and it lies less than a meter below the ground surface. Excavated over three seasons in the 1980s by Avi Gopher of Tel Aviv University and Ofer Bar-Yosef, Netiv Hagdud provides a remarkable view of the very earliest stages of agriculture in the Fertile Crescent.

Covering an area of about 1.5 hectares, the settlement is situated on the alluvial fan of Wadi Baker, where the tributary meets the Jordan Valley after descending out of the Judean Hills to the west. Within the 500-square-meter excavation area

opened up at Netiv Hagdud, Bar-Yosef and Gopher uncovered a series of superimposed layers containing the preserved floors and foundations of houses. These freestanding structures of unbaked mud brick, some oval and some circular, probably stood for a generation or so on their limestone slab foundations before they were leveled to make way for new construction.

It is difficult to know how many of these structures belonged to each family in the settlement, and how many structures and households were present at any one time during its occupation, but Netiv Hagdud was probably home to twenty to thirty families and perhaps 100 to 200 people. Some contemporaneous settlements, such as Gilgal and Gesher, were less than half the size of Netiv Hagdud, while Jericho and Aswad were probably about twice its size.

Plant parts and animal bones were well preserved at Netiv Hagdud, and flotation and dry and wet sieving of excavated soil yielded evidence that the settlement's inhabitants exploited an amazingly rich diversity of wild species of plants and animals. From a nearby spring and shallow lake they collected freshwater mollusks and moles, snails, crabs, and frogs, and caught a wide variety of ducks and other water birds, eels, and fish. The woodland belt of the hilly slopes provided chameleons and other lizards, as well as rodents and such larger game as fallow deer and wild pigs. The mountain gazelle, a grasslands grazer, was the large animal most hunted by the inhabitants of Netiv Hagdud.

The villagers collected more than fifty species of wild plants, including wild legumes and fleshy fruits and nuts—wild figs, almonds, pistachios, and acorns. A variety of tools recovered from the settlement attest to the gathering of wild grasses, as do the presence of carbonized seeds, which have been partially burned and thereby preserved. The grasses

The Netiv Hagdud site during excavation, showing house structures L.21, L.26, L.27, L.22, and L.8, all marked on the partial community plan on page 75.

Carbonized wheat grains. Seeds and other plant materials can often survive intact for thousands of years in dry caves and rock shelters or in desert zones like the coast of Peru. In the moist soils of open-air sites in nondesert zones, however, plant remains have little chance of avoiding decay unless they are accidentally burned or carbonized in part, perhaps during cooking. The 4700-year-old wheat grains shown are from Tell Gat in southern Israel.

harvested included three species of wild oats, canary grass, meadow grass, feather grass, spear grass, wild emmer, and wild barley.

Almost 200 flint sickle blades have been recovered, some still bearing traces of the asphalt adhesive that attached them to curved wooden handles. Mud brick structures a meter in diameter and smaller ones built of limestone slabs were probably storage bins for grain. Large amounts of wild oats and barley were found in such a structure at the nearby site of Gilgal. The grains of grasses, along with nuts and plant foods, were processed with a variety of stone bowls, flat grinding slabs, and slabs with cup holes.

Wild grasses were clearly important to the villagers of Netiv Hagdud, and represented a key component in their diverse economy. In fact, when investigators first analyzed the plant remains from the site, all of the grasses, including barley, were thought to have been harvested from wild stands, since they did not seem to show any morphological evidence of domestication. All the same, Ofer Bar-Yosef was convinced that these villagers had crossed over the line from an exclusively hunting-and-gathering economy and were already planting and harvesting two-rowed barley in cultivated fields. He was not that surprised, then, when further analysis revealed fragments of semi-tough barley rachises, confirming the cultivation of domesticated barley at Netiv Hagdud.

Now, Netiv Hagdud became an invaluable piece of the puzzle of the emergence of farming economies in the Fertile Crescent. This small village of mud-brick houses, dating to about 9800 years ago, provides a unique, clear view of an important landmark in the long transition from hunting and gathering to farming—the first domestication of cereals.

Taking advantage of the fertile, well-watered, and easily tilled soils of the nearby alluvial fan and lake edge, the villagers planted and harvested fields of two-rowed barley even as they continued to harvest stands of wild barley and other grasses. In contrast to Jericho, Aswad, and Abu Hureyra, where a number of domestic crops appear together, Netiv Hagdud highlights the first step toward agriculture—the addition of a single domesticate into a long-established hunting-and-gathering economy. Barley, along with emmer and einkorn, was to play an important role in the growth and increasing complexity of settlements and societies in the region: at Netiv Hagdud we see it in an earlier, less dominant role.

Before we investigate the development of later, more complex farming communities across the

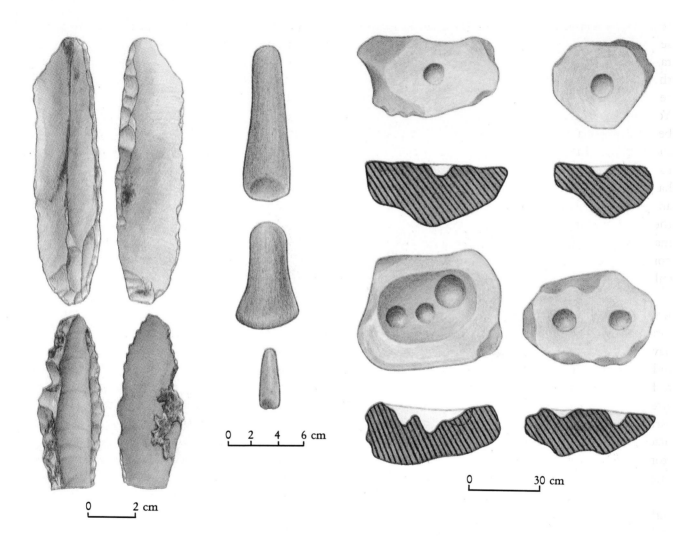

These tools from Netiv Hagdud were used for the harvesting and processing of seeds from a variety of different wild grasses and domesticated barley. At the left are flint sickle blades, which would have been hafted with asphalt in wooden handles; at the center are pestles, and at the right are grinding slabs with cup holes.

Fertile Crescent, let's first look back in time from Netiv Hagdud in search of possible reasons why hunter-gatherer societies in the southern Jordan Valley took the giant first step toward a farming way of life about 10,000 years ago. A. Belfer-Cohen of Hebrew University, and Ofer Bar-Yosef suggest that several factors were involved. Climatic change may have influenced the timing of those first efforts at cultivation. The "Younger Dryas"— a cold and dry period that lasted two centuries or so between 11,000 and 10,000 years ago—seems to have been followed about 10,000 B.P. by a rapid return to wetter conditions and the growth of the alluvial fans, springs, and lakes seemingly so central to the success of early cultivation. The Younger Dryas climatic episode could perhaps have been the external stress, reducing available wild food sources, that caused hunter-gatherer societies to turn to cultivation in efforts to increase their after-harvest reserves of grain. Even in the absence of such an external pressure, however, gradual growth in their populations and expansion of their villages may have encouraged or necessitated a variety of economic changes, including experimenting with the cultivation of wild grasses.

The hunter-gatherers in the southern Levant were certainly well positioned to undertake such efforts. No sites dating from 11,000 to 10,000 B.P. have been excavated in the region, but earlier sites indicate that many of the basic elements leading up to farming settlements such as Netiv Hagdud were already in place. Although plant remains from these early sites are not abundant, the presence of sickle blades, grinding bowls and slabs, cupstones, and storage structures indicates long reliance on wild grasses. These settlements were much smaller than Netiv Hagdud, but their inhabitants had clearly shifted to permanent year-round settlements as early as 12,500 years ago and invested considerable labor in constructing houses and storage facilities. When people established such sedentary settlements, their concepts of who owned resources likely became more restrictive as they strengthened their claim on the surrounding countryside, which they viewed more and more as being for their exclusive use. Stands of wild grasses and other animal and plant resources of the surrounding area would have become off-limits to neighboring groups as boundaries between groups became more strongly defined.

By 12,500 years ago, then, hunting and gathering societies began to adopt a way of life that set the logistic, economic, and organizational groundwork for the emergence of village farming communities. They would have been thoroughly familiar with the growing habits and other characteristics of the plants they later domesticated, for those plants were already an integral element of their economy. The hand sickle/storage silo/grinding slab technology they developed for harvesting, storing, and processing these wild cereals was also the technology they would need for successful farming.

They were also reordering the structure of their society in ways that would make the shift to a village farming way of life an easier and less abrupt transition. When they stopped moving their campsites periodically and established permanent settlements, they had to address a wide range of challenges involving the organization, coordination, and control of greater numbers of people and activities in the face of finite resources. As a result, many of the basic elements of social organization essential to village life were probably already in place before the first experiments with cultivation.

The specific context in which hunter-gatherers first began to cultivate cereal is still an open question. Did they do so in response to the stress of a growing population or of a Younger Dryas–induced decline in wild plant and animal resources or both? Did some settlements or families experiment with wild grasses during good times in an effort to expand the yield of an already reliable resource? In either case, they could store the additional grain they obtained from harvests of cultivated cereals in anticipation of lean years ahead, both reducing their own risk and giving themselves the wherewithal to increase their social standing by making gifts of their surplus to others in times of need. Whatever their motivations, the payoff for these experiments

Plaster figures being excavated at 'Ain Ghazal. Thirteen busts and a dozen full-body figures a meter in height were discovered at the 8700-year-old farming settlement at 'Ain Ghazal, near Netiv Hagdud and Jericho. These figures might represent revered ancestors and could be understood as a way of ritually reiterating the continuity of ownership of the agricultural landscape from generation to generation.

than earlier precultivation settlements, the houses were larger and more substantial, and large-scale public works such as the famous flood walls and tower at Jericho attest to the successful organization of people into larger cooperative groups.

As people began to live together in larger, more stable societies, new belief systems emerged. Small clay female figurines may point to an increasingly important role for women as cultivators in early farming societies. At the same time, the separate disposal of human skulls suggests the beginning of ancestor worship and a focus on reaffirming and legitimizing village and family claims on the landscape, particularly well-watered field plots. A few centuries later, the inhabitants of the region were

A human skull from Jericho, with cowrie shells in its eye sockets and flesh modeled in plaster. This skull of an ancestor, like the 'Ain Ghazal figures, might have been used ritually to reinforce long-standing claims of land ownership.

was both rapid and dramatic. Yields of surplus grain from well-watered fields were dependable, storable, and essentially limited only by the number of hectares a village could bring under crop.

Not surprisingly, early village settlements based on cereal cultivation were two to six times larger creating skulls coated with plaster and remarkable caches of plaster human statues (revered ancestors?), evidence that their belief systems and rituals were becoming more complex. These belief systems may have played a growing role in maintaining social cohesion as groups grew and it became important to control fixed resources, particularly fields.

The Expansion of a Village Farming Way of Life

Once established in the Levantine corridor by about 10,000 to 9700 B.P., this new village farming way of life slowly spread across the Fertile Crescent. By 9000 B.P. village settlements based on the cultivation of domesticated cereal crops had been established in favorable locations across the Fertile Crescent. Much still needs to be learned about this expansion, for relatively few settlements have been excavated that date to the eight-century span from 9800 to 9000 B.P. Cereal seed stock and information about how to use it could have easily traveled between widely scattered communities through the already well established networks of exchange for obsidian and other raw materials.

The spread of cereal cultivation between 10,000 and 9000 B.P. was by no means universal or everywhere alike. Well-watered settlements adopted the combinations of cereal crops that best matched their distinctive hunting-and-gathering economies, while settlements in less favored settings, such as Beidha in the southern Levant, continued to rely exclusively on wild plants and animals. Those societies that did cultivate cereals, however, found the innovation to be remarkably successful, for they became large and stable long before they began to domesticate goats, sheep, pigs, or cattle.

Excavations at the site of Çayönü, in the foothills of the Taurus Mountains, offer a glimpse of the long development of one such village, which was occupied from about 9300 to 8500 B.P. A sequence of four building levels documents the history of this community of twenty-five to fifty houses and perhaps 100 to 200 people. In the first two building levels, which were inhabited before domestic sheep and goats first appeared about 8700 B.P., large rectangular structures ranged in size from 5 by 10 meters to 9 by 10 meters. These early village houses were uniformly spaced and oriented, suggesting an overall community plan. Elaborate stone foundations supported floors of plaster-covered wooden beams and elaborate terrazzo pavements. Internal walls divided some of the houses into separate storage rooms and living/working areas. These people hunted wild cattle, deer, goats, and pigs, harvested wild plants, and cultivated domestic emmer and einkorn wheat.

Stable, well-organized, seemingly affluent village settlements such as Çayönü—villages that flourished even though they had no domesticated animals—underscore the long evolution of farming villages in the two western sections of the Fertile Crescent between 10,000 and 9000 B.P. At first the villagers satisfied their requirements for meat protein by intensifying the hunt for wild game. Çayönü added domesticated goats and sheep to their economy about 8700 to 8500 B.P.; domesticated pig joined them slightly later.

At other settlements in the central section of the Fertile Crescent (Gritille, Hayaz, Cafer, Assoud, and Tell es-Sinn), domestic goats, sheep, and pigs substantially replaced wild animals as sources of protein during the same general period. Together these settlements record the emergence in the region of a distinctive and powerful two-sided economy that combined various mixes of three cereal crops, peas,

Workmen excavate a rectangular mud-brick house at the early farming village of Gritille in southeastern Turkey.

and beans, with a fairly balanced dependence on three reliable and prolific herd animals. When cattle are added to the list of domesticates after 8000 B.P., the economic base is in place for the subsequent rise of cities and states in the Near East and beyond. Thus, even though the domestication of animals trails the first cultivation of cereals by a full thousand years, it is of equal importance in the development of agriculture in the Fertile Crescent.

The introduction of domesticated goats from the area in the Zagros where apparently they were first domesticated certainly provides part of the explanation for the development of a strong regional two-sided economy in the central section of the Fertile Crescent. Just as domesticated cereals had arrived from the Levantine corridor and been adopted centuries earlier, domestic goats were probably introduced from the east, along with the skills needed to

manage herds. Those skills then could well have been applied to domesticate first sheep and then pigs.

The importance of sheep and pigs as wild prey in this central section of the Fertile Crescent, and the fact that sites in the area contain the earliest evidence of their domestication, strongly suggest that this is where they were first domesticated. Only in this central section do either sheep or pigs play much of a role in early herding economies; goats were still the favored domesticated animals in both the western and eastern sections of the Fertile Crescent.

The simple introduction of goats is not the only explanation that has been proposed for the initial domestication of sheep and pigs in the central section of the Fertile Crescent. Permanent villages and the cultivation of cereal crops are seen as likely prerequisites for the domestication of animals, for field stubble and surplus straw from harvested fields would have provided the stable food supply necessary to support livestock herds.

It also has been suggested that animals, like wild grasses a thousand years earlier, were first domesticated as a necessary adaptive response to an increase in the human population. The hunting of wild animals, it is proposed, could no longer supply the ever-expanding needs of growing villages for meat. Supporting archaeological evidence for this theory, however, is very limited. An obvious response in this situation would be for a portion of the village to "bud off" and establish a new village some distance away. To make the case that population increase causes animal domestication one would first have to show that the simple safety valve of "budding off" was no longer an option because there was no longer any locally available farmland where families could easily relocate. This certainly does not seem to be the case. Farming villages do not appear to have been closely packed; on the contrary they seem to have been relatively widely scattered.

Alternatively, perhaps animals were first domesticated within a "stress-free" situation, simply as a means to reduce the uncertainties of hunting. Domestic herds would have brought the same advantages as stored surplus grain. They were a clear indication of the relative wealth, security, and well-being of the village and the family. They provided insurance against future hard times and enabled their owners to wield influence by contributing to others in times of need.

The clear economic and social advantages of domestic herds go a long way toward explaining the rapid spread of domesticated goats westward from the Zagros across the Fertile Crescent beginning about 9000 B.P. Sometime between 8700 and 8500 B.P., at the same time goats were added to the farming economies of the central third of the Fertile Crescent, they appear to have arrived in the Levant. Here goat herds rapidly replaced wild gazelles as the major source of meat, and they dominated the herding side of the powerful two-sided agricultural economies that emerged in the region.

The Emergence of Balanced Agricultural Economies

The emergence of agricultural economies followed a different historical pathway in the eastern section of the Fertile Crescent than in regions to the west. Here goats played an important role right from the beginning. The small village of Ganj Dareh, first occupied about 9000 years ago, has produced the region's earliest evidence for both domestic cereals and domestic goats.

As we have seen, Brian Hesse has presented a convincing case, based on age and sex profiles, for the presence of domestic goats in level D at Ganj Dareh, which was a small settlement of rectangular mud-brick houses. Both Uerpmann and Helmer suggest that the small size of the goats in the underlying earliest level in the settlement (Level E) indicates that they too were domesticated. In addition, Willem van Zeist has identified domesticated two-rowed barley in both levels D and E, and barley grains from Level E have been directly radiocarbon-dated by the AMS method to 9000 B.P. Thus while the earliest evidence for agricultural settlements in the eastern section of the Fertile Crescent comes as much as a thousand years or so later than in the Levantine corridor, it was in this region that domesticated field crops and domestic animals were first combined into a mixed or two-sided agricultural economy.

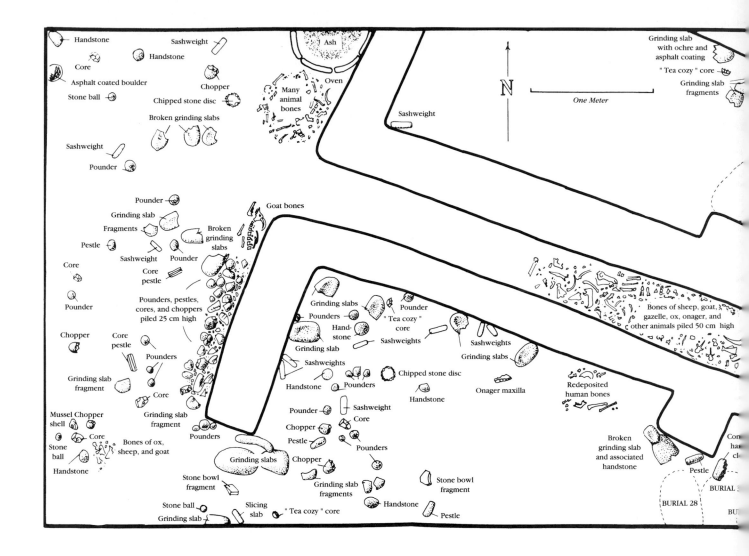

It was only with the westward spread of domestic goats and herding after 9000 B.P. that mixed economies developed in the Levant and the central section of the Fertile Crescent. It is not surprising that agricultural economies that combined both cereal cultivation and goat herding first appeared in the eastern section of the Fertile Crescent, given that hunter-gatherers in the region had long coordinated their seasonal use of wild grasses and wild goats and sheep. Each spring hunter-gatherer groups would leave their winter settlements on the valley floor and gradually relocate their campsites to higher elevations, timing their movements to both the harvest schedule for ripening stands of wild grasses and the associated seasonal migration of wild goats and sheep. As a result of this long and close relationship

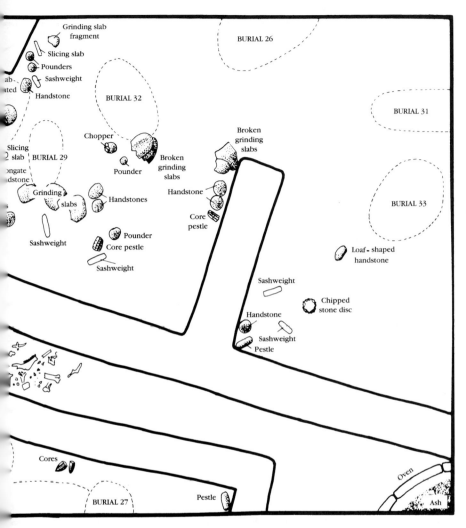

Houses at Ali Kosh. Careful excavation of portions of two house structures at the 8000-year-old farming village of Ali Kosh uncovered a dense pattern of discarded tools, animal bones, and other artifacts.

with their prey, as well as their long-maintained practice of harvesting wild grasses with sickles, these migrating hunter-gatherer societies were well prepared for the transition to closer management of these wild species that led to domestication.

In view of the strong genetic evidence that domestic barley and the emmer and einkorn wheats were each domesticated once, in a single location,

it now seems clear that the domestic cereals were introduced into the eastern section of the Fertile Crescent, rather than independently brought under domestication there.

Goats could well have been domesticated in the Zagros before cultivated cereals arrived, however, with the managed herds moving through the long-established seasonal journey to higher-elevation summer pastures much as their wild cousins did. The arrival of domesticated cereals and the beginning of their cultivation near valley floor settlements, however, would have provided field stubble and straw for domestic herds to feed on during the winter.

With the planting of field crops, these valley settlements could also have become more permanent, as the inhabitants supplemented the seasonal search for wild grasses and caprines with the cultivation of crops and in some cases eventually became largely dependent on an agricultural economy. While the small site of Ganj Dareh, with its domestic barley and bezoar goats, provides a glimpse of this transition to agriculture in the Zagros, the best picture yet available of an early farming settlement in the region is provided by Ali Kosh. This settlement was first occupied about 8500 to 8000 B.P., as agriculture expanded into more challenging, less easily farmed areas along the margins of the eastern section of the Fertile Crescent. Situated in the harsh marginal environment of the Deh Luran Plain in Khuzistan, Iran, the site was excavated in the fall of 1963 by Frank Hole of Yale University, Kent Flannery of the University of Michigan, and James Neely of the University of Texas. After excavating several test trenches in the 135-meter-diameter mound, they chose for more thorough exploration an area of 10 by 10 meters reaching down through more than 6 meters of occupational debris.

The archaeologists carefully screened excavated soil and applied flotation recovery on a larger scale than ever before. They found impressive evidence of the economic base of the early farming village of mud-brick houses that was established at Ali Kosh about 8500 to 8000 years ago. While the economy of this village shows clear continuity with earlier hunter-gatherers' adaptations to the local area, it also exhibits some dramatic similarities to an agricultural village dating more than 1300 years earlier at the opposite end of the Fertile Crescent—Netiv Hagdud.

The initial settlers at Ali Kosh, like those at Netiv Hagdud, relied on a wide variety of wild plants and animals—Flannery termed it a "broad spectrum" economy. Ninety percent of the seeds recovered from the earliest village levels were from wild legumes and small-seeded wild grasses such as oat grass, wild alfalfa, and canary grass. Not surprisingly, large grazers of the open steppe such as gazelles, onagers (wild asses and half-asses), and aurochs (wild cattle) were important prey species for Ali Kosh hunters, just as they were at Netiv Hagdud. A far more significant similarity, however, was the villagers' reliance on the animal life in and around the nearby waters. Filling a role similar to Netiv Hagdud's spring and lake habitats, a slough and associated marshy area were identified as the sources of the variety of bones of pigs, fish, shellfish, turtles, shorebirds, and migratory waterfowl recovered at Ali Kosh.

As at Netiv Hagdud, the high water table around the margins of marshy areas close to Ali Kosh allowed the villagers to cultivate domesticated cereals at little risk—in this case emmer wheat and two-rowed hulled barley, which would have been brought into the region as fully domesticated field crops. These cereals were apparently accompanied as well by several nonindigenous weeds (wild einkorn, ryegrass, goatface grass). Seeds of club rush, a marsh species, were also recovered in association with the domestic cereals, an indication that the area the farmers chose for cultivation was the moist soil at the edge of the marsh. Sickle blades, grinding slabs, and other processing tools, along with storage facilities, are also present at Ali Kosh, attesting to the important, if as yet limited, role cereal crops must have played in the broad-spectrum economy of this early farming village.

In many important respects, then, Ali Kosh is similar to Netiv Hagdud, far to the west. Both settlements were small villages of mud-brick houses. Both relied on broad-spectrum hunting-and-gathering economies centered on grazing animals, primarily gazelles, and aquatic species, along with wild seed-bearing plants. Both communities added the cultivation of domesticated cereals as another, certainly welcome, but not dominant component of the economy, and in each community the fields were situated in low-risk settings at the edge of a lake or slough, where the water table was high.

What sets Ali Kosh apart so dramatically from Netiv Hagdud is the presence of early domestic goats, which at first played an important but small role in the economy. Just as domestic cereals were added to a wide variety of wild plants, so the herding of domestic goats was added to a diverse hunting economy. Neither barley at Netiv Hagdud nor the bezoars at Ali Kosh played a dominant economic role at the beginning.

Agriculture, in fact, never did come to dominate the economy of Ali Kosh. After several centuries the village reached a size of about one hectare and a population of perhaps 100 people. Houses were larger and more substantial, fields were larger, and the contribution of emmer and barley to analyzed seed assemblages increased from less than 5 to 40 percent. But because the land of the Deh Luran Plain was only marginally suited to agricultural use, wild plants and animals remained a large part of the village diet throughout the long span of its occupation, with domestic goats and cereal crops providing an essential measure of security and reduced economic risk. At 8000 B.P., while Ali Kosh was a small farming village still heavily dependent on wild plants and animals, other villages in areas more favorable for agriculture had grown and prospered as their herds multiplied and their fields expanded.

The present-day village of Biriman, in the Euphrates Valley of southeast Turkey. This small farming village of mud-brick houses, surrounded by wheat fields, and harboring herds of sheep and goats in the foreground, is likely quite close to what early agricultural settlements looked like in the Fertile Crescent more than 8000 years ago.

By this time a rich variety of agricultural economies had emerged in various regions of the Fertile Crescent, and farming societies were rapidly approaching entirely new, more productive, and also more demanding forms of agriculture. Over the next thousand years domestic cattle and the development of the plow and irrigation technology would begin to open broad new vistas of cultural and economic development. Ali Kosh played no part in these developments, but it does provide a clear view of the transition to a farming way of life that for the first time successfully integrated both domestic plants and animals, and in so doing illuminates a final key aspect of the long and complex emergence of agriculture in the Fertile Crescent.

A Drama in Three Acts

Between 10,000 and 8000 years ago the Fertile Crescent witnessed the gradual emergence of agricultural economies based on various combinations of seven core species of domesticated plants and animals. These seven domesticates, along with the human societies that brought them under domestication, are the major players in this 2000-year-long drama that played out across the region. To understand the drama in all its complexity, we have to know the particular attributes that fitted these different players so admirably to their roles.

In clear contrast to most of the other wild plants, for example, wild emmer, einkorn, and barley grew in dense, easily harvested wild stands, produced impressive yields, and were important sources of food long before they were domesticated, so the technology necessary to harvest, store, and process them was already in place. Judging from modern field studies, these wild grasses were clearly capable of responding to human cultivation with immediate and impressive yields, even in settings very different from their natural habitat. Once they were subjected to the new selection pressures created by deliberate planting and harvesting, they quickly underwent morphological changes that happened to make them even more productive and more valuable. Clearly the wild cereals were preadapted to domestication. These were the species that most impressively responded to what must have been wide-ranging experiments in the manipulation, control, and cultivation of a great variety of wild plants. Hunter-gatherers probably auditioned many wild plant species, but only a few were given major roles.

Similarly, it is not difficult to see why they domesticated sheep, goats, cattle, and pigs but left the gazelles and other species alone. In the particular region where each species was first domesticated, it was already an important part of the human economy. Gazelles, too, were often hunted in many areas, but they were skittish and hard to control. Goats, sheep and cattle, in contrast, had star qualities. They could adjust to human management, and their very social and submissive group behavior allowed human herders to step in and usurp leadership positions. Wild pigs, too, were preadapted for human management. These plants and animals, selected for starring roles in the drama played out on the relatively small stage of the Fertile Crescent, are still major players in the farming economies that today, 8000 years later, feed much of the world's population.

Act I of this drama opens about 10,000 years ago in the Levantine corridor, when societies that had settled in permanent villages near lakes and springs began to experiment with ways to increase the harvest and dependability of wild grasses. Seeds were scattered across small prepared fields where the water table was high, on alluvial fans and at lake edges. The success of these experiments, probably both immediate and impressive, promised predictable and clearly expandable harvests in future years. Once the cultivation of grasses was begun, recognizable morphological changes in the plants themselves followed in 20 to 200 years. By 9000 B.P. cereal crops had spread beyond the Levantine corridor and around the arc of the Fertile Crescent.

While many human societies in the region, particularly in surrounding less watered and more marginal areas, continued to rely entirely on wild plants and animals, other villages in more favorable settings adopted domestic crops, adding them to their economic base. As the cultivation of cereals became more sophisticated over the centuries, villagers developed new varieties of cultigens such as six-rowed hulled barley, naked or unhulled barley, and the bread wheats, and at some point between 9800 and

9000 B.P., the practice of cultivating them likely expanded into areas of low water tables where crops were watered by rainfall alone.

While Act I, starring the cereals, begins in the western section of the Fertile Crescent, and unfolds as it expands to the north and east, Act II opens in the eastern section, in the Zagros, and unfolds westward, as the bezoar takes center stage. By 9000 years ago, communities of the Kermanshah Valley in the Zagros (Ganj Dareh) and over a larger area of the eastern section of the Fertile Crescent had begun to manage captive goat herds. We still cannot say for certain whether they began this practice before adding domesticated cereals to their hunting-gathering economies, but the peoples of the Zagros certainly have a long history of relying on caprines and vertical transhumance as a way of life. Their intimate knowledge of herd behavior patterns and seasonal movements, gained over thousands of years as they followed the annual migration cycle of goats into high summer pastures and back down again to winter grazing lands at lower elevations, would have helped them to achieve impressive results when they established the first captive goat herds. The herders would have continued following the same millennia-old annual cycle of vertical transhumance. When these small, nonsedentary societies in the Zagros added captive herds to their otherwise hunting-and-gathering way of life, they set themselves apart from all other human populations on the earth: they were managing and manipulating a major source of meat protein.

These societies soon set themselves apart in an even more important way: for the first time they combined the herding of a domesticated animal, the bezoar, with the cultivation of a domesticated cereal crop (barley and to a lesser extent emmer). It was a modest beginning but it heralded a major change in human history. After 9000 B.P., with goat herding expanding westward out of the Zagros into areas where cereals had long been cultivated, Act II draws to a close and attention shifts to center stage.

It was in the central section of the Fertile Crescent, between 8700 and 8200 years ago, that the agricultural economies took shape that subsequently fueled a long and complex developmental sequence leading up to the formation of the first city-states. These farming systems were formed by the coalescence of three major currents of innovation: first, cereal cultivation, which had expanded and diversified considerably since it was introduced from the Levantine corridor centuries earlier; second, the herding of domesticated goats, which appears to have arrived from the Zagros by 8700 B.P., and the development of two-sided economies including both plants and animals; third, the local addition of two more domesticated animals, the sheep and the pig.

With the coalescence of these three streams of innovation, agricultural economies of this region became qualitatively distinct from the earlier "cereals only" farming economies of Act I and the simpler bezoars and barley adaptations of Act II. The Act III economies have the advantage of diversity, and that advantage gives them the potential for explosive growth and expansion into a wide range of environmental settings. Farming societies now had a rich variety of strategies to choose from as they set about to combine available wild species with cultivated crop plants and domestic animals in ways that would be most advantageous to them in their particular environmental and cultural landscape.

The three areas of the Fertile Crescent thus at various times witnessed equally important episodes in the process by which agriculture emerged in the region. As Act III draws to a close, domestic cattle, the plow, and irrigation are just about to appear, and far from ending, the drama is about to explode southward along the Tigris and Euphrates and far beyond, into Africa and Europe.

5

EUROPE AND
AFRICA

 Shown here in a Roman mosaic from Saint Romain-en-Bal, France (A.D. 200–250), cattle were of central importance as draft animals and a source of food in the spread of farming across northern Europe between 6500 and 6000 years ago. Sickles for harvesting grains and adzes for shaping house timbers, shown on the facing page, also trace the agricultural colonization of Europe.

By 8000 years ago the Fertile Crescent and Anatolia had witnessed the development of agricultural economies that were remarkable both in the array of species domesticated and in the diversity of ways these species had been combined to exploit the op-

portunities presented by particular environments. Between 8000 and 7000 years ago, this flexible and multifaceted new agricultural way of life was carried westward into the Balkans and around the shores of the Mediterranean basin. In some places

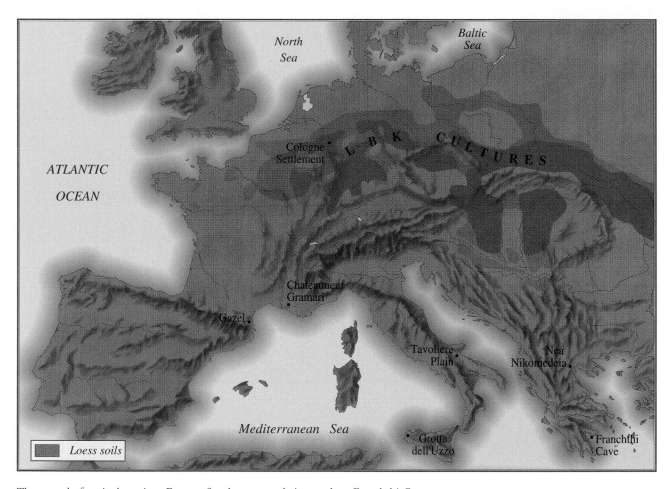

The spread of agriculture into Europe. Southern coastal sites such as Franchthi Cave, Grotta dell'Uzzo, and Gazel show the early selective adoption, by 8000 to 7800 B.P., of some domesticates but not others into long-established hunting-and-gathering economies. Fully formed agricultural societies appear in northern Greece (Nea Nikomedeia) and the Tavoliere Plain of Italy between 7500 and 7000 years ago. By 6500 to 6000 B.P., farming communities of the so-called LBK cultures (gray areas) had colonized northern Europe, where they were found in areas of rich loess soils (red areas).

individual domesticates were gradually added to indigenous hunting-and-gathering economies; in others, fully agricultural villages sprang up. The story of agriculture's beginnings in North Africa, the Nile Valley, and Europe is largely the story of the introduction into these regions of plants and animals that were first brought under domestication in the Fertile Crescent, and the subsequent tailoring of the farming way of life to different environments and climates. There were geographical limits, however, to the initial spread of agriculture out of the Fertile Crescent into Europe and Africa. To the south the Sahara at first posed a barrier to the spread of farming, while to the north the cold winters of north Europe similarly blocked early agricultural expansion.

Researchers are not in complete agreement, however, regarding the origin of some domesticated plants and animals that are of central importance in the emergence of agriculture in Europe and North Africa. Were all of the domesticates in these regions introduced from the Fertile Crescent? Or were some domesticated independently in Europe or Africa? If so, did Europe or Africa represent a second center of domestication or the only center of domestication from which the domesticated species later spread eastward into the Fertile Crescent? Pigs and cattle have been the subjects of most of the speculation on possible independent centers of domestication in Europe and North Africa. The wild ancestors of the other five core domesticates of the Fertile Crescent had restricted geographical ranges, but wild pigs and cattle ranged far across Asia and Europe. Did people in several places domesticate them independently?

Modern genetic research can often resolve such issues definitively. Genetic analysis has demonstrated that multiple domestications—the independent domestication of the same species in different places, at different times, by different societies—was more common than anyone once imagined. We now know, for example, that two species of beans (*Phaseolus vulgaris* and *P. lunatus*) were independently domesticated in Middle America and South America, and that a species of squash (*Cucurbita pepo*) was brought under domestication twice, once in Middle America and once in eastern North America. In each of these cases, scientists compared the genetic makeup of present-day wild and domesticated populations of the plants in question, and discovered that domesticated forms had been developed from separate wild populations that were geographically isolated from each other.

Most of the modern domesticated land races of the common bean (*Phaseolus vulgaris*) in Mexico, for example, contain a distinctive type of phaseolin protein that occurs in only a small number of wild *P. vulgaris* populations in southwest Mexico. This shared genetic characteristic marks these particular wild populations as the ancestors of the Mexican lineage of domesticated common beans. Similarly, modern land races of common beans in South America have a group of distinctive phaseolin proteins, different from those found in Mexico, which occur only in certain populations of South American wild beans. The differences in phaseolin protein observed in present-day Mexican and South American common beans thus indicate that they were domesticated independently in the two regions.

By employing the same general approach—establishing the degree of biological affinity between populations of plants and animals, wild and domesticated, at the molecular level—it is possible, in theory, to resolve questions about the number of times a species was domesticated, and where it was domesticated. Wide-scale genetic comparisons of wild populations and domesticates can reveal the identity of wild progenitors. While some of these new methods may be applied in the future to archaeological specimens, they are at present used only on living populations. As a result, it is difficult to apply genetic approaches if wild populations no longer exist throughout their former range.

For now, at least, the pigs and cattle of the Fertile Crescent are largely beyond the reach of genetic investigations to determine their centers of origin. Wild cattle are now extinct, and little research has been done on surviving wild pigs in Europe, the Near East, and Africa. What other kinds of information might shed light on such questions? When domesticated species such as pigs or cattle appear beyond the known geographical range of their wild ancestors, we can safely assume that they were introduced into the region. But when domesticates such as pigs and cattle show up in the archaeological record in different places within the known range of their wild progenitor, and genetic answers are not available, how can we know whether they were domesticated in one place and then introduced into adjacent areas, or if they were domesticated independently in two or more places?

In the absence of genetic answers, researchers are forced to turn to far less sophisticated kinds of information. First, did the domesticated species clearly appear earlier in one place than in others? If it did, that has to be considered the most likely place of its first domestication. Conversely, places where a domesticate shows up later have to be considered as likely to have obtained the domesticate from elsewhere, although independent domestication is still a possibility. Establishing the relative antiquity of domesticated species in different areas, then, is of crucial importance. In the 1970s the remains of domesticated pigs were recovered from the site of Nea Nikomedeia in Macedonia, and initial radiocarbon dates suggested an age of 8200 B.P., almost as old as the earliest reported domesticated pigs in the Fer-

tile Crescent. For several years the possibility that Macedonia was an independent center of pig domestication was considered. When later radiocarbon dating reduced the age of the Macedonian pigs to about 7500 years ago, however, they looked much more like immigrants than local domesticates.

Researchers also compare potential centers of domestication to determine the relative strength of the evidence. As we saw in Chapter 4, the evidence for the domestication of pigs in the Fertile Crescent is clear and convincing: the teeth found at many sites showing the reduction in size expected after domestication. A cave in southern China has also yielded evidence of domesticated pigs, but it is not as convincing. Here, mandibles indicate that 85 percent of the pigs were less than two years of age when they were killed, which could mean that humans were managing pigs for meat production. It could also indicate the hunting of wild pigs, however, since little is known about the age profile of wild pigs killed by human hunters. Unfortunately, we do not yet know if these early Chinese pigs were long snouted or short snouted. For now, the pigs from China, which date anywhere from 8500 to 6500 B.P., perhaps making them as old as the earliest domesticated pigs from the Fertile Crescent, could represent an example of independent domestication. Given the distance between the two regions and the possibility of similar time frames, it seems conceivable that *Sus scrofa* was independently domesticated in China and the Fertile Crescent.

The recovery of cattle bones from several sites in the eastern Sahara that date earlier than 8000 B.P. has led Fred Wendorf and Angela Close of Southern Methodist University to propose that this species was independently domesticated in North Africa, perhaps as early as 9000 years ago—a thousand years or more before domesticated cattle appear in the Fertile Crescent. In this case the two

This cave painting from Tassili n'Ajjer in Algeria, which may be 5000 to 6000 years old, evokes the central role of cattle in African pastoral economies. By 5000 to 4000 years ago, domesticated cattle and a pastoral way of life had extended as far south as the southern Sahara.

regions differ considerably in the evidence they provide. As we have seen, a clear reduction in the size of cattle associated with domestication has been documented at several sites in the Fertile Crescent shortly after 8000 B.P. The cattle bones recovered from the eastern Sahara, in contrast, are few and fragmentary, and in size and other morphological characteristics they cannot be distinguished from those of wild cattle. But Wendorf and Close propose that the eastern Sahara, with its lack of permanent sources of surface water, could not have supported wild cattle at that time. If humans herded domesticated cattle there, however, they could have dug dry-season wells into seasonal lake beds to provide year-round sources of drinking water. Therefore, the cattle whose bones were found in archaeological sites must have been domesticated. While this is an interesting argument, and may be correct, it is weakened by the absence of any clear evidence of a reduction in the size of the cattle. Many researchers are hesitant to accept arguments for animal domestication in the absence of supporting evidence in the form of clear size reduction and changes in age and sex profiles indicating managed herds. For now, the evidence suggests that cattle were domesticated only once, in the Fertile Crescent.

Relatively little archaeological research in Africa south of the Sahara has focused directly on agricultural origins. As a result, the emergence of distinct African agricultural economies can be sketched in only the most general way. A substantial amount of research has also been done on present-day varieties of African crop plants and their wild ancestors, providing additional insights into the early history of farming economies along the southern margin of the Sahara. First, though, let us follow the domesticates northward into Europe.

The First Domesticates along the South Coast of Europe

Domesticated plants and animals made their first appearance at a number of places along the southern edge of Europe about 8000 to 7800 years ago, not just in one but in a number of places, more than a thousand years after the peoples of the Fertile Crescent had begun to cultivate crops. How was agriculture introduced to Europe? Did agricultural so-

cieties migrate westward and settle in the continent? Or did the Europeans somehow adopt domesticates from the Fertile Crescent? Did they make a wholesale shift to a fully farming way of life, or did they accept a few domesticates into their existing subsistence strategies?

It is entirely possible that the inhabitants of southern Europe were able to learn about the domestication of plants and animals even without direct contact with agricultural peoples, through trade networks that had long been established around the Mediterranean sea. Livestock and seeds could have been passed along with other commodities down the line of exchange between neighboring societies along the coast. Although no watercraft have yet been found that date to this period, there is good indirect evidence that the people along the Mediterranean coast had considerable seafaring capabilities long before the first domesticates appeared. That they could pursue deep-water fish such as tuna, which typically weigh several hundred pounds, is indicated by the large fish vertebrae that begin to appear in coastal sites on the Greek mainland about 9200 years ago. Obsidian from the island of Melos in the Aegean also begins to show up on the mainland of Greece at the same time, attesting to successful open-water voyages of 150 kilometers or, more likely, island hops of 30 kilometers or so, a full millennium before domesticates entered the Mediterranean networks of exchange.

In fact, it is most likely that trade, not western migration, brought agriculture to southern Europe. The story of the first European farmers and herders can be read in the excavations at five cave sites: Franchthi Cave in southern Greece, Grotta dell'Uzzo in western Sicily, and Chateauneuf, Gazel, and Gramari caves in southern France.

The Franchthi Cave contains an extraordinary record of human prehistory: the cave was occupied

Franchthi Cave, on the southern coast of Greece. Excavation of this large cave and the shoreline in front of it, has documented that Near Eastern domesticates were adopted by local hunter-gatherers around 8000 B.P.

for 15,000 years, from 20,000 to 5000 B.P. Since those years bracket the introduction of domesticates, the remains in the cave offered archaeologists the opportunity to follow a society as it made the transition to an agricultural way of life. A study of the cave was launched by T. W. Jacobsen of Indiana University, who excavated the site from 1967 to 1974. During this time, Jacobsen's team carried out one of the most intensive archaeological sieving and flotation efforts ever undertaken.

Before 8000 B.P., the occupants of the cave survived entirely from hunting and gathering. They ate wild barley and lentils, wild cattle and pigs, deer, shellfish, and fish. Then, around 8000 B.P., their way of life began to change. The people of the cave began to herd sheep and goats in a limited way and to plant emmer wheat and two-rowed hulled barley, while retaining their dependence on hunting and gathering. At this time they also expanded their settlement out of the cave and along the nearby shoreline.

These early experimenters were clearly not new arrivals. The pottery and the blade and ground-stone tools that appear about the same time as domesticates clearly developed from the stone and bone tools of earlier levels. Around 8000 years ago then, a group of people who had lived in Franchthi Cave a very long time added some domesticates to their well-established hunting-and-gathering way of life, but did not change that way of life in any substantial way.

Like Franchthi Cave, the Grotta dell'Uzzo on the northwest coast of Sicily, west of Palermo, was occupied for many thousands of years. And like Franchthi Cave, it sheltered a society of hunter-gatherers who adopted domesticates between 8000 and 7800 years ago. Indeed, although the cave is more distant from the sources of domesticates in the Fertile Crescent, its inhabitants raised even more types of domesticates: archaeologists have recovered both einkorn and emmer wheat, barley, and lentils from layers dating to 7900 B.P. And not only goats and sheep, but domestic cattle and pigs have been tentatively identified in deposits dating to the same period.

The wide array of domesticates at Grotta dell'Uzzo, however, does not mark an abrupt transition to an agricultural way of life. The wild plants and animals relied on by the earlier hunter-gatherers— red and roe deer, wild pigs, birds, sea mammals, tuna and other fish, acorns, and wild olives and legumes—continued to form a large part of the diet. These people, like those at Franchthi Cave, apparently enriched their hunting-and-gathering way of life with a few domesticates but otherwise lived much as they had done before.

Still farther west, along the south coast of France, archaeologists have found perhaps the clearest evidence of selective adoption of Near Eastern domesticates by hunter-gatherers. In caves at Chateauneuf and Gramari in southeast France and at Gazel in the Aude River valley in southwest France, the bones of clearly domesticated sheep, but no other domesticates, show up in layers dating from 8000 to 7800 years ago. The people who lived in these caves seem to have come back to them year after year to gather wild plants and hunt wild pigs and deer in the forests. The herding of domestic sheep on a small scale was compatible with this subsistence pattern, and sheep bones consistently account for from 2 to 20 percent of the animal remains recovered.

Sheep gradually increased in importance over the next thousand years along this portion of the Mediterranean coast, but the people here did not complete the transition to a fully sedentary agricultural way of life until after 7000 years ago. The people in some coastal plain areas of the eastern Mediterranean, however, took a very different route to agriculture perhaps 500 years earlier.

Early Farming Villages in Italy and Greece

Warfare has most often proved a bane of archaeologists, as on occasion their explorations have been interrupted by the flaring of hostilities in a region of study. But we now come to an example of how an activity of warfare actually helped archaeologists make a discovery. During World War II, allied photographers flying in military aircraft took aerial photographs of much of Italy. The photographs of the

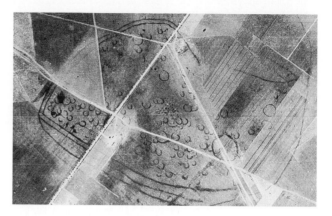

An aerial view of Passo di Corvo, a 7000-year-old farming settlement on the Tavoliere Plain of southern Italy. A series of ditches tracing the settlement perimeter enclosed the smaller circular ditches and walls, which were family compounds containing house structures and providing ample room for corralling livestock.

Tavoliere Plain in southeastern Italy proved to be of more than military interest. Those photographs revealed hundreds of large circular features on the landscape, each containing numerous smaller ring-like features.

Archaeologists were intrigued by the circles. When they excavated at the sites, they found the small partial circles to be ditches and earthen walls. The walls probably enclosed family compounds, since excavations in some of them uncovered one or more house structures. The larger circles also turned out to be ditches, this time encircling distinct communities. Some enclosures, such as the site of Passo di Corvo, are 500 meters or more in diameter and contain more than 100 house compounds. These enclosures were not all contemporaneous, but rather span a considerable period of time, beginning about 7200 to 7000 years ago and ending about 6500 B.P. Buried in the remains was evidence of the full complex of Near Eastern domesticates—emmer and einkorn wheat, two-rowed barley, lentils, sheep and goats, cattle and pigs.

The communities on the Tavoliere Plain, as well as comparable communities on the fertile plains of Macedonia and Thessaly in Greece, are the remains of complex, fully formed agricultural societies that seem to have appeared abruptly between 7500 and 7000 years ago. Both the Italian and Greek societies showed little continuity with local hunting-and-gathering groups in economy, material culture, or settlements. In the absence of any known evidence of indigenous development, these agricultural villages are thought to have been colonized by farming societies from other parts of southeastern Europe, but just where has not been identified.

Interestingly, these settlements are in areas that apparently held little appeal for hunter-gatherers, but that had excellent potential for the cultivation of cereals. Rather than being scattered at random across the landscape, the settlements of the Tavoliere Plain are situated adjacent to small pockets of light, well-drained, and easily tilled soils, which cover less than 20 percent of the whole plain. Here, on these lighter soils, people cultivated their cereals. In the winter, no doubt, they grazed their sheep and goats on the grasslands that dominated the Tavoliere, and in the spring moved their flocks to the better-watered pastures in the nearby uplands. This farming economy of 7200 years ago, which combined cereal cultivation with herding of sheep and goats on extensive summer and winter pastures, flourished in southeastern Italy right up into the historic period. As recently as the 1600s the Tavoliere Plain and adjacent uplands supported enormous flocks of sheep and goats, which were also herded back and forth between summer and winter pastures.

To the east, on the Macedonian and Thessalian plains of Greece, comparable farming villages first appear at about 7500 B.P., three to five centuries ear-lier than in Italy. These early farming communities grew much the same range of crops as those in Italy, and also herded sheep and goats. These small settlements ranged in size from one-half to one hectare and were usually situated in deciduous forests at the edges of coastal alluvial plains near their juncture with upland zones. Here the best arable soils were found—well drained, fertile, and easy to cultivate with simple light plows and hand tools. Although mountainous hinterlands and nearby river floodplains provided summer and winter pasturage for livestock, these farming villages are thought to have depended primarily on cereal grains and legumes that were intensively cultivated in small clearings in the forest. By rotating crops and fertilizing their fields with human and livestock manure, farming villages of 50 to perhaps 200 people could grow enough to sustain themselves on fields covering 10 to 50 hectares.

Among the many farming villages that have been studied so far, the site of Nea Nikomedeia provides the best evidence of this early agricultural way of life. Named after a nearby modern village, the low-lying mound of Nea Nikomedeia was investigated by Robert Rodden and a team from Cambridge and Harvard universities from 1961 to 1963. During the 1963 season the team excavated over half an acre of the site's thin 18-inch layer of occupational debris and clay from collapsed house walls, exposing a number of superimposed rectangular structures that had been built during two different periods. Of the seven structures of varying size and organization erected during the earlier period, six are thought to be ordinary houses while the seventh structure apparently served some ritual purpose. Centrally located and considerably larger than the other structures, this "shrine" yielded five female ceramic figurines, which presumably were fertility symbols.

The farming economy at Nea Nikomedeia was based primarily on emmer wheat, accompanied by einkorn, barley, and legumes. Sheep and goats accounted for 70 percent of the animal bones, cattle and pigs contributed another 20 percent, and wild species (primarily deer and wild pigs) accounted for the remainder.

The seemingly abrupt appearance, and impressive success, of fully farming settlements such as Nea Nikomedeia on the fertile coastal plain regions of Greece by 7500 years ago, and along the Dalmatian coast as well as in Italy by 7000 B.P., can be explained at least in part by the ease with which Near Eastern agriculture could be transferred around the Mediterranean. The climate and growing seasons of the coastal plains of southern Europe were similar to those of the Fertile Crescent and Anatolia, so long-established Near Eastern farming technology

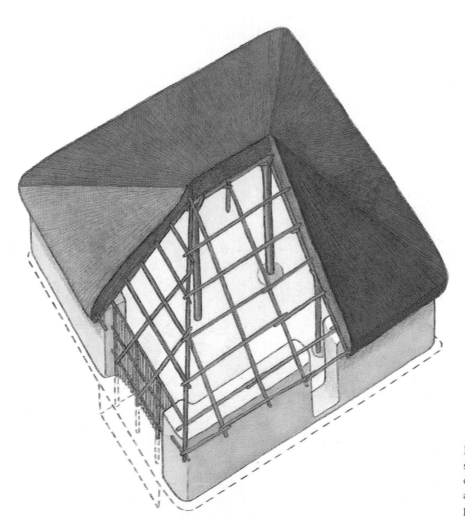

Houses at Nea Nikomedeia were substantial structures, with thick walls of clay plastered onto frames of saplings and reeds. Interior posts supported a pole-and-thatch roof.

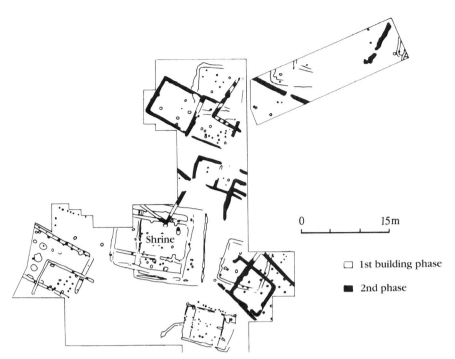

Part of the community plan at Nea Nikomedeia, showing houses constructed during two phases of building (the second in black) and the central shrine that yielded female figurines.

0   15m

☐ 1st building phase

■ 2nd phase

and practices required few modifications when they were introduced into the region. Of particular importance was the fact that crops could still be planted in the fall and harvested in the spring. And because farming zones on the coastal plains of southern Europe had access to summer grazing areas at high elevations and abundant winter pasturage closer by, it was easy to introduce the vertical transhumance herding schedules of the Fertile Crescent into these regions.

Many parts of southern Europe were not so accommodating, and here hunting-and-gathering ways of life persisted for many centuries. Eventually they were replaced by various specialized forms of farming and herding, which in time evolved into the complex mosaic of traditional Mediterranean agricultural economies.

The Expansion of Agriculture into the Temperate Latitudes

Just as many parts of southern Europe could not accept Near Eastern farming systems in unmodified form, so too did the more northerly latitudes of Europe present a series of barriers to the expansion of agriculture. The vast expanse of northern forests held little promise for large-scale herding of sheep and goats, and the harsh winters offered little in the way of cold-season grazing. Whatever livestock was raised would have to be sustained on a food supply stored through the long winter months. The cold winters also made impossible the autumn planting and spring harvesting of crops that had so successfully spread across the coastal plains of southern Europe.

By 6700 years ago, however, a set of solutions to these problems had emerged, and they became the basis of a new, uniquely European, and remarkably standardized agriculture that rapidly expanded over a vast area. In general outline, the solutions seem straightforward enough. Emmer wheat continued to play a central, even dominant role, along with einkorn, legumes, and in some areas barley, but the schedule of planting was shifted to take advantage of higher spring rainfall and a spring-summer growing season. Crops were planted in the spring rather than the fall, and fall harvests replaced the spring harvests of southern agricultural systems.

At the same time, the climate and vegetation of temperate Europe clearly favored cattle and pigs over sheep and goats, which preferred the milder winters and more open grasslands of the Near East and Mediterranean. Cattle not only became a significant source of meat, but also served as draft animals and as a prolific source of manure for fertilizing the fields after the fall harvests. Cattle consistently account for more than half of the mammal bones recovered from the settlements of these first farmers of temperate Europe, but surprisingly the remains of pigs are only rarely found. Comfortable in close quarters, able to thrive on human leavings, producing large numbers of young that grow rapidly, pigs would seem to be obvious candidates to raise in temperate-forest agriculture. But instead of pigs, we find sheep and goats in a distant second

place behind cattle in the new farming system. Pigs are only occasionally present.

Once these modifications to the "southern cool-season" agriculture were in place, farming spread rapidly across central and western Europe. By 6500 to 6000 years ago, thousands of farming villages appeared as far east as Russia and as far west as northern France. Although these agricultural settlements were established over a vast area of Europe, they were almost always situated in a very specific setting. Just as was the case earlier in Greece and Italy, the key to the placement of these farming settlements was the right type of farmland. The wind-deposited loess soils that stretch in irregular and widely scattered bands across Europe are fertile, well drained, and easily tilled. These were the soils that the first farmers of temperate Europe consistently sought out and colonized. The early agricultural societies that settled the loess soils of northern Europe also shared a large number of other similarities in

Ceramic vessels such as these from southern Germany, with their distinctive linear bands of decoration, are the hallmark of LBK societies.

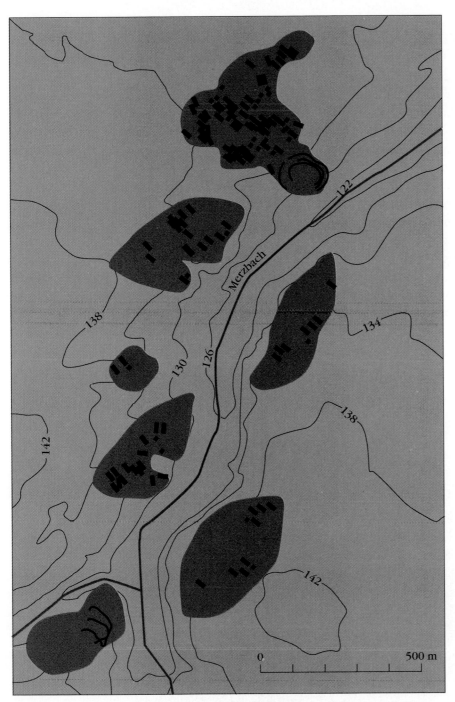

LBK settlements along the upper slopes of the Merzbach Valley near Cologne, Germany. The black rectangles are individual longhouses, and the curved black lines represent earthworks.

technology and in the placement and organization of their settlements. These numerous similarities over such a broad area underscore both the rapidity of the agricultural colonization of the loess lands, and the degree to which it was a standardized adaptation that was successfully repeated again and again across Europe.

Among the artifacts most frequently recovered from these farming settlements is a distinctive type of pottery with linear bands of designs. The German term for linear-band ceramics—*Linearbandkeramik* (abbreviated as LBK)—provides the general label that is applied to this remarkably uniform, broadly distributed group of societies. Other items of LBK material culture, such as distinctively shaped shoe-last adzes, are also very similar in form over broad areas, providing further evidence that these pioneers adhered rather conservatively to a particular way of life that opened up vast areas of Europe to agriculture.

LBK societies followed a generally consistent

pattern in locating their settlements, organizing their communities, and establishing their food production strategies. The typical LBK settlement was situated on the higher terrace or gently sloping upper margin of a secondary stream or river, very near or on upland loess soil. It was often within a few kilometers of another LBK site and part of a small regional cluster of ten to twenty settlements. These valley-margin farming "villages" have as their most distinctive feature large timber-framed longhouses.

Built with substantial internal support posts and wattle-and-daub walls, these structures measured 5 to 7 meters wide and anywhere from 12 to 45 meters long. Perhaps the houses varied in dimension to accommodate extended families of different size or degrees of affluence, or perhaps families had different requirements for the storage of field crops or the shelter of cattle, sheep, and goats. These extended-family longhouses were the basic social and economic building blocks of LBK society.

How socially and economically independent

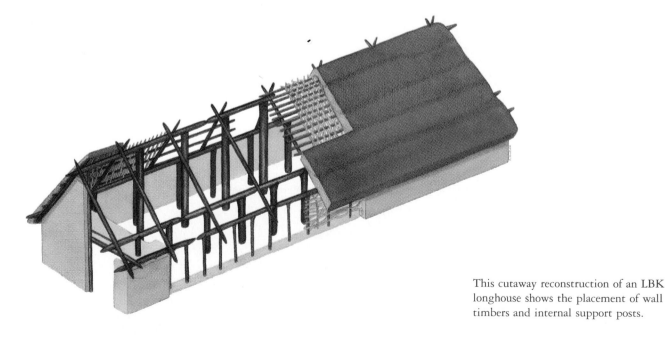

This cutaway reconstruction of an LBK longhouse shows the placement of wall timbers and internal support posts.

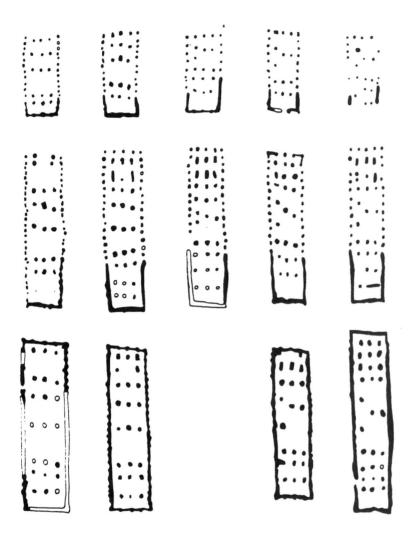

As these houseplans show, LBK long-houses varied considerably in size, reflecting differences in the size and social standing of the families that occupied them, as well as the space needed by those families for storing grain and perhaps sheltering livestock.

were these individual longhouse kin groups? To what extent were they enmeshed in various larger networks of cooperative community undertakings? For now, these questions remain largely unanswered. The longhouses of a particular locale, sometimes numbering more than 100, are often distributed rather widely across both space and the span of a settlement's sometimes long occupation, making it difficult to ascertain the number of structures oc-cupied at any one time, and their degree of social and economic integration.

With simple systems of manuring and crop ro-tation, the fields of LBK settlements were probably relatively small (perhaps 10 to 30 hectares, for pop-ulations of perhaps twenty to sixty), and relatively permanent, being cultivated for a number of years in succession. Although plant remains are generally poorly preserved and excavations yield only small samples of carbonized seeds, some of the weeds represented at LBK sites suggest small forest clearings and the presence of hedgerows and fixed fields. Emmer wheat is the most commonly recovered cereal and clearly the single most important crop, followed by einkorn. Barley is found only infrequently. LBK farmers also grew legumes, lentils, flax, fruits, and opium poppies.

Appearing rapidly across temperate Europe between 6700 and 6000 years ago, these thousands of small scattered clearings in the vast unbroken expanse of forest marked the beginning of a long transformation in the landscape and lifeways of the region. But the origins of agriculture in Europe are not solely a story of LBK colonization and the introduction of a fully integrated farming way of life. For LBK societies did not reach all the way to the Atlantic or the North Sea. In northern and western Europe and the British Isles, where soil and climate were less optimum, farming took hold more slowly. In these areas we find no abrupt appearance of a fully formed agricultural way of life. Hunting-and-gathering societies adopted a few domesticates—cereals, legumes, and livestock, especially sheep and goats—as minor additions to their way of life, in much the same way that domesticates were first adopted along the Mediterranean coast of Europe. Gradually farming economies that were finely tuned to the particular challenges and opportunities of different local environments emerged, creating complex patterns of quite diverse agricultural and pastoral adaptations across the region.

Indigenous African Agriculture

By 6500 years ago, about 1000 years after full farming economies had first emerged in southern Europe, they also appeared in the Nile Valley of northeastern Africa. The introduction of barley, sheep, goats, and cattle helped to fuel the remarkable development of civilization along the fertile floodplains of this great river. Independent of events along the Nile, other, uniquely African, farming economies also emerged along the southern margins of the Sahara about 5000 to 3000 years ago.

Most people think of the Sahara as a vast desolate desert of shifting sand dunes, but such was not entirely the case between 7000 and 4000 B.P., when parts of it offered some of the most favorable landscapes for human hunter-gatherers in all of Africa. Rainfall was greater then, and the Sahel grassland belt that borders the Sahara on the south extended farther north, displacing most of the southern part of the desert and a large portion of its central parts. During the rainy season the extensive grasslands of this area became dotted with shallow lakes and swampy depressions. Hunter-gatherer societies located their settlements at the edges of lakes and marshes, and people fished, hunted savannah herd animals, including wild cattle, and harvested wild grasses and other plants.

In this vast extension of the savannah, economies based on the herding of domesticated cattle emerged by about 5000 B.P., judging from the analysis of animal bones recovered from a number of archaeological sites dating to that time (Adrar Bous, Arlit, Meniet). The domesticated cattle whose bones have been identified at these sites were most likely introduced from northern Africa and the Nile Valley of stock initially domesticated in the western half of the Fertile Crescent, but some scholars argue for the independent domestication of *Bos* in the Sahara. Pastoral economies also became established on the savannahs of east Africa by about 4000 B.P. Diane Gifford-Gonzales of the University of California, Santa Cruz, has identified domesticated cattle and goats in several sites of that age in Kenya.

A pastoral village scene in the Sudan. Cattle have been at the center of North African herding economies for 5000 years.

Similarly, the herding of cattle and goats had reached the Dhar Tichitt region along the southwestern edge of the Sahara by about 3500 years ago.

While the other Near Eastern animal domesticates—sheep and pigs—do eventually become part of African herding and farming economies, it is cattle that gain early and lasting prominence as the most important domesticated animal south of the Sahara. The prominence of cattle in Africa parallels in an interesting way their prominence in temper-ate Europe, where cattle were essential to the success and spread of LBK agricultural societies.

There is a striking difference, however, between the early agricultural economies that swept across temperate Europe and those that developed in the Sahara-savannah zone of Africa. In Europe the wheats and barley introduced from the Near East were the major crop plants. In Africa, in contrast, it was three indigenous crop plants, not wheat and barley, that formed the basis of an agricultural way of life. These three African crop plants—millet, sorghum, and African rice—are today important sources of food for millions of people across Africa and Asia.

Of the three, African rice (*Oryza glaberrima*) has the most limited range of cultivation: today it is grown only in West Africa (Ivory Coast, Mali, Nigeria), where a number of tribes are heavily dependent on rice crops. In recent years, this African crop has been largely replaced in these areas by Asiatic rice (*Oryza sativa*). Although African and Asiatic rice belong to the same genus, and resemble each other, they were independently domesticated from different wild plants. African rice is grown today in upland forests, west of the Niger River, but its wild ancestor is a savannah plant that grows in water holes that fill up during the rains and then dry out in the dry season. The earliest evidence of domesticated African rice, dating to about A.D. 200, comes from the site of Jenne-Jeno near the bend of the Niger River, suggesting that this is the general area where it was brought under domestication.

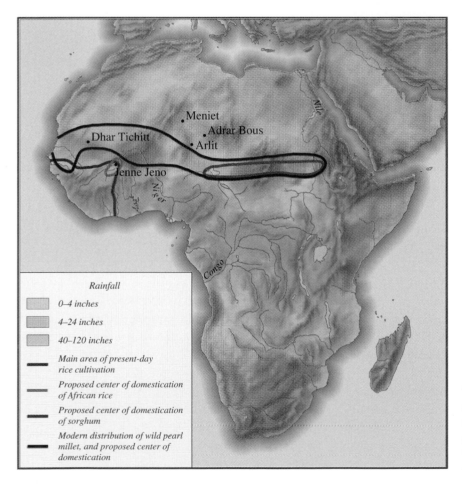

Rainfall

☐ 0–4 inches

☐ 4–24 inches

☐ 40–120 inches

— Main area of present-day rice cultivation

— Proposed center of domestication of African rice

— Proposed center of domestication of sorghum

— Modern distribution of wild pearl millet, and proposed center of domestication

The proposed areas of domestication of African rice, pearl millet, and sorghum, and the archaeological regions and sites that have yielded the earliest evidence of indigenous African agriculture.

A woman carries a bundle of rice after the harvest in Madagascar.

Patrick Munson of Indiana University has investigated sites of the Dhar Tichitt region along the southern margin of the Sahara, where he found evidence that pearl millet (*Pennisetum glaucum*) was being cultivated in the southwestern Sahara by about 3000 B.P. Earlier, by about 3500 years ago, societies in the Dhar Tichitt had established settlements at lake edges supported by cattle and goat herding, fishing, hunting, and the harvesting of wild plants. The plants in the ancient diet at Dhar Tichitt were recorded in the form of grain impressions preserved

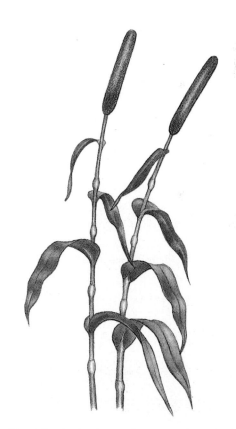

Pearl millet. The distinctive panicle, or seed head, of some varieties of this important African crop plant are more than a meter in length, while those of its wild ancestor are only 10 centimeters long.

The grasslands origin of African rice links it to the two other major African cereal crops—millet and sorghum, both of whose ancestors were drought-resistant savannah plants. There is little archaeological evidence for the early history of domestication of millet and sorghum, and it comes from the same central and southern Sahara areas that have yielded early evidence of domesticated cattle. The earliest evidence of domesticated sorghum (*Sorghum bicolor*) consists of a single impression of a grain in a piece of pottery from the site of Adrar Bous, dating to about 4000 B.P.

109

These pot sherds from the Niemilane site in the Dhar Tichitt region, Islamic Republic of Mauritania, contain grain impressions of domesticated millet. They document the initial cultivation of this crop in the southern Sahara by about 3000 years ago.

in pottery. Ninety-nine percent of the impressions recovered by Munson from sites dating between 3500 and 3000 B.P. were of a single wild plant— "kram-kram" (*Cenchrus biflorus*), which is widely collected in the region even today. At 3000 to 2900 B.P., however, domesticated pearl millet makes an abrupt appearance in the Dhar Tichitt economy, as 61 percent of the 121 grain impressions from this period exhibit definite characteristics of this domesticated crop plant.

Clearly in the Dhar Tichitt region cattle and goat herding economies had been established by 3500 B.P., and the cultivation of pearl millet was begun about 3000 years ago. The result was a mixed economy that was uniquely African in character. Similarly, in the central Sahara, at Adrar Bous, cattle were being herded by 5000 B.P., and the cultivation of sorghum seems to have begun by 4000 years ago. Although the archaeological evidence for the emergence and early history of agriculture in Africa

is admittedly meager at present, the information we do have would seem to indicate that mixed farming economies emerged in different parts of the Sahara between 5000 and 3000 years ago, as the herding of domesticated animals was first introduced into the region, and local seed crops were later domesticated.

A number of researchers have suggested that the timing of initial domestication of millet and sorghum was tied to the southward expansion of the desert, which intensified about 4000 years ago, displacing people south and forcing innovations and experimentation that led to plant cultivation. Alternatively, it is possible that in the future archaeologists will show that millet and sorghum were domesticated earlier than the evidence now indicates, during a period of abundant wild resources rather than a period of climatic stress. The climatic stress theory and its stress-free alternatives, similar to those proposed as leading to plant domestication in the Levantine corridor, are both worthy of further consideration.

At the same time that archaeologists have been searching for evidence of early African agriculture in ancient settlements of the Sahara, Jack Harlan has been tracing the early history of millet and sorghum by studying present-day types of these two crops and their wild relatives. Harlan, professor emeritus at the University of Illinois and the leading authority on the evolutionary history of African crop plants, has traveled extensively across Africa and studied herbarium collections around the world in order to map the present-day distribution of different varieties of millet, sorghum, and other crop plants and to reconstruct their history of development.

Harlan has identified three distinctive and long-established crop complexes that form a broad band stretching across Africa between 5 and 15 degrees north latitude. The Forest Margin complex, at the western end of this band, and the Ethiopian complex, at its eastern end, cover relatively small areas in comparison with the Savannah complex, which stretches across Africa from the Atlantic coast east to the upper Nile, along the dry southern edge of the Sahara desert. Little is known of the antiquity or history of the Forest Margin and the Ethiopian agricultures, and it is the crops of this Savannah complex—African rice, millet, and sorghum—that have been a main focus of Harlan's research.

Today sorghum is grown far beyond this Savannah complex zone, across a broad expanse of sub-Saharan Africa. In their research on this most important of African crop plants, Harlan and his colleagues visited most of the areas where it is now under cultivation, collecting plant specimens and

recording information about the morphology of the plant's large and distinctive seed head. Their work was not limited to living plants, however, for they also studied museum collections across Africa and in Europe. During the course of their field and herbarium research they analyzed more than 10,000 sorghum seed heads.

Based on differences in the morphology of the seed heads they studied, Harlan identified five basic types or races of sorghum: bicolor, guinea, kafir, caudatum, and durra. By looking at the geographical distribution of these five different types of sorghum, and the extent to which each was different from wild sorghum, Harlan was able to trace the evolution of this African cereal back through time to its initial domestication. He found that the seed heads of four of the five modern races of

Ripening seed heads of sorghum.

sorghum were highly evolved and very different from those of their wild ancestor, and that each of these specialized races was largely limited to a particular region of Africa. The guinea type dominates fields in West Africa, kafir predominates in South Africa, durra in Ethiopia, and caudatum in Chad and the Sudan.

The fifth modern race of domesticated sorghum, in contrast, had a very different pattern of regional distribution and abundance. Harlan found this bicolor type in almost every area where sorghum is cultivated today, but rarely was it ever abundant. The seed head of the bicolor race was also found to be quite primitive compared to the other four cultivated types of sorghum—it was much closer in appearance to wild sorghum than to durra, guinea, kafir, or caudatum.

This bicolor race, Harlan concluded, was the modern remnant of an early primitive form of domesticated sorghum that had spread widely and rapidly across Africa from its heartland of domestication thousands of years ago. After becoming established in different regions of Africa, bicolor developed into the four distinct sorghum races of today, while also surviving as a minor constituent of cultivated fields.

Where was the heartland of domestication of this primitive bicolor type? Harlan believes that sorghum was domesticated in the Chad-Sudan savannah region, along the southern margin of the Sahara. Today this is the region of greatest abundance of *Sorghum verticilliflorum,* the primary wild ancestor of the bicolor race. Here, in the tall-grass savannah landscape that stretches, pristine and largely undisturbed, across hundreds of kilometers, the wild ancestor of sorghum, growing to a height of 4 meters and remarkably productive, is still present today in enormous quantities.

Interestingly, Harlan's proposed savannah heartland of domestication of *Sorghum verticilliflorum* comes very close to the site of Adrar Bous, which has yielded the earliest evidence of sorghum cultivation, and in the climate of 7000 to 4000 years ago this savannah heartland could well have extended far enough north to include it. As is the case with African rice in West Africa, then, the archaeological and biological evidence points to sorghum being domesticated within the southern Sahara-savannah zone at about the time the desert started moving south.

In the case of pearl millet, too, archaeological excavation and research on modern plant populations suggests that this crop plant was domesticated somewhere along this almost continent-wide band of the southern Sahara that was once savannah but is now desert. The Dhar Tichitt region has produced the only early evidence of domesticated pearl millet, at 3000 B.P., but the present-day distribution of both wild and cultivated forms suggests that the plant could have been domesticated in any one of a number of other areas within the southern Sahara zone.

The wild ancestor of pearl millet (*Pennisetum violaceum*), whose 10-centimeter-long grain heads are less than 5 percent as long as those of some domesticated varieties, is a drought-resistant plant that grows across the southern desert from the Atlantic to the upper Nile. The major band of cultivation of domesticated varieties of pearl millet also follows this desert-savannah boundary across Africa.

While research on present-day plant populations indicates the general environmental zone within which the three major African cereals were domesticated, and these indications agree with the limited archaeological information, it is clear that additional excavation of early settlements is needed to clarify the timing, location, and cultural context of agricultural development in the region. What is known at present regarding the settlements and subsistence patterns of the societies that lived in the southern and central savannah zone some 5000 to 3000 years ago, however, does provide at least a partial picture of how plant domestication might have taken place.

Settlements were located along the margins of permanent lakes that would have enlarged in size during the rainy season and shrunk during the dry season. The lakes provided water for people and livestock, and fish and other wild species living in or along the lakes were important sources of food. Wild plants of the lake margin and savannah, including grasses, were also harvested, and of these, wild African rice, millet, and sorghum were probably important in the diet of these pastoral societies.

A number of scholars, including Jack Harlan and Patrick Munson, have suggested that domestication of these plants could well have taken place around the edges of these lakes, close to village settlements. The first plantings may have been synchronized with the regular seasonal fluctuation of lake levels. The French term *decrue,* meaning "the period when the floodwaters recede," is used to describe a method of cultivation that is today practiced widely in sub-Saharan Africa: seeds are planted along lake margins soon after the water begins to recede at the beginning of the dry season, and the crops grow to maturity solely on the water that is available in the soil. This method could have been employed by hunter-gatherers to expand the yields of wild rice, millet, and sorghum, leading to cultivation and domestication. It is interesting to note that the decrue method has parallels both to the groundwater cultivation used in the initial domestication of cereals in the Levantine corridor and to the initial cultivation of rice in East Asia, a crop and region to which we now turn.

6

EAST ASIA

Lowland wet rice agriculture, Lombok Island, Indonesia. In a setting much like this, and with the help of tools such as the 6400-year-old spades shown on the facing page, rice was first cultivated along the Yangtze River in South China more than 8000 years ago.

Extending for thousands of kilometers across northern China, the Great Wall has stood for more than 2000 years as a monumental boundary line between two very different ways of life and two very different environments. To the north and west of the wall, grasslands and deserts stretch away across the arid interior of Asia. Here lay the center of the Mogul dynasties and the heartland of the pastoral economies of the past. To the east and south of the wall, within reach of the warm, moisture-laden winds that blow in off the Pacific in the summer, vast forests once extended all the way to the coast. In this eastern woodlands zone, farming societies have flourished for more than 7000 years, the forests inexorably giving way over time to an ever-expanding agricultural landscape.

Originating in the Tibetan Plateau, two great eastward-flowing river systems drain most of the vast eastern woodlands of China—the Huang Ho, or Yellow River, in the north and the Yangtze in the south. It is along the banks of these two rivers that teams of Chinese archaeologists have uncovered the earliest evidence of agriculture in East Asia. In Honan and adjacent provinces, where the Yellow River completes its great loop and is joined by the Wei River, farming settlements based on the cultivation of drought-resistant millets and other crops date back as early as 7500 years ago. To the south, in the Hupei basin along the middle Yangtze, as well as along the coastal plain of Hang-chou Bay, in the Yangtze delta region south of Shanghai, sophisticated farming societies were cultivating domesticated rice by about 8500 to 6500 years ago. At the same time that the domesticates and farming systems of the Fertile Crescent were being introduced along the Mediterranean coast of southern Europe and spreading across the loesslands of northern Europe, China was witnessing the independent and parallel emergence of two quite distinct agricultural ways of life along its two great river systems.

The Yangtze River and the Rise of Rice Agriculture

Stretching from east to west at about the 34th parallel, the Ch'in Ling mountain range and its eastern extensions separate the Yellow River system of north China from south China and the Yangtze. Sheltered by these mountains from the cold, dry winter winds blowing out of Central Asia, and open to the weather patterns of the Pacific, south China has a moister, more stable climate than the north. Year-round rainfall is both much higher in the south, with a pronounced summer peak, and far less variable, with far fewer droughts and floods. In this moist temperate to subtropical climate, the Yangtze River valley offered an ideal environment for the development of rice-centered agricultural societies.

Today rice (*Oryza sativa*) accounts for half of the food eaten by 1.7 billion people and 21 percent of the total calories consumed by our species. It stands out from the other major food crops in that it is in large part grown in flooded fields, or "paddies." "Dryland" or "upland" varieties of rice that are watered only by rain account for about 10 percent of the rice cultivated, and "deep-water" varieties grown at depths greater than 50 centimeters account for another 15 percent. A full three-fourths of today's rice crop is grown in shallow water (5 to 50 centimeters) in lowland settings. Some of these paddies are surrounded by dams and artificially flooded, and others are flooded by rainfall.

Based on plant characteristics and genetic analysis, it is thought that the varieties of rice grown both

Narrow rice terraces step up a steep slope near Guilin, China.

on dry land at higher elevations and in deep-water settings were most likely developed some time after rice was first domesticated and grown in lowland paddies. To develop upland and deep-water rice, early farmers had to relocate the plant out of its wild shallow water habitat. The cultivation of rain-fed lowland rice, in contrast, closely approximates the growth of wild rice in its natural habitat, and it is most likely in this setting that rice was first farmed.

A variety of annual and perennial forms of "wild" or "free-living" rice survive today without human care across a broad belt of South Asia. Because rice has been cultivated for thousands of years in South Asia and so much potential wild-rice habitat has been transformed into cultivated paddies, it has proved difficult so far to establish the identity of the wild progenitor of domestic rice. Similarly, it has been difficult to determine whether present-day free-living rice populations are truly wild, or just escapes from cultivation, or something in between. Eight thousand years of continual cross-pollenization and genetic exchange between the cultivated plants of an ever-expanding agricultural landscape and the wild plants of a shrinking natural habitat have blurred the genetic distinctions between wild and cultivated rices. To compound the confusion, weedy forms have also evolved over the millennia, flourishing at the edges of the agricultural landscape, sometimes "escaping" as feral populations back into unmanaged natural habitats, and exchanging genetic material with both wild and cultivated populations. Although present-day free-living populations of wild/weedy rice are genetically blurred, they do provide an opportunity to reconstruct the general habitat and seasonal growth cycle of the wild progenitor of domestic rice.

Studies of free-living annual rice populations in South Asia indicate that this wild ancestor occupied a very distinct habitat and had a life cycle closely tied to the seasonal ebb and flow of shallow water. Stands of annual wild rice could successfully compete with other plants in habitats that were gradually inundated during the rainy season to depths of half a meter or so. At the end of the rainy season, mature seeds would be dispersed onto drying ground, where they would lie dormant until the ground was inundated at the beginning of the next rainy season. The wild ancestor of domesticated rice, then, was a plant of seasonally flooded areas, flourishing in the border zone between permanently dry and permanently flooded lands.

The first efforts to cultivate rice could have begun with nothing more than deliberate attempts to extend this seasonally inundated habitat by constructing encircling dams that would trap and contain rainy-season runoff, flooding out the existing dry-land vegetation. By breaking these dikes at the end of the rainy season, the early cultivators could ensure that rice seed would have the drying soil it needed to germinate. These cultivators could have

Rice, which today provides 21 percent of the total calories consumed by our species, stands out from the world's other major crop plants in that it is usually grown in flooded fields at depths of 5 to 50 centimeters.

accelerated the expansion of wild rice by casting seeds they had harvested from wild stands in their newly created paddies at the end of the rainy season. The key subsequent step toward domestication—the deliberate annual sowing and harvesting of paddies—would have closely mimicked the seasonal germination and growth cycles of wild rice.

Such efforts to modify the environment, then, were the likely first steps in the transformation of south China peoples from hunter-gatherers who harvested wild rice from natural habitats to rice farmers who cultivated rice in rain-fed rice paddies. By intentionally transforming dry land into the seasonally flooded habitat of wild rice, early cultivators would have increased their yields and established "laboratories" for experimenting with further interventions in the life cycle of rice. The deliberate planting and harvesting of rice in these shallow water laboratories would be the key innovation that then led to the domestication of this plant.

This scenario calls for an ideal setting, one that combined extensive seasonally flooded wild-rice habitat with considerable adjacent drier land that could be diked, transformed, and appropriated for rain-fed rice paddies. Regions of both the middle and lower Yangtze River fit this profile closely: both receive heavy summer rainfall and both have substantial seasonally flooded lowlands that are bordered by gently sloping areas of dry land easily transformed into rain-fed rice paddies. It is thus no accident that throughout the long history of agriculture in China, the middle and lower Yangtze have been among China's most important rice-producing regions.

Annual rainfall along the Yangtze is between 100 and 150 centimeters, almost twice that of North China, and nearly half of it is concentrated in three summer months. Within the valley of the middle and lower course of this great river, including the delta region, a vast wetland corridor was formed in the late Mesozoic, more than 70 million years ago. At that period the gradual uplifting of the Asiatic continent began, and a shallow sea gave way to an almost continuous series of lakes connected by waterways and interspersed with gently sloping plains and surrounding uplands. Fed by summer rains and the nutrient-rich floodwaters of the Yangtze, this huge freshwater environmental system is unique in the temperate world. The valley of the Yangtze River was a vast, east-west corridor of shallow water and seasonally flooded environments having both extensive expanses of wild-rice habitat and seemingly limitless adjacent lowlands that could be converted to paddy fields. It would be difficult to imagine an area that held greater promise for the rapid emergence of rice agriculture.

It is therefore not surprising that since the 1970s a number of archaeological sites along the middle Yangtze and in the Yangtze delta region have yielded evidence of sophisticated rice-farming societies that predate any signs of rice cultivation elsewhere in East Asia by a thousand years or more. Yet some scholars still argue that rice was first domesticated farther south and that rice agriculture was then introduced northward into the Yangtze region.

Before the early rice-farming settlements of the Yangtze were discovered, it was generally assumed that rice farming had begun farther to the south. This scenario was based both on the geographical range of wild rice, which was not thought to extend as far north as the Yangtze River, and on archaeological records of very early domestic rice from Southeast Asia and India (now known to be not so old as first reported). Present-day proponents of the southern-origin theory point out that the early rice-farming societies along the Yangtze were already highly developed and that evidence for the first

The Yangtze corridor stretches more than 1000 kilometers from the Hupei basin in the west to Hang-chou Bay in the east. This vast freshwater landscape of shallow lakes and marshes contains both extensive wild rice habitat and broad expanses of adjacent lowlands suitable for conversion to paddy fields.

stages of rice cultivation is missing. They argue that the first hunter-gatherers to develop rice agriculture must have done so in this southern zone, within the apparent present-day geographical range of "wild" rice.

This argument, however, is tenuous in several respects. While most of the stands of "wild" or free-living rice reported in a 1984 survey of south China were concentrated to the south of the Yangtze drainage, two northern outlier populations were also

discovered in provinces along the middle and lower Yangtze. These stands would seem to indicate that the present-day geographical range of "wild" rice extends northward to the Yangtze River valley, although they could alternatively be discounted as representing feral escapes of crop companion weeds rather than truly wild plants. Similar arguments have been used to discount early historical accounts of "wild" rice growing in the middle and lower Yangtze River valley—that such references refer not to wild stands but to cultivated or weedy varieties of rice that had either survived in abandoned paddies or escaped from cultivation.

From an opposing perspective, however, these sightings could be viewed as evidence that the rich wetlands of the Yangtze do in fact fall within both the present-day and historically described geographical range of rice's wild ancestor. Perhaps in the past, during warmer climatic episodes, wild rice was far more abundant along the Yangtze and throughout the northern portion of its range. There is the substantial evidence from studies of ancient

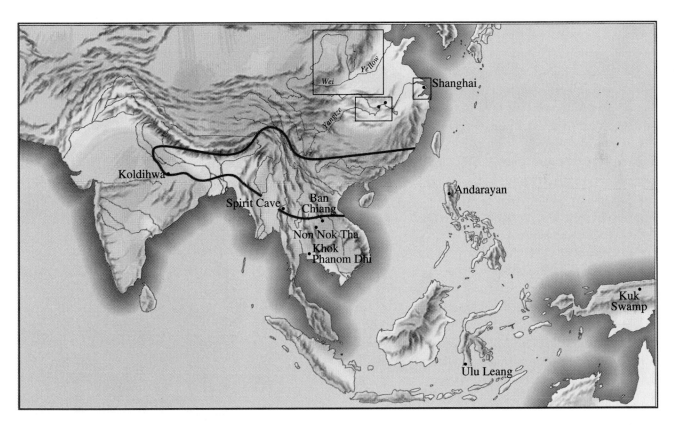

Rice was more than likely first domesticated in the Yangtze Valley, even though until recently its heartland of domestication was thought to be within a broad band that stretched from India across Southeast Asia (outlined area). This proposed southern heartland of rice domestication was based on the present-day distribution of wild rice and on early evidence of domesticated rice recovered from archaeological sites in India and Southeast Asia. The geographical range of wild rice, however, has recently been extended north to include the Yangtze Valley (red dots), and rice remains from Southeast Asia and India are now known to be not nearly as old as the materials recovered from the Yangtze Valley. The black boxes enclose the three centers of agricultural origin in East Asia, one for millet in North China along the Yellow River and two for rice in South China along the Yangtze River.

pollen found in the Yangtze delta that temperatures in the region were distinctly higher 9000 to 6000 years ago than they are today. Plant and animal remains from a more humid subtropical environment have been recovered from early farming villages in the Yangtze delta region dating to about 6500 years ago. At that time a variety of species such as elephant, rhinoceros, and water deer that today have a more southern geographical range were present in the Hang-chou Bay region just south of the mouth of the Yangtze. This evidence, combined with historical and present-day records of "wild" rice growing in the Yangtze River valley, provides strong support for the idea that the Yangtze was within the geographical range of wild rice. Chinese scholars such as Yan Wenming of Beijing University, believe that the rich wetlands of the Yangtze supported both extensive stands of the wild ancestor of domesticated rice and hunter-gatherer societies well positioned to experiment with them.

As researchers in the future search for earlier signs of the initial transition to rice cultivation, the middle and lower Yangtze must be considered the most likely heartland of rice domestication. While it is of course possible that evidence of the earliest domestication of rice will be recovered to the south of the Yangtze, the information currently available appears to argue otherwise.

In archaeological sites investigated over the past three decades in China south of the Yangtze, in Southeast Asia, and in India, all indications of the cultivation of rice, whether solid or speculative, consistently date later than 6000 to 5000 years ago. Pollen cores taken close to the site of Khok Phanom Di in Thailand contain charcoal fragments that might be evidence of field burning; they also show an increase in grass pollen, possibly from rice-field weeds. This evidence has led Charles Higham of the University of Otago in New Zealand to speculate that rice cultivation might have begun on the coast of the Gulf of Thailand as early as 6000 B.P. Clearer evidence of cultivation, however, does not appear either in coastal Southeast Asian sites such as Khok Phanom Di or in the famous northeast Thailand sites of Ban Chiang and Non Nok Tha until after 5000 to 4000 years ago.

Ban Chiang and Non Nok Tha certainly appear to be the permanent settlements of well-established agricultural societies, given their elaborate burials, which are rich in ceramic and metal grave offerings. But was their economy based on wet rice agriculture? Analysis of the 5000-year-old rice from Ban Chiang and Non Nok Tha illustrates how the use

A 4000- to 5000-year-old vessel from Ban Chiang displays an advanced ceramic technology, suggesting a complex agricultural way of life.

of different criteria can give rise to disagreements as archaeobotanists attempt to distinguish between wild rice and domesticated varieties. The remains of rice recovered from early archaeological contexts almost always consist of fragments of carbonized grains and husks and of impressions of them preserved in ceramics and clay. Two sets of morphological characteristics have been used to determine whether the burned remains of rice recovered from archaeological sites, or their ceramic impressions, were seed gathered from wild stands or from harvests of cultivated crops.

The first of these morphological markers is an increase in grain size. Once rice had been deliberately planted in prepared seedbeds, strong selective pressures would favor those seeds that were larger and had greater food reserves, enabling them to outgrow their competitors and put them in the shade. The initial cultivation of rice, then, could be marked by rice grains that were longer and wider than those produced by wild plants. Carbonized large-grained rice was found embedded in pottery sherds at Ban Chiang and Non Nok Tha, a seeming indication that domesticated rice and an agricultural economy were present.

The absence of a second morphological marker of domestication, however, leads T. T. Chang of the International Rice Research Institute, Manila, to believe that the Ban Chiang and Non Nok Tha rice was not domesticated. Chang has examined wild and domesticated varieties of rice extensively under the microscope and has found that cells on the husks, or glumes, and on the thin outer pericarp covering of domesticated rice seed are more regularly aligned and present a smoother profile than those of wild rice. In view of the irregularity of the glume surface of the Ban Chiang and Non Nok Tha rice, he has classified it as intermediate between wild and weed varieties.

These conflicting views of the rice from Ban Chiang and Non Nok Tha underscore our need to better understand the sequence and full range of morphological changes associated with the domestication of rice and the likely variety of wild, weedy, and domesticated forms that could be expected to be present in early agricultural settlements. If the rice from these two northeast Thailand settlements does in fact turn out to be domesticated, it would represent, at 5000 to 4500 B.P., the earliest evidence of rice agriculture outside of the Yangtze River region.

Several apparently early occurrences of domesticated rice in India and Southeast Asia have proved to be far more recent than they were first thought to be. For example, rice from the site of Koldihwa in Managara, India, once thought to be 8500 to 6500 years old, now appears to date to about 3500 B.P. Similarly, the clearly domesticated rice recovered from Ulu Leang Cave in Celebes, Indonesia, which had been tentatively assigned a date of 6000 B.P., was later found to be only 2000 years old. An accelerator radiocarbon date of 3400 B.P. on rice from the Andaryan site in Philippines provides the earliest solid date for rice in that region.

The quite limited and scattered archaeological evidence that is currently available, then, indicates that about 5000 to 3000 years ago, domesticated rice and rice agriculture became established over broad areas of India and Southeast Asia. The evidence for earlier cultivation of rice in these regions, perhaps as far back as 6000 years ago, is tantalizing but tenuous. In contrast, the evidence for early rice farming along the middle Yangtze River valley and in the Hang-chou Bay region of the Yangtze delta is solid. As the number of excavated sites in these regions has steadily increased, the age of their agricultural societies has been steadily pushed back, first to 6400 B.P. and now to more than 8000 years ago.

Hang-chou Bay

South of the modern city of Shanghai and the mouth of the Yangtze River, Hang-chou Bay extends westward for a hundred kilometers, gradually narrowing to meet the Ch'ien-t'ang River. Sixty-five hundred years ago this river appears to have formed a boundary between two societies that occupied the broad coastal plain along Hang-chou Bay. The settlements to the north of the river, scattered between the north

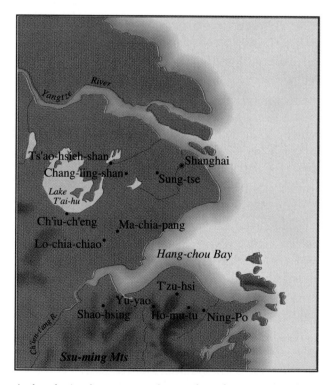

Archaeologists have excavated a number of settlements of the Lake Tai-hu and Ho-mu-tu societies, which are scattered across the rich freshwater wetlands of the coastal plain of Hang-chou Bay. The excavations provide a clear picture of the way of life of these aquacultural communities 6500 years ago.

shore of the bay and Lake Ta'i-hu, share many similarities in material culture and technology, and are often grouped under the general label "Lake Ta'i-hu culture." South of the river, along the narrower coastal plain that extends south from the shore of Hang-chou Bay to the Ssu-ming Mountain range, more than twenty early rice-farming settlements have been discovered that are contemporary with the Lake Ta'i-hu culture sites. Only one of these settlements, the Ho-mu-tu site, has been excavated to any extent, and its name is applied to all the other sites on the southern coastal plain. The Ho-mu-tu and Lake Ta'i-hu cultures are distinctly different in their ceramics and other types of artifact, yet they also were similar in a number of respects.

Most important, all of the societies in the Hang-chou Bay region about 6500 years ago had adapted in a generally similar way to the subtropical, freshwater wetlands environment of the coastal plain. Crisscrossed by rivers and streams and dotted with large and small lakes, ponds, and freshwater marshes, this rich mosaic of habitats offered a wide range of wild plants and animals, both aquatic and terrestrial. The peat deposits in which some of these settlements were found preserved abundant plant and animal remains, which provide a clear view of these societies' reliance on the wildlife they found both on dry land and in the water. At the Ma-chia-pang site, for example, potsherds, the most commonly found items of material culture, were outnumbered ten to one by animal bones.

A variety of wooden, bamboo, and bone spear and arrow points, along with bone fishhooks and net fragments, attest to the hunting and fishing skills of these wetlands societies, and so do the long list of species represented among the animal remains. As one might expect, fish (primarily freshwater carp), mollusks, wetland birds, and waterfowl (including a variety of ducks and geese) are abundant,

Along with rice, a number of shallow- and deep-water plants were apparently important in the diets of early farmers of the Yangtze corridor. They include water caltrop, which are members of the genus *Trapa* (*Trapa natans* is shown on the left with its "nut"), and the foxnut (*Euryale ferox*), shown on the right. Both were cultivated for their succulent nutlike fruits.

as are small mammals of wetland habitats, alligators, and turtles. Among the medium-sized and larger animals are several species of deer, along with monkeys, wild pigs, foxes, elephants, rhinoceroses, tigers, and bears.

Few wild plant remains other than acorns have been recognized, probably because the Hang-chou Bay societies relied on cultivated crops, primarily rice, along with water caltrop (*Trapa* sp.) and fox nut (*Euryale ferox*), two other shallow-water, apparently domesticated plants of their unique agricultural (or aquacultural) way of life.

Built on higher ground or on artificial mounds near rivers and ponds, the houses of Lake Ta'i-hu culture settlements were substantial rectangular structures supported by timbers connected by mortise-and-tenon joints. The walls were of reed and clay, and the floors of clay and shells. These houses, along with storage pits and middens (deposits of refuse), contained the bones of three likely domesticated animals—dogs, pigs, and water buffaloes—along with fragmentary remains of domesticated crop plants—bottle gourds (*Laganaria siceraria*), water caltrop, and rice. Yet even though the settlements of the Lake Ta'i-hu culture provide consistent evidence of rice cultivation, none of them can compare in richness of deposits to the remarkable water-logged settlement of Ho-mu-tu.

Situated along the shore of a pond or river and facing north across the flat coastal wetlands that stretched away to Hang-chou Bay, the Ho-mu-tu site was surrounded by forests and a rich variety of shallow-water habitats and peat deposits. Excavators probing deep into the peat formations at Ho-mu-tu in 1973–74 and again in 1977–78 found remarkably well preserved cultural deposits that extended down almost 4 meters. These deposits provide a detailed record of more than a thousand years of human habitation. In the lowest layer at Ho-mu-tu, dating to about 6300 B.P., wooden posts and planks were exposed—the remains of at least three long wooden houses, each measuring about 7 meters wide by more than 23 meters long. The houses show the same careful mortise-and-tenon joinery found in houses of the Lake Ta'i-hu culture, but they were raised on piles, so that their plank floors rested about a meter above the shallow waters of the river or pond margin along which the settlement was located. For the inhabitants of this village, the disposal of refuse was a simple matter of dumping it off their house platforms into the slowly forming peat deposits that preserved it. Vast amounts of wild plant and animal

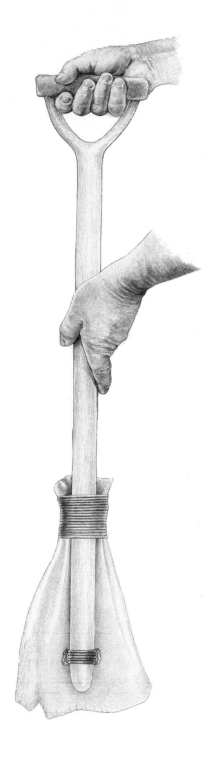

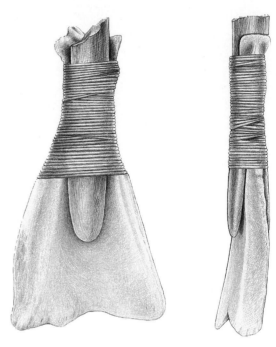

An artist's reconstruction of two agricultural digging implements of the Ho-mu-tu culture, based on remarkably preserved artifacts recovered in the peat deposits of that site. Carved wooden handles and water buffalo shoulder blades were combined to make efficient spades for preparing rice paddies.

remains were recovered here, along with the bones of dogs, pigs, and water buffaloes, all probably domesticated, and three aquaculture crop plants: water caltrop, possibly fox nut (*Euryale ferox*), and most importantly—rice.

Stalks, leaves, husks, and grains of domesticated rice were found throughout the Ho-mu-tu deposits, sometimes in concentrations that have never been matched at any other archaeological site. In one place there is a vertical layer of rice husks a meter thick. In another, a large quantity of both husked and unhusked rice extends over an area of 400 square meters. Two radiocarbon dates from this layer place it at 6500 to 6000 years ago. Ho-mu-tu has produced more rice than any other archaeological site of any age, and until relatively recently these massive rice deposits also represented the earliest known record of rice agriculture.

These well-preserved rice assemblages should provide an unmatched opportunity to document the microscopic changes in morphology that accompany the domestication of rice, as well as the proportions of wild, weedy, and domesticated varieties in harvests early in the history of rice agriculture. Such studies have not yet been undertaken, but we do know that both of the major races of rice grown in Asia today were apparently already being cultivated at Ho-mu-tu 6500 years ago. A sample of rice recovered there has been described as consisting of 80 percent long-grain *indica* (*Oryza sativa* var. *indica*) and 20 percent short-grain *japonica* (*Oryza sativa* var. *japonica*). Similarly, the rice from the nearby and contemporary Lo-chia-chiao site has been characterized as being 76 percent *indica* and 24 percent *japonica*. These identifications, it should be noted, are complicated by a substantial overlap in grain size between the *indica* and *japonica* varieties; sorting studies of modern grains show a 39 percent probability of misclassification.

Today *indica* dominates the rice paddies of southern China, while *japonica* is the only variety grown in north China, Korea, and Japan. *Indica* is better adapted to tropical and subtropical lowlands, and is cultivated south of 33 degrees north latitude and up to 2000 meters above sea level. *Japonica* is adapted to the shorter growing seasons and colder temperatures north of 33 degrees north latitude and at higher elevations in south China. Gene flow between *indica* and *japonica* is restricted, so we know that they were established as separate domesticated varieties very early. Their early evolutionary relationship, however, is still not clear.

Because of its greater diversity of forms and its morphological similarity to wild rice, *indica* has long been regarded as the founder variety of domesticated rice, and *japonica* as a temperate-zone variety that was later developed from it. More recently two alternative scenarios have been proposed: (1) that *indica* and *japonica* both developed out of an ancestral domesticate form; and (2) that *indica* and *japonica* emerged as domesticates either in separate locations or together as different wild varieties were brought under domestication at the same time. Weedy and perhaps wild forms of rice similar to *japonica* grow today in the lower Yangtze, and it is interesting to note that the east-west Yangtze Valley corridor falls in the boundary zone where both the southern *indica* and northern *japonica* will grow. It is quite possible, then, that both the *indica* and *japonica* varieties of domesticated rice were first developed by societies living in the middle and lower Yangtze River regions.

As archaeologists continue to excavate on the coastal plain, they should uncover evidence of emerging agricultural economies even earlier than 6500 B.P. The technological sophistication of the Ho-mu-tu farmers, as reflected in their ceramics, architecture, and agricultural implements, points to earlier stages of rice cultivation not yet discovered. The likely existence of such earlier farming societies has been underscored by discoveries in the Hupei basin of the middle Yangtze River. Here rice-farming settlements of the Ta-hsi culture, roughly contemporaneous with Ho-mu-tu and exhibiting a similar level of technology, have been known since the 1960s, but in 1988 evidence of an earlier rice-farming society was uncovered, and recent dates of 7800 to 8500 B.P. place it a full 2000 years earlier than either the Ta-hsi or Ho-mu-tu cultures. This is the earliest instance of rice cultivation known to date.

The Hupei Basin

Eight hundred kilometers west of Hang-chou Bay, the present-day city of Yi-ch'ang stands at the dramatic point of transition between the upper and middle valleys of the Yangtze River. Here, at the boundary between two major environmental zones, the eastward-flowing Yangtze escapes the narrow gorges and rugged country of the Wu-shan Mountains and enters the flat wetlands of the Hupei basin. Once the Yangtze enters the Hupei basin, its long meandering journey of more than 1000 kilometers

to the sea will take it through a seemingly endless and unbroken landscape of lowlands and extensive shallow-water habitats formed by lakes, marshes, and numerous tributary streams. Early rice-farming communities probably extended the full length of the corridor along the middle and lower Yangtze, but the earliest evidence of rice agriculture comes from Hang-chou Bay at its eastern end, and from the Hupei basin at its western end.

Other rivers, including the Han, Yuan, Li, and Hsiang, flow into the Hupei basin from the uplands that border it on the west, north, and south. These rivers feed into the extensive system of lakes,

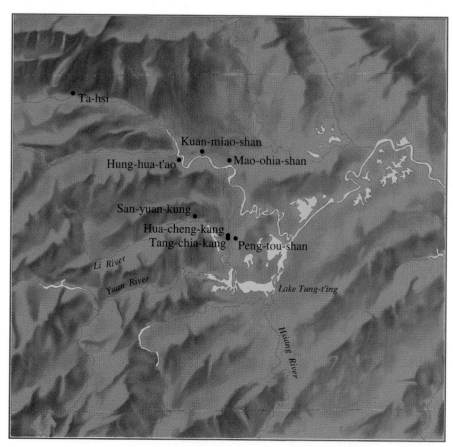

Early rice-farming settlements of the Ta-hsi and Peng-tou-shan cultures, in the rich wetlands of the Hupei basin.

marshes, and waterways that provided a rich environment for early rice-farming societies. The lakes of the Hupei basin today are meager remnants of the much larger area of lakes and marshes that once existed here. Extending outward from the margins of these central wetlands, gradually sloping plains reach to the foothills of the surrounding mountain ranges. Between 6000 and 5000 years ago, the farming settlements of the Ta-hsi culture were scattered across these low-lying plains, within easy reach of shallow-water rice habitats.

Only a small number of these settlements have been excavated, and these only to a limited extent, but the information recovered from them does provide a window on their way of life. Many Ta-hsi sites have midden deposits a meter or more deep, and the complex layers of debris, pits, and house floors tell us that the sites were permanently occupied over a long period by people of the Ta-hsi and later Ch'u-chia-ling cultures. At the San-yuan-kung site, bones of pigs and cattle are said to have been recovered from the numerous storage and refuse pits typical of Ta-hsi sites, but it is not yet documented whether either of these species had been domesticated.

The 208 burials excavated at the Ta-hsi site indicate both that these village settlements were relatively large and that there was apparently some variation in the wealth and social standing of the villagers. Some burials were not accompanied by any grave goods, while others were accompanied by more than thirty items, including ceramic vessels, stone axes and sickles, and ornaments.

The Kuan-miao-shan site has provided the best information about houses in Ta-hsi farming settlements. Measuring 6 by 6 meters, the best preserved of the two house floors found here had a central hearth and clay-plastered floor. Walls were constructed of wood and bamboo posts set in shallow trenches and then covered with clay mixed with

The early rice-farming communities of the Hupei basin manufactured ceramic vessels in a variety of shapes, including the beaker, jar, and bowl forms shown here.

bamboo and wooden sticks. Few intact house floors have been recovered so far, but clay fragments from structures that were torn down or collapsed are plentiful in the midden deposits of Ta-hsi villages. These ubiquitous floor and wall fragments provide compelling evidence of rice agriculture, since they often contain straw and husk fragments of domesticated rice. Stone sickles for harvesting rice are also common in village middens and provide additional evidence for the way of life of these as yet only partially documented agricultural societies.

Up until the late 1980s, the earliest evidence of rice-farming villages in the Hupei basin came from the lower Ta-hsi culture layers at the Tang-chia-kang, Hung-hua-t'ao, and Kuan-miao-shan sites, dated at 5500 to 6000 years ago, and perhaps some-

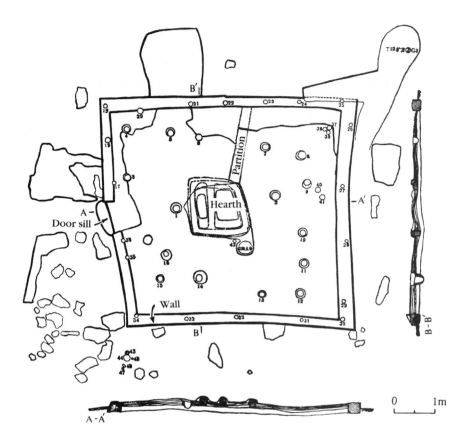

Ta-hsi houses, like this one excavated at the Kuan-miao-shan site, were square in shape, 6 meters on a side, with a central fire hearth and clay-plastered bamboo and wood walls. Earlier houses recently excavated at the 8500-year-old Peng-tou-shan settlement were similar to Ta-hsi structures.

what earlier. In November and December of 1988, however, the Archaeology Research Institute of Hunan Province excavated the site of Peng-tou-shan and uncovered evidence of rice agriculture dating to 7800 to 8400 B.P., a full 2000 years earlier than Ta-hsi settlements. Detailed reports on the site are not yet available, and only a few short preliminary articles have been published in English.

Located on the Li-yang Plain, along the northwest shore of Lake Tung-t'ing and overlooking the Li River, Peng-tou-shan is within 200 kilometers of most of the Ta-hsi culture sites so far excavated. The midden at Peng-tou-shan is of impressive size: it covers an area of about 10,000 square meters and rises 3 to 4 meters above the surrounding plain, sug-

gesting the existence of a large permanent village over a long period of time. Three conventional and three AMS radiocarbon dates from the midden range in age from 7815 to 8455 B.P. These dates tell us that Peng-tou-shan may have been occupied for six centuries or more, about the same time that Çayönü, Abu Hureyra, 'Ain Ghazal, and Ali Kosh were flourishing in the Fertile Crescent.

In the lowest level of the midden the research team uncovered the earliest house structures yet to be discovered in China. With walls constructed of posts covered by clay and with floors of yellow sand, the structures did not differ markedly in size or shape from later Ta-hsi houses. Ash pits and human burials were also found in association with these houses, but plant and animal remains were not well preserved, so we do not yet have a detailed picture of the way of life of these Peng-tou-shan villagers. We do not know if they had domesticated animals, nor can we say which species of wild plants and animals were important in their diet. We can confidently say, however, that they cultivated domesticated rice. Rice husks are plentiful in fragments of red-fired earth recovered from the site, and they were also used as a tempering agent in some ceramic wares. Preliminary analysis of the rice husks shows that the grains were large and similar in form to modern cultivated rice. Whether the rice is *indica* or *japonica,* or both, however, has yet to be determined.

Since the discovery and excavation of Peng-tou-shan, sites similar to it have been found on the Liyang Plain northwest of Lake Tung-t'ing, and future research in the region holds the promise of providing a detailed description of this early rice-farming society. As is the case in the Hang-chou Bay region, Chinese archaeologists in the Hupei basin have just begun to uncover the very early stages of

Members of the joint Sino-American research team excavate the Wang-dong site in the fall of 1993.

Present-day rice cultivation near Wang-dong Cave in Jiangxi Province, China.

a deep and complex history of rice agriculture in East Asia.

I would hazard a guess that research along the 1000-kilometer Yangtze corridor that stretches from the Hupei basin to Hang-chou Bay will reveal evidence of a rich spectrum of rice-farming societies long before rice agriculture developed elsewhere in the world. A joint Sino-American research team began to look for just such evidence of early rice farming in the fall of 1993. Headed by Yan Wenming of Beijing University, Richard S. MacNeish of the Andover Foundation for Archaeologi-

cal Research, and Peng Shifan of the Jiangxi Archaeological Institute, the research team has begun excavating two deeply stratified cave sites in Jiangxi Province. Lying about 150 kilometers south of the Yangtze River, Xian-ren-dong and Wang-dong caves are near the modern city of Wan-nian and within 2 kilometers of each other. The investigators have made preliminary excavations down through more than 2 meters of cultural deposits, and their findings suggest that hunter-gatherer groups may have begun to occupy both caves more than 12,000 years ago, and that people continued to live there perhaps up to 5000 B.P. These two caves appear to span the transition from hunting and gathering to the initial cultivation of rice, and could well shed new light on the origins of rice farming along the Yangtze.

The First Millet Farmers

Six hundred kilometers north of the Hupei basin and the Yangtze Valley heartland of rice farming, across the Ch'in Ling mountain range, lies a second center of East Asian agricultural origins. This northern center shares several interesting similarities with the Hupei basin. Just as the Hupei basin is located where the Yangtze leaves the mountainous region of western China, the North China center is located where China's other great river, the Yellow, descends out of the western highlands onto the low-lying plains of eastern China. Here, the earliest farming settlements yet discovered in North China occupy locations on the landscape similar to those occupied by the Ta-hsi and Peng-tou-shan villages of the Hupei basin. Many are situated near watercourses on lower terraces, along the foothills and sloping plains that mark the transition between two major environmental zones—the semi-arid highland steppe to the west and the temperate deciduous forests of the great plain to the east. These early farming settlements also fall into the same general time frame as

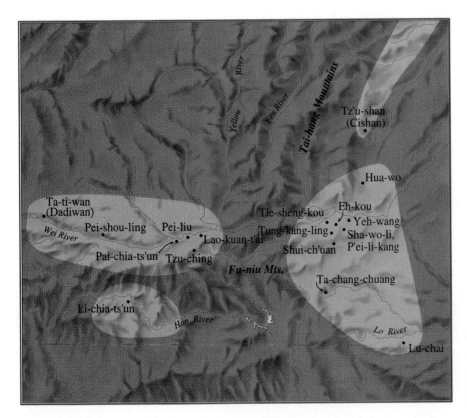

The North China center of millet agriculture. Early millet-farming settlements of the four subregions of the P'ei-li-kang culture were scattered along four different rivers.

those discovered in the Hupei basin and Hang-chou Bay: they are older than Ho-mu-tu (6500 B.P.) but younger than Peng-tou-shan (7800–8400 B.P.). Just to the south of the Yellow River, along the lower terraces of the Fu-niu Mountains, more than forty early farming settlements have been identified that date from 7500 to 7200 years ago.

Other farming settlements of a similar age have also been discovered in three adjacent areas: north of the Yellow River along the eastward-facing foothills of the Tai-hang Mountains, and west along the Wei River and the Han River, where they extend into the highlands. Although settlements of these four areas exhibit differences in ceramics and other tool types, they share enough similarities to be grouped together under a single label, as the P'ei-li-kang culture. Like the Hupei basin, this northern center also exhibits a deep and rich cultural continuity up through time, with the different geographical variants of the P'ei-li-kang culture developing directly into distinct clusters of the much better known Yang-shao culture of 6800 to 4500

years ago. A little later we will briefly consider several of these Yang-shao village settlements that provide a remarkable picture of an early farming way of life in North China.

Our understanding of the P'ei-li-kang farming societies must be pieced together from the results of limited excavations at a number of settlements, the most important being the P'ei-li-kang site itself. P'ei-li-kang villages were large, covering as much as 20,000 square meters. Houses were round or occasionally square, 2 to 3 meters across, with plastered floors either at ground level or sunk into the ground. Numerous storage pits were scattered among the houses; some had straight walls, others the outflaring bell-shaped vertical cross section that suggests they had been repeatedly renewed and enlarged. The excavators frequently encountered the remains of grain crops stored in the pits. Burials often contained a variety of grave goods, including pottery vessels and a range of tool types associated with agriculture: stone axes for clearing the forest, stone hoes for tilling the sandy loess soils, distinc-

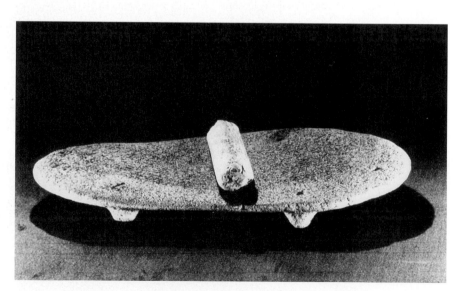

A footed grinding slab used for processing millets and other seed crops, excavated at the Shui-ch'uan site.

tive footed stone mortars and pestles for grinding grain, and remarkable serrated stone sickles for harvesting.

P'ei-li-kang settlements seem generally similar to the Ta-hsi and Peng-tou-shan villages of the Hu-pei basin, far to the south. Granted, there are very distinct differences between the two regions across the spectrum of material culture, indicating that the two cultures developed independently and in isolation. But their agricultural development and social and political organization are comparable. By 8000 to 7500 years ago, large, stable village-based societies had emerged in both regions. In both the north and south, communities built substantial houses, held richly appointed burials, made elaborate ceramic vessels, and fashioned advanced agricultural technologies. This generally parallel development of farming societies in the two regions is all the more remarkable because the agricultural economies of North and South China centered on very different crop plants.

In the south, the aquaculture of rice developed in rich subtropical wetlands where winters were mild and rain was reliably abundant in summer. Water played a critical role in shaping the northern agricultural economy too, but in quite different ways. Situated between the semi-arid loess highland steppes to the west and the temperate broadleaf deciduous forests of the great plain to the east, the northern center was probably somewhat warmer and wetter 9000 to 6000 years ago, and probably supported a variety of grassland and temperate forest habitats. It is safe to say, however, that winters were most likely harsh and summer rains unreliable. Winters today are severe, with little precipitation, mostly snow. The vagaries of monsoon weather patterns would have made rainfall highly variable during the growing season, and the possibility of floods or droughts would have been a constant threat.

Below the rim of the western highlands, the wild plants successfully targeted for domestication were drought-resistant species of the highland steppes, which were preadapted to cultivation in zones of marginal rainfall. Two species of millets have been identified as the main crops cultivated by P'ei-li-kang communities: broomcorn millet (*Panicum miliaceum*) and foxtail millet (*Setaria italica* sp. *italica*).

The wild ancestor of foxtail millet is thought to be green bristlegrass (*Setaria viridis*), which today grows across a broad expanse of northern and southwestern China in uplands of low rainfall. No single progenitor of broomcorn millet has been identified, and several North China species may have contributed to the genetic composition of this domesticate. While foxtail millet is certainly adapted to arid growing conditions, broomcorn millet has one of the lowest water requirements of all cereals.

Evidence for the domestication of these two millets is based not on morphological markers, but on the obvious fact that the excavated settlements were agricultural villages. Hunting-and-gathering economies could not have supported communities of this size and permanence. Grain identified as broomcorn or foxtail millet has been frequently recovered. It was present in eighty pits excavated at the Tz'u-shan site, for example, and the single sample analyzed so far has been identified as foxtail millet. Broomcorn millet may well have also been cultivated at Tz'u-shan, however, since the grains of the two millets are difficult to distinguish, and the plant remains from P'ei-li-kang and Yang-shao settlements have yet to be analyzed in detail. Similarly, although only broomcorn millet has been identified at the village sites of Ta-ti-wan and P'ei-li-kang, foxtail millet was probably also grown. Both millets were the central agricultural crops of North China up through the historic period, though foxtail millet was the more important of the two.

Seed heads of foxtail millet (right) and its likely wild ancestor, green bristle-grass (left), show the increase in size of the seed head that took place with domestication.

There is still much to be learned about the initial domestication of millet and the development of farming economies in North China before the appearance of the P'ei-li-kang culture. The transition from a hunting-and-gathering way of life to the cultivation of millets was probably accomplished by the societies that preceded P'ei-li-kang in the Yellow River region during the poorly documented centuries from 9000 to 7500 years ago. When Chinese archaeologists find and investigate the settlements of these societies, they are likely to discover that foxtail and broomcorn millets were important wild food sources before they were domesticated. I also think it highly likely that the people who first domesticated and cultivated millets were "affluent" hunters and gatherers who lived in permanent settlements and relied on a rich variety of wild plants and animals in addition to millets. These hunter-gatherers would have at first cultivated millet as a supplement to the existing hunting-and-gathering economy, in an effort to increase the yield and reliability of a wild resource that was already important to them.

Some evidence of this earlier stage of agriculture can be seen in the lifeways of P'ei-li-kang societies 7500 to 7200 years ago. Although these peoples were farmers, they were still hunter-gatherers as well. We know from the plant and animal re-

mains at P'ei-li-kang villages that they harvested a variety of woodland nuts and fruits, including walnuts, hazelnuts, hackberries, acorns, and the Chinese juijuibi dates. Fish remains are abundant, as are a number of medium-sized and large mammals. Three species of deer (sika, elaphure, and water deer) were the most important species hunted.

Domesticated animals were also important to P'ei-li-kang societies, as well as to the rice farmers of the Yangtze River valley. We still have much to

A woman feeding her pigs in Yunnan Province, China. Domesticated pigs have been an important part of the agricultural landscape in China for more than 6500 years.

A boy riding a water buffalo through the monsoon rains in Yunnan Province, China.
Detailed morphological studies documenting the domestication of this important animal species in East Asia have yet to be carried out.

learn, however, about where and when the primary agricultural animals of East Asia—pigs (*Sus scrofa*), chickens (*Gallus gallus domesticus*), and water buffaloes (*Bubalus bubalis*)—were first domesticated. Archaeologists have not yet been able to compare in detail the skeletal remains of these species from different regions and time periods, as they must do in order to establish morphological markers and population profiles indicating domesticated status.

The large quantity of chicken bones recovered from the P'ei-li-kang village settlements of T'zu-shan have been identified by the Chinese archaeozoologist Chao Ben-shuh as representing domesticated birds. Although the morphological basis for identifying these bones as being from domesticated fowl has not been outlined, they provide, at 7400 to 7200 B.P., the world's earliest proposed evidence for domesticated chickens (*Gallus gallus domesticus*).

Similarly, although the criteria for assigning domesticated status are not detailed, domesticated pigs have also been reported as abundant at T'zu-shan and other P'ei-li-kang villages dating from 7500 to 7200 B.P., and at the Ho-mu-tu site (6400 B.P.) on the coastal plain of Hang-chou Bay. *Sus scrofa* was also artistically rendered in clay in both regions.

With twelve radiocarbon dates ranging from 8500 to 6500 years ago, the Tseng-p'i-yen Cave in southern China provides the best documented and perhaps the earliest evidence to date for domesticated pigs in East Asia. In their analysis of sixty-seven pig mandibles from this site, forty of which were intact enough that scientists could estimate the ages of the animals when they died, Y. H. Li and T. F. Han determined that a full 85 percent of the animals were younger than two years, and 20 percent were under a year old. This age profile is consistent with that of a domesticated herd of pigs managed for meat production. Most animals in such herds are culled once they reach adult size, between one and two years of age. It is also possible, however, that the Tseng-p'i-yen Cave pigs were wild, since very little is known about what kind of age

Animal pens

Road Surfaces

Cemeteries

Lin-bo River

0   15 m

Community plan of the 6500-year-old village at Chiang-chai, belonging to the Yang-shao culture. Cemeteries were placed outside the defensive ditch system, which protected the square and round houses of individual families and larger communal structures. A central plaza contained corrals for domesticated animals.

profile might be expected from the hunting of wild pigs. It will be interesting to learn if these mandibles and teeth are from long-snouted pigs comparable to present-day wild pigs in China, or if they show the size reduction one would expect in domesticated pigs.

If the Tseng-p'i-yen cave pigs are domesticated, it is possible that they were introduced into East Asia from the Fertile Crescent, where they were domesticated between 8500 and 8000 B.P. Given the distance involved, however, I think that it is more likely that *Sus scrofa* was independently domesticated in the two widely separated regions about the same time. The apparently domesticated pigs from the Tseng-pi-yen cave may date as early as 8500 B.P. or as recently as 6500 B.P. When we have morphological analyses of Peng-tou-shan animal remains from the Hupei basin, which date between 8400 and 7800 B.P., they should help to shed new light on the domestication of both pigs and water buffaloes (*Bubalus bubalis*).

The Ho-mu-tu site, dating to 6500 years ago, appears to provide the earliest evidence for the domestication of water buffaloes, which would have been used as draft animals. After analyzing water buffalo remains from Southeast Asia, Charles Higham of the University of Otago concluded that domesticated *Bubalus bubalis* was not present in the region until about 3500 years ago.

The cultivation of foxtail and broomcorn millet and the raising of domestic pigs and chickens steadily increased in importance over time, and by 6800 years ago the Yang-shao descendants of P'ei-li-kang farming societies flourished over a broad expanse of North China. Two Yang-shao settlements that have been extensively excavated provide a clear picture of what appears to be a fairly standardized social and community organization. Only kilometers apart, both the Chiang-chai and Pan-po sites

A reconstructed circular house at the Yang-shao village of Pan-po.

cover about 30,000 square meters, and are oval in outline, and the outer boundaries of their dwelling areas are defined by deep defensive ditches. Beyond these surrounding ditches lie burial areas. Within these protective ditches, single-family dwellings, along with storage and refuse pits, are organized around a central plaza. At Chiang-chai, excavated from 1972 to 1979, more than 100 houses were uncovered, along with 300 storage pits. Larger communal structures were also exposed, along with communal animal pens located in the central plaza. Such community plans indicate that by 6500 years ago a strongly developed agricultural way of life centered on large kinship-based farming communities had emerged in North China. This ancient pattern of rural life has endured across the millennia right up to the present day.

Early Agriculture in Southeast Asia

Although some scholars speculate that rice was brought under cultivation south of the Yangtze, along the coast of Southeast Asia, as early as 6000 B.P., current evidence suggests that wet rice farming was introduced into the region from South China by about 5000 to 4000 years ago. But as rice farming spread across Southeast Asia, did it gradually supplant an older form of agriculture? Were Southeast Asian societies already cultivating locally domesticated tropical species—primarily root crops and fruit and nut trees—long before rice arrived?

As early as the 1930s it was suggested that Southeast Asia may have been an ancient center of plant domestication and agricultural innovation, and since then numerous botanists, geographers, and archaeologists have supported the idea. In the absence of any clear evidence, these theories rested largely on two quite tenuous lines of argument. First, since it would be simpler to reproduce tubers and trees by planting shoots and cuttings than to reproduce other plants by planting seeds, it was argued, trees and tubers were probably domesticated before seed plants, including rice. Second, since root crops and fruit and nut trees were much more broadly distributed across Southeast Asia than rice, they must have been domesticated and widely diffused before rice farming arrived in the region. What, then, is the identity of the root and tree crops that are thought to have constituted a Southeast Asian farming economy of such great antiquity?

Southeast Asia today contains a rich variety of root and tuber crops, fruits, nuts, and of course spices (cloves, black pepper, nutmeg, and so on) that were derived from wild plants native to one or more of the region's diverse environments. Southeast Asia's root and tuber crops, the staples that could be vegetatively reproduced, include aroid tuber (*Amorphophallus* spp.), taro (*Colocasia esculenta*), elephant ear (*Alocasia macrorrhiza, Cytosperma chamissonis*), arrowroot (*Tacca leontopetaloides*), and yam (*Dioscorea alata, D. esculenta*). Important fruit- and nut-producing species include the coconut (*Cocos nucifera*), sago palm (*Metroxylon*), citrus trees (orange, lime, lemon, tangerine, grapefruit), banana (*Mangifera acuminata*), breadfruit (*Artocarpus communis*), and jackfruit (*A. integrifolia*).

What was the origin of these and other indigenous crop plants of Southeast Asia? Where and when were they first brought under domestication, and how were they cultivated and combined into crop

A harvest of yams in the Santos Islands. Evidence of yams and other Southeast Asian crops is rarely preserved in archaeological sites.

complexes across the varied mainland and island environments? Were some of them domesticated together, by the same Southeast Asian societies, as part of the same developmental process, or were they domesticated for the most part at different times in different places? Unfortunately, we have no answers at present. Very little information is currently available regarding where and when any of these Southeast Asian plants were first domesticated.

In some cases it is possible to identify the type of environment in which a species was first domesticated by determining the habitat occupied by its likely wild ancestor (often still unidentified). Since root crops are adapted to survive long dry seasons, for example, they must have been first domesticated in zones where dry seasons were more than two to three months long. Similarly, banana, orange, and other fruit and nut trees grow on the margins of forests, along streams and clearings, and in other open habitats where sunlight can reach them. Yet even when investigators identify the general environments where Southeast Asian crop plants were first domesticated, their efforts still leave broad geographical zones as potential heartlands of tropical agriculture.

Plant remains can disintegrate quickly in the tropics, so although the number of archaeological excavations in the region is increasing, little primary evidence of Southeast Asian domesticates in the form of plant remains has yet been recovered.

In the 1960s, considerable excitement was generated by the plants recovered during the excavation of Spirit Cave in northwestern Thailand. When Chester Gorman of the University of Pennsylvania excavated the cave in 1966 and again in 1973–74, he found that the site had been occupied by hunter-gatherers from about 11,000 to 7500 years ago. Spirit Cave yielded well-preserved remains of candle nuts, canarium nuts, butter nuts, almonds, water chestnuts, cucumbers, lotuses, and several types of beans. At first some of these remains seemed to represent domesticated plants, or at least plants well on their way to being domesticated. As a result, for a short time Spirit Cave appeared to finally provide the long anticipated evidence for the ancient Southeast Asian tropical agriculture that preceded rice farming. Detailed analysis, however, revealed that the Spirit Cave plant remains were wild plants that had been collected rather than cultivated.

Since Spirit Cave, no other Southeast Asian archaeological site has produced plant remains to prove the existence of an indigenous agriculture before rice was introduced into the region. Other kinds of evidence, however, have been proposed as indicating the presence of early agriculture in Southeast Asia.

Probably the most tantalizing evidence comes from the Kuk swamp in a highland basin of New Guinea. There a series of buried, meter-deep channels was discovered, leading away from where a main tributary stream entered the basin. Ranging in width from 1 to 10 meters, the channels extended across the basin for considerable distances. Were they drainage canals dug with digging sticks by early farmers, or were they natural features of the landscape? Some of the channels followed a straight line, suggesting human construction, and most were thought to be about 5000 years old or less. One of them, however, measuring 2 meters wide by 1 meter deep, and bending across the basin a distance of perhaps 500 meters, was assigned an age of 9000 B.P., based on a radiocarbon date obtained on charcoal recovered from channel fill. Was this feature dug by early root crop cultivators, or was it just the continuation of the streambed that emptied into Kuk basin? It would have taken substantial effort by many people to dig this channel by hand 9000 years ago, yet no settlements have been located that

Part of the later canal systems and associated island garden beds unearthed in the Kuk basin. The curved canals date to perhaps 5000 B.P., the straight ones to perhaps 2500 B.P.

stone axes appeared around 26,000 years ago. Both developments have been seen as evidence that hunter-gatherers tried to encourage the growth of favored food plants. Hunter-gatherers, however, commonly use axes and other woodworking tools for a variety of tasks that have nothing to do with encouraging the growth of plants, and changes in the pollen sequence are likely to have been caused by natural factors rather than large-scale efforts to clear the forest.

Since so many investigators have speculated so long about Southeast Asia as the place where plants were first domesticated, researchers are likely to continue to look for and to find evidence, however tenuous, that seems to support such a scenario. But establishing where, when, and by whom Southeast Asian crop plants were first domesticated will be a long and challenging process. Biological research has just begun to identify wild ancestors of the numerous crop plants, and to define their geographical ranges. Similarly, archaeologists have only just started parallel efforts to recover plant remains from suspected areas of initial domestication, establish morphological markers of domestication, and directly date specimens identified as domesticates. I suspect that it will be several decades at least before the general outline of Southeast Asian agriculture is known. Perhaps the most interesting and promising body of evidence that is slowly building across Southeast Asia—one that rarely draws the attention it deserves—is the increasing number of excavated archaeological sites in the region that have *not* yielded evidence of domesticated crop plants. As more and more sites from different times and different areas across Southeast Asia are excavated and found to contain no domesticates, this negative evidence will go a long way toward defining the true boundaries, both in space and in time, of the emergence of agriculture in Southeast Asia.

date earlier than 6000 B.P., nor has any evidence of the plants thought to have been cultivated in the Kuk basin been recovered. Clearly further research is needed to confirm the age, origins, and purpose of the enigmatic Kuk basin "canal," and to establish the identity of the crops that were grown and the people who grew them. Until then the Kuk canal cannot be considered to be substantial evidence that agriculture existed in the highlands of New Guinea at such an early date.

Some archaeologists point to even older indications of efforts to modify the New Guinea landscape. These have been proposed as evidence that the early inhabitants manipulated plants and "domesticated" the forest environment, but this evidence too is tenuous. Pollen sequences show disturbance of the forest some 30,000 years ago, and large ground-

7

MIDDLE AND SOUTH AMERICA

 The "foot plow," the tool on the facing page, has long been used in South America in the planting of potatoes, which were probably domesticated in the south-central Andes more than 4000 years ago.

The long history of human occupation of the Americas began about 20,000 to 15,000 years ago, when hunter-gatherers moved across the broad Bering Strait land bridge that then connected Siberia and Alaska. Created during the Pleistocene epoch when polar ice caps formed and lowered sea levels, this connecting corridor provided a gateway to a new world that was as yet uninhabited by humans. How quickly and in what directions did these first colonizers expand across the vast open landscapes of the Americas? When did they arrive in different regions? These questions are still a matter of debate. However, the Monte Verde site in south-central Chile, excavated by Tom Dillehay of the University of Kentucky and firmly dated by conventional and AMS radiocarbon methods, provides an important benchmark: it indicates that human colonization of the Americas had reached all the way to southern South America by 12,000 years ago.

As the last ice age drew to a close, the chilly climates of the Pleistocene were giving way to the warmer, more seasonal patterns of the Holocene. By 11,000 to 10,000 years ago each of the many human societies of the Americas were adjusting their hunting-and-gathering ways of life to the changing plant and animal communities of their particular regions of this new world. Over the next 10,000 years these societies developed along a variety of paths,

In 1613, Poma de Ayala sent the King of Spain a lengthy description of the Inca way of life in the Andes, which included his remarkable drawings of agricultural practices. Left: The traditional foot plow is being used to plant potatoes. Right: Workers use short-handled hoes to cultivate high-altitude fields.

Maize was the central crop plant in agricultural economies of ancient Mexico. This market scene in Tenochtitlán—the capital of the Aztec empire—is depicted in a 1945 mural by Diego Rivera, *La Grande Tenochtitlán*.

leading in some regions to the eventual development of large states. Along the spine of the Andes, in the thin air of high-altitude valleys and grasslands, the Inca state began its long history of expansion around A.D. 1400 and flourished until the arrival of Francisco Pizarro in 1532. In the forests of Central America, a series of Maya city-states followed a complex historical trajectory from A.D. 200 onward. Farther north, in the semi-arid central highlands of what is today Mexico, the Aztec empire extended its control far beyond its capital city of Tenochtitlán in the Valley of Mexico, until it fell to the Spanish conquistadores in 1521.

Although they were founded in very different environmental settings and emerged out of quite different historical backgrounds, the Inca, Maya, and Aztec states were alike in one basic respect: they were fueled by well-established and productive agricultural economies. These three New World civilizations, however, were far from the only pre-Columbian agriculturalists of the New World. Farming societies had been long established throughout many regions of the Americas by the time the first Europeans arrived. The economies of most of these groups, like those of the Maya and Aztec, were centered on the triad of squash, beans, and maize, the paramount crop plant of the Western Hemisphere. From Argentina to Ecuador, up through Central America and Mexico, and as far north as southern Ontario, maize, beans, and squash were the primary crops of societies that otherwise were widely diverse in language, culture, sociopolitical organization, and history.

Not all agricultural economies in the Americas,

however, were centered on these three crops. In the vast tropical lowlands of South America, for example, hunter-gatherers had domesticated a wide variety of plants, principal among them such roots crops as manioc (*Manihot esculenta*) and sweet potato (*Ipomoea batatas*). The archaeological record of this lowland rain-forest agriculture, however, is still almost nonexistent, and the early history of these crops is largely unknown.

In contrast, biological and archaeological research has provided considerable information on the emergence of a distinctive high-altitude agriculture in the central Andes between 5000 and 4000 years ago. Forming an economic base that would support the long sequence of Andean cultural development leading up to the emergence of the Inca, this highland agriculture was unique in the Americas in that animals (llamas, alpacas, guinea pigs) as well as plants (potatoes, quinua) played important roles. But before we consider the evidence for the domes-

tication of these high-altitude plants and animals, let us turn first to the maize/beans/squash agriculture that had its origins in what is now Mexico more than 5000 years ago, and that then expanded to transform the economies of societies across the Americas.

The Caves of Mexico

In 1948 a number of remarkably well preserved maize cobs and squash seeds were recovered from the lowest levels of Bat Cave, 2021 meters up in the Mogollon Highlands of New Mexico. The then very new radiocarbon method was called upon to date charcoal found in apparent association with the maize: it was found to be more than 6000 years old. This discovery provided the earliest record of these two domesticates in the southwestern United States,

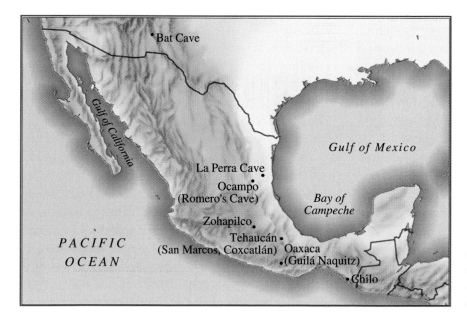

The cave and rock shelter sites of Tamaulipas, Tehuacán, and Oaxaca, which have provided the evidence of early agriculture in Middle America.

where they had been introduced from Mexico, and demonstrated the remarkable potential of dry caves for providing evidence of the early history of an agricultural way of life in the Americas. The location of Bat Cave in the Mogollon Highlands suggested that cave sites in similar semi-arid, intermediate-altitude environments in Mexico might be promising places to look for evidence of early farming.

Support for this idea came in early 1949 from the state of Tamaulipas in northeastern Mexico. Excavating in La Perra Cave in the Tamaulipas Mountains, only some 150 kilometers south of the Texas border, Richard MacNeish, now with the Andover Foundation for Archaeological Research, recovered well-preserved early plant remains, including maize. Following his success in La Perra Cave, in the early 1950s, MacNeish excavated Romero's Cave, along with a second nearby cave, in the Sierra Madre near the town of Ocampo in southwestern Tamaulipas. Here he uncovered additional abundant evidence that early crop plants had been added to preexisting hunting-and-gathering economies.

La Perra and Romero's caves, along with similar cave sites in Mexico, have also yielded a picture of the hunting-and-gathering way of life that led up to the first cultivation of domesticated plants. Excavating down through the soil and human refuse that accumulated in caves over thousands of years, MacNeish and other archaeologists have exposed thin habitation layers stacked one on top of the other. Each thin layer marked a brief seasonal occupation of the cave by a small hunter-gatherer group that probably consisted of an extended family. Plant remains and the bones of wild animals, discarded broken tools, along with fire hearths and storage pits, tell the story of small groups moving from place to place with the changing seasons, hunting antelope and deer, rabbits and other small prey, and harvesting pinyon, hackberry, and a variety of other

wild plants. After his success in the caves of Tamaulipas, MacNeish decided to continue his search for the origins of agriculture farther south.

Just as Braidwood had selected the foothills of the Zagros as a likely heartland of agriculture in the Near East, MacNeish theorized in the 1950s that the heartland of agriculture in Middle America lay in the central highlands of Mexico. His search for agricultural origins in the central highlands would parallel Braidwood's Near Eastern project in a number of important respects. In addition to identifying a likely heartland for agriculture based on the apparent natural habitats of the wild ancestors of maize, beans, and squash, MacNeish also targeted sites that showed promise of being the right age and of containing well-preserved early evidence of domesticates. In addition, he attracted scientists from a number of disciplines to study the climate and environment of the likely heartland region, and to analyze the plant and animal remains recovered during excavation.

From 1960 to 1964 MacNeish directed a remarkable interdisciplinary project in the Tehuacán Valley in the central Mexican state of Puebla. Here, MacNeish and other archaeologists recovered abundant well-preserved plant remains in a series of well-stratified caves, particularly in two caves called Coxcatlán and San Marcos. The remains of maize, squashes, and beans recovered from the Tehuacán Valley caves were analyzed by botanists who were both authorities on the species in question and committed to documenting the evolution of these domestic crop plants in the Americas. Hugh C. Cutler of the Missouri Botanical Garden and Thomas Whitaker of the U.S. Department of Agriculture analyzed the squash (*Cucurbita*) remains; Paul Mangelsdorf and Walton Galinat of Harvard University analyzed the maize; and Lawrence Kaplan of the University of Massachusetts in Boston studied the

In the early 1960s, careful excavation down through the occupation layers of Coxcatlán Cave, in the Tehuacán Valley of Mexico, yielded abundant evidence of early domesticated plants.

beans (*Phaseolus*). Since the pioneering Tehuacán project these researchers have studied a substantial percentage of the maize, squashes, and beans recovered from archaeological sites in Mexico and South America. Whitaker and Kaplan also analyzed the squash and beans recovered from Guilá Naquitz Cave in the southern Mexican state of Oaxaca, excavated in 1966 by Kent Flannery of the University of Michigan, who had been a member of the Tehuacán research project.

These dry caves excavated by MacNeish, Flannery, and their colleagues provide all of the early evidence as yet available for the domestication of maize, squash, and the common bean in Middle America. In contrast to other areas of the world such

as the Fertile Crescent, where a large number of excavated settlements tell us about early agriculture, in Mexico all our knowledge of early crop plants comes from a half dozen sites—Guilá Naquitz, the Tehuacán Valley caves, and the Tamaulipas caves. Yet few as they are, these carefully excavated dry caves have yielded much of the story of the emergence of agriculture in Middle America.

Maize

More than 24,000 specimens of maize (*Zea mays*) have been found during the excavation of the dry

Early maize cobs from San Marcos Cave in the Tehuacán Valley (actual size). The kernels have been removed, but the long, soft glumes that enclosed them are still visible.

mesticated maize was derived. Since the late 1930s a spirited debate had surrounded the ancestry of this crop plant, with Mangelsdorf steadfastly championing a now-extinct wild maize as the progenitor and George Beadle of the University of Chicago and others consistently arguing that teosinte, an annual grass that still grows today in Mexico, was the ancestor of maize. To Mangelsdorf, the small cobs from Tehuacán provided clear support for the existence of a wild maize.

We now know, however, that teosinte is the true ancestor of maize, and that the early cobs from the Tehuacán caves are in fact from domesticated plants. In a detailed reanalysis of the early maize from San

caves of the Tehuacán Valley—almost 21,000 cobs and cob fragments, 797 kernels, and smaller amounts of husks, leaves, tassel fragments, roots, and so on. This remarkable assemblage documents a long sequence of maize evolution. The sequence begins with seventy-one small cobs recovered from the lowest levels of San Marcos Cave (zones E and F) and from deep in the deposits of Coxcatlán Cave (zones 11–13), in contexts then considered to be 7000 to 5500 years old. These cobs, representing the oldest and most primitive maize yet recovered in the Americas, are less than 2 inches long (19 to 25 millimeters). Morphologically they are quite uniform, characteristically having eight short rows of six to nine kernels each. Individual kernels are partially enclosed by distinctive long, soft glumes—outer husklike sheaths. Sometimes found folded back, probably as the result of the removal of the kernels, these glumes, along with other characteristics, seemed to set these early cobs apart from those found higher in the cave deposits.

Paul Mangelsdorf considered these small corncobs to predate the domestication of *Zea mays,* and in fact to represent a wild maize from which do-

Reconstruction of an early ear of corn from San Marcos Cave in the Tehuacán Valley.

151

Marcos Cave, Bruce Benz of the Universidad de Guadalajara and Hugh Iltis of the University of Wisconsin have confirmed that the small primitive cobs display morphological features characteristic of a domesticated plant. Most important, they found that the early Tehuacán maize lacked a basic feature essential to the survival of any seed plant in the wild—the ability to disperse its kernels naturally.

The primitive early maize from the Tehuacán valley caves was domesticated in the fullest sense of the term: it could have survived from one growing season to the next only through the active intervention of human hands stripping cobs of their tightly held ("nondisarticulating") kernels and storing some of them as seed stock for the next planting.

Benz and Iltis also located a modern race of

Modern ears of corn differ widely from race to race in size, shape, and color, the result of thousands of years of human selection. The ear in the lower right corner is U.S. Corn Belt dent, the world's most productive corn. To the left of it is an ear of Cuzco Gigante, a Peruvian race with the world's largest kernels. Above the Cuzco ear is the tiny Lady Finger Pop, or Argentine popcorn, thought to be a present-day relict of the early Tehuacán maize.

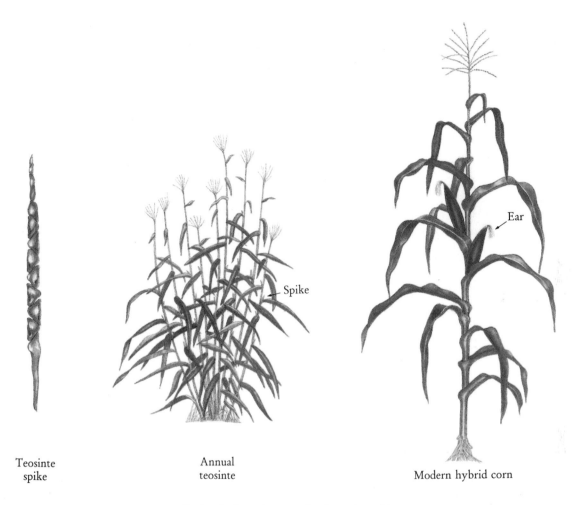

Teosinte
spike

Annual
teosinte

Modern hybrid corn

Present-day maize, with its single main stalk, has its kernels conveniently packaged in a few large, easily harvested cobs. In contrast, its wild ancestor, teosinte, had numerous small stalks, each having several small grain spikes.

maize that looks much like the early San Marcos maize—Argentine popcorn. Still being grown today in Argentina on a small scale, this popcorn is thought to be a relict of the maize initially dispersed south out of Mexico and across South America. It has long been replaced by specialized and higher-

yielding maize races, and now survives only in isolated patches on the southern periphery of maize cultivation. Interestingly, it was introduced and grown in the United States as early as the 1920s under the name "Lady Finger Pop."

Argentine popcorn retains a number of primitive

characteristics and so provides an excellent proxy for the early maize cultivated in the Tehuacán Valley. Judging from Argentine popcorn, early Tehuacán corn would have been relatively small, up to 1.2 meters high. Each plant typically would have had from one to five ear-bearing lateral branches, and most of these branches would have had not only an ear at the end, but also several additional ears growing along its length. One of these plants could have produced ten to fifteen or more short ears that were only slightly larger than those of the largest-grained annual teosinte in Mexico.

Although clearly primitive in a number of respects, the small-cob, eight-row popcorn grown in the Tehuacán Valley was at the same time morphologically quite distinct from teosinte, its wild ancestor. It is not yet clear how much further back in time along the evolutionary pathway leading up to the Tehuacán Valley maize we will have to travel to reach the point at which teosinte was transformed

into domesticated maize, but it does appear that the search should be directed west from Tehuacán into the river valleys that flow west out the central highlands to the Pacific. It is here, at elevations of 400 to 1700 meters, that today grow the populations of annual teosinte that show the greatest biochemical similarity to domesticated maize.

Throughout the twentieth century botanists have been seeking out new populations of teosinte across rural and often remote areas of Mexico and Central America. By 1980 three perennial and three annual teosintes had been identified by Hugh Iltis, John Doebley, and other researchers, and their geographical distributions had been plotted. Within this group of six potential ancestors of maize, two of the annuals (*Zea mays* subsp. *mexicana* and *Zea mays* subsp. *parviglumis*) were found most similar to maize in their morphology and other characteristics, and they became the focus of further research by John Doebley, a biologist at the University of Min-

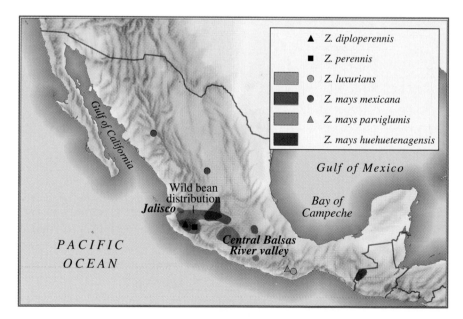

The Jalisco cluster of *Zea mays* subsp. *parviglumis,* in second place behind the central Balsas cluster as the likely wild ancestor of maize, overlaps in geographical range with the Guadalajara population cluster of wild *Phaseolus vulgaris* beans having S-type phaseolin. This was the cluster that gave rise to the domesticated common bean in Mexico.

nesota. The *mexicana* subspecies grows today between 1800 and 2500 meters above sea level in the valleys and on the plains of central and northern Mexico, while *parviglumis* is adapted to wetter and warmer zones and grows at elevations of 400 to 1700 meters on the upper slopes of the river valleys of more southern and western Mexico.

Both of these subspecies of teosinte also vary somewhat from north to south, and each was further broken down into three natural subdivisions or population clusters. John Doebley included samples of all six of these geographically separated subspecies of *mexicana* and *parviglumis* in his genetic search for the wild ancestor of maize, along with samples from all other annual and perennial teosintes. Having brought together all of the known wild forms of *Zea*, Doebley was now ready to examine their genetic profiles and to compare each with domesticated maize. The ancestral teosinte would be the type of teosinte most similar to maize. In comparing specific proteins in the wild teosintes with those in maize, Doebley found that the subspecies *parviglumis* could not be distinguished from maize and in fact was much more similar to it than it was to any of the other teosintes.

Having identified *parviglumis* as the wild progenitor of maize, Doebley turned to a closer consideration of the three present-day geographical clusters of this subspecies. He found the populations biochemically most similar to maize to be growing at an elevation of 400 to 1200 meters along the upper slopes of the central Balsas River drainage, more than 250 kilometers west of the Tehuacán Valley. While it is possible that this population cluster may have had a more extensive geographical range when maize was brought under domestication than it does today, its present-day range still seems to suggest a promising region to look for evidence of the first cultivation of corn. Another population cluster of

the subspecies *parviglumis,* however, to the north in the state of Jalisco, also deserves consideration. Although the Jalisco population cluster is not as similar to maize as the central Balsas cluster, it is located in the same area as the population cluster of wild *Phaseolus* beans now identified as the wild ancestor of the domesticated common bean (*Phaseolus vulgaris*). This area around the modern city of Guadalajara, shared by the apparent ancestors of maize and beans, would seem to hold considerable promise for future archaeological research.

Since the Tehuacán caves are several hundred kilometers east of the modern range of the wild ancestor of maize, and since no teosinte was recovered during their excavation, the early cobs found there appear to mark not the initial domestication of maize in Middle America but the introduction of a plant that had already been domesticated somewhere else. Yet it is still important to determine when domesticated maize was introduced into the Tehuacán Valley for several reasons. First, its arrival establishes a temporal benchmark from which we can search back in time for evidence of the initial domestication of maize. Second, it provides an opportunity to consider the way of life in place when this crop plant was adopted. Third, it provides a starting point from which to track the spread of maize agriculture through the Americas.

Fortunately, at the same time that researchers were showing that the early maize from Tehuacán was domesticated rather than wild, efforts were also underway to establish its antiquity by the direct AMS radiocarbon method. Since the AMS method requires only a very small sample, the primitive cobs from San Marcos and Coxcatlán caves could be dated directly for the first time. Their age had previously been estimated at 7000 to 5500 B.P., based on conventional large-sample radiocarbon dates of charcoal recovered from the same cultural levels as the maize

Stands of a perennial species of teosinte (*Zea perennis*) in the state of Jalisco, Mexico. It is in Jalisco, in settings similar to the one shown here, that the populations of the annual teosinte *Zea mays* subsp. *parviglumis* grow today which rank second behind the central Balsas populations as being biochemically most similar to maize.

and thought to be of the same age. When Austin Long of the University of Arizona and his colleagues dated twelve of these early cobs by the AMS method (six each from Coxcatlán and San Marcos), however, they were found to range in age from about 4700 to 1600 B.P. The four oldest (all from San Marcos) were 4700 to 4600 years old. The earliest of the Tehuacán cobs, then, were at least 800 to 2300 years younger than previously thought. The new AMS dates thus provide a new time period for the arrival of maize in the Tehuacán Valley. The new dates do not, however, change the cultural context of its adoption in the Tehuacán Valley: the people who adopted maize were still small, seasonally mobile, hunter-gatherer societies, who added it into their way of life without changing that way of life radically. Neither do the new dates alter the documented sequence of subsequent cultural development in the region. But they do extend the hunter-gatherer way of life in the Tehuacán Valley up to 4700 B.P., and thereby considerably foreshorten the developmental sequence of farming societies.

AMS dates on the Bat Cave maize have shown it, too, to be about half as old as first thought. In the interval between the appearance of maize cultivation in the Tehuacán Valley at 4700 B.P. and its arrival in the southwestern United States at 3200 B.P., maize cultivation appears to have spread widely throughout Mexico. At the Zohapilco site on the shore of Lake Xochimilco in the Valley of Mexico, the arrival of maize is tentatively placed at 4300 to 3500 B.P. on the basis of pollen evidence. From carbonized kernels recovered at the site of La Venta on the Gulf coast, we know that maize first arrived there about 3400 B.P. Kernels and cob fragments from the Chilo site provide the earliest evidence to date of maize cultivation along the southern Pacific coast of Mexico, at 3500 B.P. Much of this Mexican maize has yet to be directly dated, however, so this sketchy timetable is open to revision.

South of Mexico, in Central and South America, two different categories of evidence now suggest two alternative scenarios for the southward expansion of maize cultivation. The first alternative is the small-kernel popcorn scenario, and it gains strong support from actual cob fragments and kernels recovered from archaeological sites in northern South America. This kind of evidence indicates that a small-kerneled, small-cob popcorn similar to the Tehuacán maize made the 3000-kilometer journey from its suspected heartland of domestication in the Balsas drainage of southwestern Mexico and reached northern South America by about 3000 to 2800 B.P. (1000 to 800 B.C.), about the same time it reached the southwestern United States. Carbonized kernels and cob fragments of this primitive Tehuacán-like popcorn appear in contexts dated at 2800 to 2400 B.P. at two sites along the Orinoco River in Venezuela, and are present in numerous flotation samples dating at 3200 to 2800 B.P. at the La Ponga site on the Valdivia River, close to the Pacific coast in Ecuador. Farther inland in Ecuador, the Nueva Era site has yielded small-kernel popcorn maize from hearths dating to 2710 and 2620 B.P.

Additional support of the idea that this maize from Ecuador and Venezuela represents the expansion of a primitive popcorn out of southwestern Mexico comes from farther south, high in the Mantaro River valley of the central Andes. Here, at an elevation of 3400 meters, the Pancan site provides a thousand-year-long developmental history of maize varieties in highland Peru. The earliest maize in this sequence, dating to 1500 B.P. (A.D. 450), is a small-kernel popcorn.

The second alternative scenario for the introduction of maize into South America has been proposed by Dolores Piperno of the Smithsonian Institution Tropical Research Institute and Deborah Pearsall of the University of Missouri. They argue that maize had been domesticated in Mexico early enough to have reached Central and South America by 8000 to 7000 years ago. Such an early arrival did not seem that out of line when maize was thought to have been domesticated in Mexico about 7000 years ago, but with the date now pushed up closer to 4700 B.P., the Pearsall and Piperno chronology of maize dispersal appears far less likely. How can maize have reached South America 2300 to 3300 years earlier than it first shows up as a domesticated plant in the region where it was probably first domesticated? Perhaps, one could argue, proof will eventually be found that maize was domesticated much earlier than the evidence now suggests. Let's look at the evidence from South America that supports the arrival of maize by 8000 to 7000 years ago.

In part the early-arrival chronology for maize rests on four maize kernels recovered from three sites in Ecuador. As is the case with most of the maize recovered from sites in Mexico, Central, and South

America, these four kernels have not yet been directly dated by the AMS method. Two of the kernels come from deposits dating at 5200 to 4700 B.P. at the Loma Alta site, and another from a context assigned a date of 3500 B.P. at San Isidro. In addition, a kernel fragment has been found imbedded in a ceramic vessel from deposits assigned an age of 3900 to 3800 B.P. at the San Pablo site in Ecuador. This single kernel is cited as evidence of the presence in South America of a variety of maize having large cobs and large and broad kernels, long before 3000 B.P. and the arrival of a primitive popcorn maize. Pearsall and Piperno propose that this larger-grained, larger-cobbed, clearly advanced maize must have had a long developmental history in South America, and therefore must have diffused out of Mexico at an even earlier date.

Evidence for this even earlier arrival comes not from preserved cob or kernel fragments but from microscopic opal phytoliths. These are small, hard particles found in the epidermal cells of some plant groups, and believed to add structural strength. Composed of silica, they can remain preserved in archaeological soils long after organic plant tissue has decayed away. Phytoliths vary in size and shape, and Pearsall and Piperno have conducted a wide-ranging comparison of phytoliths in maize leaves with those found in the leaves of wild grasses, especially the panicoid grasses, the group of wild plants that produce phytoliths most similar to those in maize.

Cross-shaped phytoliths provided Pearsall and Piperno with what they were looking for—a possible way of distinguishing maize from wild grasses in archaeological soil samples. They defined eight types of cross-shaped phytoliths and found maize to contain more type-1 cross-shaped phytoliths than do wild grasses, which in turn contained a greater abundance of type 2 and type 6. In addition, they learned that the type-1 cross-shaped phytoliths found in maize were larger than those in the wild grasses. In wild grasses, type-1 cross-shaped phytoliths only occasionally exceeded 16 microns in

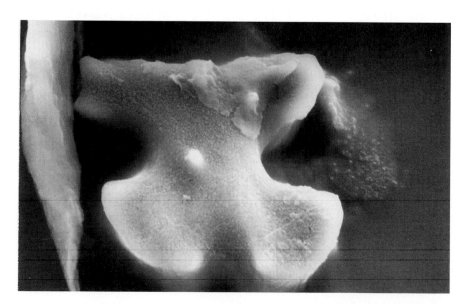

Cross-shaped phytoliths occur in the leaves, stalks, and other parts of maize and some wild grasses.

length and were never larger than 20.5 microns (one micron is a millionth of a meter). In maize, however, type-1 phytoliths larger than 20.5 microns occasionally did occur. Using these differences, Pearsall and Piperno developed a formula for distinguishing between phytolith samples produced by modern maize and those produced by wild grasses.

Armed with the formula, they then analyzed soil samples containing thirty to fifty cross-shared phytoliths recovered from fifteen different locations in the Real Alto site and the Las Vegas culture type site of coastal Ecuador. Of the fifteen samples that were analyzed, ten had scores too low to qualify as maize, but five yielded scores in the low end of the range for maize. Pearsall and Piperno looked at the conventional radiocarbon dates assigned to the deposits that had produced these five samples and concluded that maize was present at Real Alto by 4500 B.P. and that it had arrived at the Las Vegas culture type site between 8000 and 7000 years ago. The average size of the type-1 cross-shaped phytoliths was clearly critical in the identification of maize at these two sites. If the average size of the type-1 crosses, as measured through a light microscope, was reduced by only 0.1 to 0.4 micron, the five maize samples would no longer qualify as maize.

This does not appear to be very strong evidence for the presence of maize. Other questions further weaken the case for maize arriving in South America before 7000 years ago. How can we be sure of the age of these phytolith samples, for example? Because of their small size, phytoliths could have easily been moved down through sediments into deposits of a much earlier age. The AMS dates on the Bat Cave and Tehuacán maize, as well as the AMS dates on early domesticated beans, have highlighted the problems of dating small objects by association, and in the process they have essentially established a new standard of proof. Any kind of evidence for the presence of domesticates, including phytoliths, that is not dated directly, but is based only on age by association, carries far less weight today than it once did.

Another question is the absence of any cobs or kernels from domesticated maize in sites dating between 8000 and 4700 years ago. If maize was present as a domesticated plant in South America by 8000 to 7000 years ago, and was therefore domesticated earlier in Mexico, where are the kernel and cob fragments from this early time period? If such evidence of maize is preserved so well and found so widely in sites dating to 4700 to 3000 B.P., why doesn't it show up in excavated sites occupied earlier, such as the Tehuacán caves, Guilá Naquitz, and Zohapilco?

In the future, as more AMS dates are run on proposed early maize, as more early sites are excavated in the search for kernel and cob fragments, and as more and larger samples of phytoliths are analyzed, we will be in a better position to choose between these two scenarios. But for now, the evidence best supports the scenario that has maize spreading out of southwestern Mexico by about 5000 B.P., reaching Tehuacán by 4700 B.P., appearing on the southern Pacific and Gulf coasts of Mexico by about 3400 B.P., and arriving in South America and the southwestern United States by 3200 B.P.

I suspect that when the first morphological indications of the transformation of *Zea mays* subsp. *parviglumis* into domesticated maize are found, they will date between 6000 and 5000 B.P. Speculating further, I suspect that the societies that first brought maize under cultivation will be found to have occupied river valley settlements not very different from those of the first farming societies documented in the Tucson area of the Southwest and in eastern North America. Buried somewhere in the alluvial sediments of the Balsas and other westward-flowing rivers of western and southwestern Mexico, these settlements should differ from the small, seasonally occupied cave sites of mobile hunter-gatherers that have been the focus of investigation so far. They should be larger and have been occupied by a more sedentary people, and they should have deep midden deposits holding the remains of an abundant variety of wild plants, including teosinte, and animals on which these people would have long relied.

Although the site of Zohapilco in the Valley of Mexico is at the edge of a lake rather than in a river valley, and although it is at a much higher elevation, it does in a general way tell us what to expect from the settlements of the first maize cultivators. Here, from 7000 to 6000 B.P., hunter-gatherers lived in a zone with a high water table and rich soils. Scholars disagree as to whether the site represents a permanent settlement or a series of seasonal campsites. The plant and animal remains recovered from the midden deposit are the relics of an economy based on a broad spectrum of activities, especially fishing, hunting (primarily deer, rabbits, and water birds), and the harvesting of wild plants, including the seed plants *Chenopodium,* amaranth, and teosinte. This, I suspect, is close to what we can expect the settlements of the early river-valley maize farmers of western and southwestern Mexico to look like, once they are excavated.

Beans

Today more than a hundred different cultivated varieties of common beans (*Phaseolus vulgaris*) are grown. They come in a rich variety of different shapes, sizes, and colors—pinto, red, kidney, navy, Anasazi, and so on. It is this rich and diverse species

that became a favored crop in the New World. Three other species of *Phaseolus,* however, were also domesticated in the Americas. Two of these, the runner bean (*P. coccineus*) and the terary bean (*P. acutifolius*), are only rarely encountered in archaeological sites, and appear to have played little if any role in the lives of early farmers in the Americas. In contrast, the lima bean (*P. lunatus*), along with the common bean, were being cultivated over broad areas by the time Europeans arrived. The origins and early history of both these beans have been studied by a number of researchers, who have applied biochemical techniques to identify wild ancestor populations and direct AMS dating to determine the ages of early domesticated beans. Their findings have dramatically changed our understanding of the early history of beans in the Americas.

Because the wild ancestor of the common bean grows across such a broad geographical range, its present-day distribution is of little help in establishing where it was first domesticated. Wild populations of *Phaseolus* grow at elevations from 1500 to 2500 meters all the way from northern Mexico to northwestern Argentina. Nonetheless, Paul Gepts of the University of California, Davis, and his colleagues have studied wild bean populations throughout this vast geographical range and have found a way to identify where the common bean was first domesticated.

In order to trace the ancestry of the various cultivated varieties of common beans grown today in Mexico and South America, Gepts and his colleagues systematically analyzed seeds (beans) collected from both wild and cultivated plants growing throughout Mexico, Central, and South America. Their aim was to identify the different types of phaseolin present in the beans they studied. Phaseolin, a protein that is abundant in beans, takes a number of different forms. mon beans growing today in Mexico and Central America contain types of phaseolin (types S, M) that are distinctly different from the types of phaseolin present in wild populations growing in the northern Andes (types CH, B, I) and in the southern Andes (types T, C, H, J).

When Gepts looked at the types of phaseolin that were present in the beans of domesticated varieties, he found a very similar pattern. The type S phaseolin that was found in some wild populations in Mexico was also the dominant phaseolin type in Mexican cultivated varieties of the common bean. Similarly, the type T, C, and H phaseolins of south Andean wild populations dominated in the South American domesticated varieties.

These results indicated that *Phaseolus vulgaris* had been independently domesticated twice: in Mexico, from an ancestor population of type S phaseolin, and in the southern Andes, from ancestor populations having types T, C, and H phaseolin. A parallel investigation of lima beans has uncovered a similar division into Mexican and Andean groups, indicating that this species, too, was domesticated independently in the two regions. By showing that both of these plants were actually domesticated independently in both Mexico and the southern Andes, this research opens up a number of possible developmental scenarios. Were common beans and lima beans domesticated together in both South America and Mexico, or were there four separate processes of domestication, in different areas, at different times? And how was the domestication of beans related to the domestication of other crop plants, particularly maize and squash? Were they all domesticated together, as part of the same process, or in isolation, only later to be combined to form a distinctive and remarkably successful agricultural triad?

Most of the answers to these questions will have to come from analyses of plant remains recovered from archaeological sites rather than from research on present-day plant populations, but Gepts' research has nonetheless shown a tantalizing geographical link between the wild ancestors of maize and the common bean in Mexico. The type S phaseolin that dominates the domesticated varieties of common beans grown today in Mexico and Central America is found in only five of the ninety populations of wild common beans that occur today across the region. It was from these five populations—or rather from their remote ancestor populations—that the Mexican lineage of domesticated *P. vulgaris* was derived thousands of years ago. These five progenitor populations survive today in a small, well-defined area surrounding the modern city of Guadalajara, in the state of Jalisco. This area is about 500 kilometers north of the central Balsas River valley, the homeland of the populations of *Z. mays* subsp. *parviglumis* identified as giving rise to maize. Interestingly, the cluster of populations of *Z. mays* subsp. *parviglumis* that ranked just behind the Balsas populations as the possible progenitor of maize is located in Jalisco, and its range overlaps with that of the population cluster of wild common beans that gave rise to the domestic common bean in Mexico.

The close proximity of the present-day ranges of the wild ancestors of maize and the common bean would seem to support the possibility that they were domesticated together as part of the same developmental process. But that possibility will remain a conjecture until further archaeological research is focused on the river systems along the western slopes of the Mexican highlands, particularly the large Balsas drainage system, and smaller rivers to the north of it in Jalisco.

Both wild and domesticated beans are less likely than numerous other plants to be preserved in archaeological sites, so it is more difficult to trace the early history of this crop plant. The most commonly employed marker of domestication is an increase in the size of the seeds—or beans—determined either

In wild beans (left), seeds are expelled as an inner layer of stringy tissue dries out and the pod splits, leaving strongly twisted pod walls. In domesticated beans (center), this inner tissue layer is reduced and seeds are held in the pod until harvested. In beans cultivated for their "stringless" pods (green beans) (right), the total absence of fibers leads to shriveled pods that do not open.

by measuring the seeds directly or by measuring the pod that carries them. Pods also carry another frequently encountered morphological marker of domestication—a reduced dehiscence, or capacity to split open. The two halves or valves of wild pods forcibly expel the seeds when they split open along their connecting sutures as an inner layer of tissue dries out. This inner layer is reduced in domesticated plants, and the pods split open much less easily, if at all. Without a natural mechanism to disperse them, the seeds are held in the pod until someone comes along to harvest them.

In both Mexico and South America, almost all we know of the early history of the domesticated common bean we have learned from large seeds and associated pods recovered from deep deposits in dry caves. The age of these early domesticated beans was first established by radiocarbon dating of materials found in association with them and thought to be contemporaneous with them. But now Lawrence Kaplan of the University of Massachusetts in Boston, who has analyzed the vast majority of the beans recovered from sites in the Americas, has begun a comprehensive program to redate early *Phaseolus* specimens by the direct AMS method. The first two direct dates he obtained were run on specimens representing the oldest known domesticated common beans in Mexico and in South America. The results were no less stunning than those obtained on the early Tehuacán maize.

When Thomas Lynch, then of Cornell University, excavated Guitarrero Cave, located at an elevation of 2500 meters in the Callejón de Huaylas Valley in the Andes, he recovered abundant well-preserved plant remains, including the oldest evidence for domesticated common and lima beans in South America. Large seeds, clearly from domesticated crop plants, were found embedded in organic debris. A sample of this organic matrix yielded a radiocarbon date of 7680 B.P. At first these early dates were not considered out of line. In view of the present-day range of wild populations of these species along the eastern slopes of the Andes and phaseolin studies that confirmed their progenitor status, it was reasonable to assume that they were first domesticated in valleys high in the southern Andes, in a setting like that of Guitarrero Cave. At the same time, common and lima beans had also been found along the dry desert coast of Peru and Chile, in association with organic material whose age could be assessed by the standard large-sample radiocarbon dating technique. The results appeared to indicate that these two higher-elevation crop plants had reached sea level by 5000 to 4600 B.P.

Among the mass of organic debris in Guitarrero Cave that had produced a date of 7680 B.P., however, a single common bean selected by Kaplan for direct AMS dating yielded a date of only 2430 B.P. Not only does this date reduce the known age of the domesticated common bean in South America by more than 5000 years; it also calls into question the age of the domesticated lima bean found in the same mass of organic debris, as well as the dates when these two species arrived on the Pacific coast. Clearly the initial domestication in South America of a wide variety of plants, including *Phaseolus,* must be put on a firm chronological footing, along with questions regarding the cultural context of agricultural origins. Such a solid temporal framework does not now exist, and can be established only through comprehensive AMS dating programs such as the one being undertaken by Lawrence Kaplan. The same can be said, of course, for Mexico.

At the beginning of Kaplan's AMS dating program, the earliest evidence for domesticated common beans in Mexico was a single pod fragment recovered from zone 11, deep in the cultural deposits of Coxcatlán Cave in the Tehuacán Valley. Zone 11 produced a conventional radiocarbon date of 6975 B.P., but Kaplan's direct AMS age determination on the pod valve itself proved it to be only 2285 years old. This AMS date, it should be noted, adds to the wide range of dates obtained on corncobs from zones 11 to 13 in this cave, which extend from 1860 B.P. to 4090 B.P. The most likely explanation seems to be that the small directly dated *Phaseolus* pod, as well as some of the maize material, was carried down from higher layers in the cave by rodents or some other disturbance.

For now, this pod valve must stand as the earliest firmly dated evidence for domesticated *P. vulgaris* in Mexico. This plant was certainly domesticated before 2285 B.P., however, and earlier beans showing morphological markers of domestication are sure to be found, both as Kaplan extends his program to other potentially early specimens such

as the beans from Tamaulipas, estimated to be 6000 to 4000 years old, and as excavation uncovers new material, particularly, perhaps, in areas closer to the Jalisco heartland of the wild progenitor of *P. vulgaris.*

This future research may narrow the 2400-year gap that now separates the earliest directly dated domesticated maize in Mexico (San Marcos Cave, Tehuacán Valley, 4700 B.P.) from the earliest evidence of domesticated common beans (Coxcatlán Cave, Tehuacán Valley, 2285 B.P.). While the close proximity of the present-day wild progenitors of maize and *P. vulgaris* suggests that they might have been domesticated together in a shared process, other evidence provides less support for such a close relationship. Even though maize and beans are often found together in later crop complexes, they do not appear to have traveled together very often early in their history. For example, beans arrived about 900 years later than maize in both the southwestern and eastern United States. How closely their domestication coincided in time and cultural context, before they arrived in the Tehuacán Valley to make their first appearance in the archaeological record, fully domesticated, won't be known until excavation of earlier settlements successfully documents their transformation from wild to domesticated plants. Nor do we know how much of the developmental history of the third member of the Middle America agricultural triad, squash, was shared with maize and the common bean.

Squash

Of the five different species of squash (*Cucurbita*) that were domesticated in the Americas, the best known today is *Cucurbita pepo*. There are many dif-

Modern specimens of *Cucurbita moschata,* grown in Tamarindo, state of Veracruz, Mexico (top), and modern specimens of *Cucurbita maxima,* grown in Santa Cruz, Bolivia (bottom).

ferent cultivated varieties of *C. pepo,* including the jack-o'-lantern pumpkins and the green and yellow acorn, zucchini, marrow, spaghetti, and patty pan squashes. This most popular of all the squashes is also by far the most common in the archaeological record. Before we turn to it, however, let's briefly consider the other four domesticated squashes of the Americas. None of these four is very well documented in the archaeological record, and biological research has yet to illuminate their developmental history or locate all of their wild ancestors. Three are thought to have been domesticated in South America, since that is where most of the cultivated varieties are grown today and where their known or suspected wild ancestors are found. *Cucurbita maxima* is known to have been derived from *C. andreana,* a weedy species of warm temperate climates that grows today in Uruguay and Argentina. The undiscovered wild ancestor of *C. moschata* is suspected to survive in northern Colombia, in an area that boasts a high diversity of cultivated forms, some of which

have primitive-looking fruits. *Cucurbita ficifola,* found in medium to high altitudes, is thought to have a wild ancestor somewhere in the Andes, and a potential wild progenitor has been reported from near La Paz, Bolivia. *Cucurbita sororia,* the wild ancestor of *C. agyrosperma,* grows today in lowland thorn-scrub along the Pacific and Gulf coasts of Central America from southern Mexico south to Nicaragua.

In contrast to these relatively poorly known squashes, *Cucurbita pepo* has been the subject of considerable biological research. Taxonomic and biochemical studies carried out by Deena Decker-Walters of the Fairchild Tropical Garden in Florida indicate that all of the varieties of *C. pepo* squashes grown today can be sorted into two distinct lineages, and that these two lineages reach back across the millennia to independent centers of domestication. Interestingly, the color of a squash seems to provide a good indication of which of the two lineages it belongs to. The green and yellow squashes

Rediscovered growing in notheastern Mexico, *Cucurbita fratera* is a hardball-sized wild gourd that, until recent genetic research showed otherwise, was thought to be the wild ancestor of *Cucurbita pepo.*

belong to the lineage that originated in what is now the eastern United States, and the orange pumpkin forms belong to the lineage rooted in what is now Mexico.

The wild ancestor of the eastern North American *pepo* squash lineage (*C. pepo* subsp. *ovifera* var. *ozarkana*) has been discovered growing along rivers and streams of the Arkansas Ozarks, but the wild progenitor of the Mexican lineage has not yet been identified. Until recently the leading candidates were two wild gourds, one growing in northeastern Mexico (*Cucurbita fraterna*) and one in Texas (*Cucurbita texana*), but biochemical analysis has now ruled both of them out. Part of the reason these two wild gourds were prime suspects was their proximity to the caves excavated by Richard MacNeish near Ocampo in southwestern Tamaulipas, which have yielded some of the earliest evidence of possible domesticated *C. pepo* in the Americas.

Excavators at these caves recovered an abundance of *C. pepo* remains: they found both seeds and pieces of rind and peduncle (where the vine attaches to the fruit) scattered through the sixteen occupation layers of Romero's Cave and in the eight cultural layers of another nearby cave, known as Tm c 248. Many of these seeds, rind fragments, and peduncles were from a wild *Cucurbita* gourd. Harvested from nearby wild populations for their small seeds, these hard-walled gourds, the size of a hardball, may be the wild ancestor of the Mexican lineage of *C. pepo,* although they may be one of several wild gourds that did not become domesticated. The challenge for any archaeobotanist looking at the *Cucurbita* material recovered from these two caves is to identify and sort out the rind fragments and seeds of domesticated *C. pepo* from this background of harvested wild gourds. Rind fragments from wild and domesticated forms of *Cucurbita* sometimes be distinguished by their thickness and curvature (domesticated fruits are larger and have thicker rinds), but seed size is likely to have increased earlier than fruit size, and seed size is therefore a better morphological marker of the early stages of domestication.

When the Ocampo caves material was first analyzed in the 1950s, three squash seeds present in the earliest occupation layers were deemed large enough to be from domesticated plants. These layers were thought to date between 9000 and 7000 years ago, based on radiocarbon dates of 8540 and 8200 B.P. Higher in the caves' deposits, thirteen more seeds thought to be from domesticated plants were found in layers estimated to date between 6000 and 4300 B.P.

Since these seeds were first studied, however, AMS dating has been devised as a way of establishing ages directly, and more rigorous methods of comparative analysis have been developed for assessing whether seeds represent wild or domesticated plants. Once the squash seeds from these two sites have been directly dated, and their morphology has been studied in more detail, we will be in a much better position to determine if and when domesticated squash was added to the diet of the people who occupied the Ocampo caves. A similar program of reanalysis and redating has just been undertaken for the *C. pepo* materials recovered from Guilá Naquitz Cave in Oaxaca. The squash fragments recovered from this cave are especially interesting, for they have been proposed as perhaps representing the oldest domesticate in the Americas.

Excavated in 1966 under the direction of Kent Flannery of the University of Michigan, Guilá Naquitz is a small cave in the Oaxaca Valley of Mexico's southern highlands. One of the most carefully excavated and comprehensively analyzed dry caves in the Americas, Guilá Naquitz was found to contain a deposit 60 to 80 centimeters deep compris-

Excavation of Guilá Naquitz in 1966.

ing seven cultural layers or living floors. The uppermost layer (zone A) was dated to about A.D. 620–740 and was occupied by a fully agricultural group, judging from the presence of maize, beans, squash, avocados, chiles, cotton, and other crop plants.

The cultural layers directly beneath zone A were much older. These lower living floors represented at least six brief seasonal occupations, when the cave was inhabited in the late summer to late fall by small family groups, or "microbands." The occupations were spaced several hundred to several thousand years apart: the earliest (zone E) appears to date to about 10,800 B.P., while the uppermost (zone B1), directly beneath zone A, is assigned an age of about 8700 B.P.

Maize makes its first appearance in the thin ash lenses between zones A and B1 of Guilá Naquitz, and common beans show up in zone A and in deeper deposits where human or animal activities may have moved them down from zone A. *Cucurbita* material, in contrast, was found in all six of the early living

167

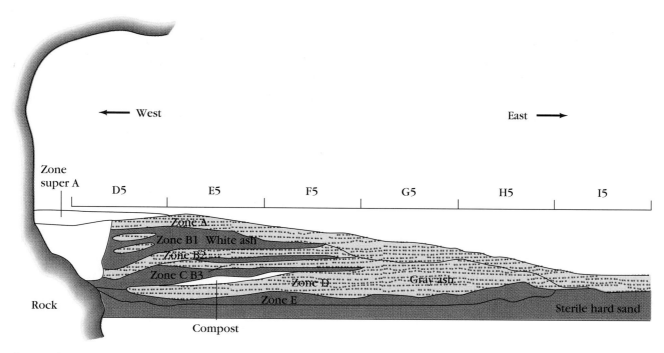

A vertical cross section of Guilá Naquitz, showing the different occupation zones.

floors dated between 10,800 and 8700 B.P. (zones E, D, C, B3, B2, B1). When Thomas Whitaker and Hugh Cutler analyzed the *Cucurbita* materials from these early living floors, they found that a wild species of *Cucurbita* gourd had been consistently collected, probably for its small protein-rich seeds, by the small family groups that sporadically occupied Guilá Naquitz in the fall of the year. A total of seventy-six rind fragments, small seeds, and peduncles found in zones E through B1 were identified as being from wild gourds.

In addition, a total of nine seeds and six peduncle specimens recovered from these six lower layers were proposed as being from domesticated *C. pepo* plants. The earliest of these specimens is a 10-millimeter-long seed recovered from zone D. A charcoal sample from layer D, found within a meter of this seed, yielded a radiocarbon date of 9800 B.P. If in fact from a domesticated squash plant, this seed would be more than 4000 years older than any other domesticate in the Americas. In zone C, dated to about 9300 B.P., three more seeds and two peduncles were identified as being from domesticated *C. pepo* plants. Curiously, zones B2 and B3 produced wild *Cucurbita* remains but nothing considered as possibly domesticated, while zone B1, directly below the overlying fully agricultural zone A, yielded five seeds and four peduncles identified as being from domesticated squash.

The very early age assigned to these materials thought to be from domesticated plants did not seem to be too out of line before AMS dating, when domesticated common beans in Middle America were thought to be 7000 years old, and domesticated maize had been assigned an age of 7000 B.P. But once the antiquity of the other two members of the agricultural triumvirate had been so substantially reduced, attention turned to the early *Cucurbita* remains from Guilá Naquitz. Were these seeds really from domesticated plants, or could they have come from wild gourds? Could some of the seeds found in zone B1 have been displaced down from zone A? In order to resolve these questions, Kent Flannery has initiated a program to restudy the *Cucurbita* material from the six early living floors at Guilá Naquitz. Squash seeds and other plant materials from all layers of the cave will be directly dated by the AMS method. At the same time, a comparative reanalysis of the ninety-one *C. pepo* specimens from Guilá Naquitz is under way. It will not be an easy task, however, to separate out any seeds or peduncles belonging to domesticated plants from those of wild plants, since an important baseline of comparison—the wild ancestor of the Mexican lineage of *C. pepo*—has not yet been identified. Until this reanalysis and redating is completed, the Guilá Naquitz squash material must remain in limbo. Flannery suspects, however, that the two largest squash seeds, measuring 17 and 12 millimeters in length, clearly from domesticated plants, likely filtered down from zone A, and that the remaining squash remains from the lower layers could well be from wild plants.

Thus, as in the case of maize and the common bean, the timing and cultural context of the initial domestication of *C. pepo* still remains to be established. The search continues for the wild ancestor of the Mexican lineage of *C. pepo,* and comprehensive programs are under way to reanalyze and directly date the third member of the Middle American agricultural trinity.

The parallel efforts to define and directly date the morphological changes that mark the transformation of maize, beans, and squash from wild to domesticated represent only one part of the research necessary to understand how, when, and why hunter-gatherers began to grow crops in Middle America. The other essential ingredient in this undertaking is a continuation and expansion of the research begun decades ago by Richard MacNeish in Tamaulipas: the careful selection of promising sites and the meticulous excavation and detailed analysis of recovered materials by a range of specialists. In my opinion, the most promising direction to take is out of the dry caves of the central and southern highlands of Mexico into the westward-flowing mid-elevation river valleys that empty into the Pacific, particularly the homelands of the present-day wild ancestors of maize and the common bean. I suspect that settlements dating at 6000 to 5000 B.P. in such river valley settings should span the transition from hunting and gathering to the cultivation of maize, beans, and squash, and that they will provide the information we lack on the emergence of agriculture in Mexico. I suspect, too, that when we learn the details of time and place we will find that the emergence of agriculture agrees in general with the scenario outlined by Kent Flannery in his interpretation of Guilá Naquitz Cave.

In brief, Flannery sees the deliberate planting and early cultivation of maize, beans, and squash in Middle America as logical extensions of hunter-gatherers' wide-ranging exploratory efforts to increase the predictability and abundance of resources and reduce the difference between good and bad years. Rather than maintain a rigid strategy for survival in environments where resources vary in abundance from one year to the next, hunter-gatherers were constantly experimenting, trying out innovations that might make resources, and life in general, more predictable. While the first experiments with deliberate planting of seeds and limited cultivation of maize, beans, and squash would have been a very small innovation, they quite likely would have produced clear positive results very quickly, and in this respect would have differed significantly from the vast majority of efforts in other directions. Both the landscape and the future would have become more predictable, as the creation of small patches of cultivated plants would have concentrated storable food resources in known nearby locations. The food gathered from more widely scattered and annually variable wild plants would thus have been supplemented in small but significant ways. By producing a small hedge against uncertainty, such early efforts would have encouraged further investments of time and effort. From the beginning, cultivation also differed in a far more important way from other experiments: it not only was successful on a small scale in the short run, but it also held the promise of much larger returns. Increased investment would have been linked in a positive-feedback loop with ever-increasing yields, and over time, what began as a small-scale extension of the usual hunter-gatherer experimentation would transform the world and the lives of many of its species, especially our own.

Although Flannery's model was developed to explain the emergence of plant cultivation in highland semi-arid zones, with their unpredictable cycle of wet and dry years, it can also apply to other, less harsh Mexican environments.

High-Altitude Agriculture of the Andes

Just as scholars have speculated for many years that Southeast Asia was an early center of tropical forest agriculture, so too have the vast rain forests of the Amazon lowlands long been proposed as the earliest center of agriculture in the Americas. Even though no clear evidence of early root crop cultivation has been found in either of these regions, they continue to be the subject of some speculation. But in South America attention has now largely been focused on the central spine of the Andes, and with good reason. Research carried out high in the valleys, basins, and grasslands of the Andes has shed considerable light on the emergence of distinctive agricultural economies based on high-altitude species of plants and animals.

At least five Andean species would come to define these high-altitude food production economies: llama (*Lama glama*), alpaca (*Lama pacos*), cuy or guinea pig (*Cavia porcellus*), potato (*Solanum*), and quinua (*Chenopodium quinoa*). We still have much to learn about when, where, and in what circumstances these and other Andean species such as the common bean and lima bean were domesticated. Nor do we know whether these plants and animals were domesticated separately, by different societies, or together as part of the same developmental process.

Quinua

The grain crop quinua (*Chenopodium quinoa*) is cultivated today in a band that stretches south out of Columbia along the Andes at elevations above 1800 meters, through Peru and Bolivia, and into Chile and Argentina. Free-living populations can also be found all along the Andean range of this domesticated plant. These free-living plants do not represent the wild ancestor of domesticated quinua, however; rather they are companion weeds that have developed in association with the domesticated plants over a long period of time.

Multicolored seed heads of *C. quinoa,* showing the dense terminal clusters of seeds in this Andean domesticate.

Hugh Wilson, a plant biologist from Texas A&M University, has extensively studied these cultivated and free-living populations and, based on protein analysis as well as fruit and leaf morphology, has found that they can be divided into northern and southern groupings. He has also identified a third group of quinua cultivated along the south coast of Chile, at low elevation. Wilson has shown that the populations of the southern Andes exhibit considerably more genetic variation than the other two, each of which contains a distinctive subset of the genetic variation that is present in the southern Andes. He suggests that this spatial pattern reflects quinua's developmental history: it was first domesticated in the south-central Andes of southern Peru and Bolivia, and then rapidly diffused as a domesticate north along the Andes and south to the Pacific coast.

This proposed south-central Andean heartland of initial quinua domestication is also contiguous with the western margin of the geographical range of *Chenopodium hircinum,* a broadly distributed wild chenopod that Wilson identifies as a top candidate for the wild ancestor of quinua. The earliest archaeological evidence for the domestication of this crop plant comes from the Junin basin of Peru, on the northern boundary of the proposed heartland of domestication.

Today quinua is a major crop in the high-altitude basins and valleys of the Andes.

Excavated by John Rick of Stanford University, Panaulauca Cave overlooks the Junin basin at an elevation of 4150 meters, 150 kilometers northeast of Lima. en Carol Nordstrom and Christine Hastorf of the University of Minnesota and University of California, Berkeley, set out to reanalyze the *Chenopodium* seeds recovered from Panaulauca Cave and a number of other Andean sites, they searched for a specific morphological marker of domestication—a reduction in the thickness of the seed coat or testa. Such a thinning of the testa, which, as we saw earlier, is associated with a reduced ability to delay germination and with seedbed competition, had already been shown to mark the initial domestication of *Chenopodium* in eastern North America.

Using a scanning electron microscope at the University of Minnesota, Nordstrom was able to measure the thickness of the seed coats of *Chenopodium* recovered from the occupation layers of Panaulauca Cave; she found them to be far thinner

(10 to 17 microns) than those of modern wild Andean *Chenopodium*. These seeds were in fact comparable in thickness to those of present-day domesticated varieties of *C. quinoa*. Although none of this thin-testa domesticated quinua has been directly dated, it has been recovered from occupational layers that date between 5000 and 4000 B.P. A single thin-testa domesticated seed was identified from layer 34, which has been assigned an age of 5000 B.P., and eleven more thin-testa seeds were present in levels 21 and 22, which date to about 4000 B.P. Thin-testa chenopod seeds increased in abundance in higher levels of the cave, and were also present in a number of other younger sites. While the age of the Panaulauca specimens will have to be confirmed through direct AMS radiocarbon dating, these preliminary results from the Junin basin suggest that quinua had been brought under domestication in the southern Andes by 5000 to 4000 B.P.

Interestingly, the Junin basin also provides ev-

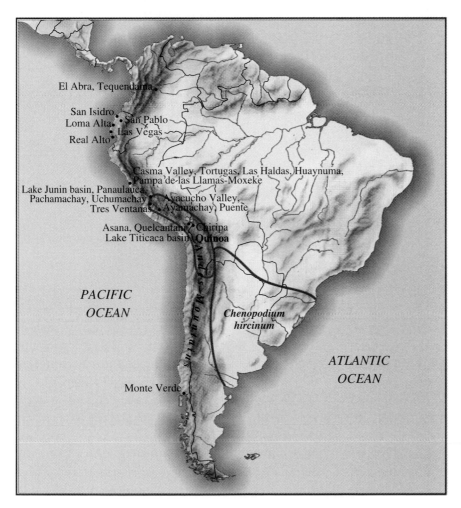

The proposed heartland of quinua domestication and the geographical range of its wild ancestor, *C. hircinum.* Also shown are the archaeological regions and sites of the south-central Andes that have provided evidence of early agriculture and of the domestication of quinua, potatoes, llamas, alpacas, and guinea pigs, as well as sites in Ecuador that have provided evidence in support of the phytolith chronology of early dispersal of maize into South America.

Panaulauca Cave, near Lake Junin, has yielded the earliest evidence of domesticated quinua in the south-central Andes.

idence that llamas were domesticated by 5000 to 4000 B.P., and a number of researchers have proposed that quinua and llamas may well have been brought under domestication together. Wild species of *Chenopodium,* including the ancestor of quinua, are highly favored forage plants for llamas. The ingested seeds often pass through the digestive system of llama undamaged, to be deposited far from where they were eaten, accompanied by a quantity of natural fertilizer to speed their growth. When humans began to control the movements of llama herds, and

to corral them at night near their settlements, stands of *Chenopodium* would flourish in the organic soils of corrals. By simply relocating corrals occasionally, and using the old corrals to protect the thriving new stands of *Chenopodium* from grazing by llamas, early herders could have established and maintained large, well-fertilized stands of this plant close to their settlements. Wild *Chenopodium* was also an important food source for Andean hunter-gatherer and early herding societies, and these corral stands would have provided not only a nearby supplement to the wild stands that they would seek out farther afield, but also an opportunity to further expand yields by deliberately planting and domesticating the plant.

Llamas and Alpacas

The high-altitude puna grasslands in the Andes are the primary habitat of the domestic llama (*Lama glama*) and its wild ancestor the guanaco (*Lama guanicoe*), as well as the smaller domestic alpaca (*Lama pacos*) and its wild ancestor the vicuña (*Lama vicugna*). All are camelids, members of the same family as the camel. Guanacos and vicuñas differ somewhat in the habitats they require: vicuñas live at higher elevations, do not migrate, and require water frequently, whereas guanacos range over wider areas and require water less frequently, and some populations migrate. Both species, however, fit the profile of preadaptation to domestication quite closely: they are gregarious, strongly social animals, and both species form herds that establish strong dominance hierarchies. As we have come to expect, their dominance hierarchies leave them open to control by human herders, who can step in at the top of the pecking order and take advantage of the pre-existing social structure to manage and manipulate the herds. Once these species were domesticated, llamas became extremely useful as pack animals, and both llamas and alpacas as sources of wool and of meat.

A number of cave sites in Peru document the specialized hunting of vicuna and guanacos as early as 9000 B.P. and also provide evidence of their domestication. Elizabeth Wing of the University of Florida and Jane Wheeler of Camelid Consultants International, along with a growing number of other researchers, are documenting the early history of human interaction with these species.

Some, but not all, of the criteria that are used to identify domesticated herd animals in the Fertile Crescent can be successfully applied in the Americas. With the possible exception of the development of a broader back in the llamas as a result of deliberate selection for better pack animals, no clear morphological markers of domestication in the camelids have yet been identified, nor do they appear to

Guanaco, the wild ancestor of the llama, was an excellent candidate for domestication because of its gregarious, strongly social nature and the strong dominance hierarchy of its herds.

Llamas were domesticated not only as a source of meat and wool, but also as a means of transporting goods across the high Andes. A broadening of the back may have resulted as breeders selected those animals better able to carry cargo; in fact, broader backs may provide a morphological marker of domestication in this species.

undergo any reduction in size as they become domesticated. As a result, the only way to recognize initial herding of these animals is to look for changes in age profiles and in the relative abundance of their remains in archaeological sites, along with other indirect indications of human control such as corrals.

In a series of caves in the Lake Junin basin, an increase in the abundance of camelids in relation to deer is proposed as evidence of early herd management and domestication. Here, in occupation layers of Panaulauca and Uchumachay caves dating earlier than 7000 B.P., camelids accounted for 26 to 42 percent of the animal bones. Between 7000 and 4500 B.P. camelids increased dramatically in importance,

now accounting for 82 to 98 percent of the bones recovered from occupation layers in Pachamachay, Panaulauca, and Uchumachay caves.

Accompanying this increase in the representation of camelids was a parallel increase in the proportion of newborn and young animals, which averaged about 22 percent of the total camelid remains in ten occupation layers in the Lake Junin area before 7000 B.P. and more than 50 percent in layers dating from 7000 to 3000 B.P. This increase in young animals is thought to be evidence that humans were managing domestic herds, since many infants would die from the spread of infectious diseases, particularly enterotoxemia diarrhea, among animals confined to crowded corrals. Even though abrupt changes in the weather, such as an unexpected snowfall, could cause a similar high mortality among the young in wild herds, it would not be very likely that the young animals killed by such a natural disaster would be found in the settlements of either hunters or herders. These dramatic shifts in both the general abundance of camelids and the number of very young animals provide good evidence that by 4500 B.P. societies in the Lake Junin basin had begun to exert control over camelid herds.

Eight hundred kilometers to the south, the Lake Titicaca basin has also yielded early evidence of camelid domestication. Today this area is a major center of alpaca herding. Camelids account for 98 percent of the animal bones recovered from deposits dating as early as 3500 B.P. in the Chiripa site, at the southern end of Lake Titicaca, providing good evidence for the herding of domesticated llamas by this early date. Mark Aldenderfer of the University of California, Santa Barbara, has recovered even earlier evidence for camelid domestication from the Asana site, located southwest of Lake Titicaca in the Rio Asana Valley. Analysis of the soil in this open-air settlement yielded the clear chemical signature of dung within an area defined by a series of post holes—the remains of a corral. The layer containing the corral has been dated to 4000 B.P.—clear evidence for managed herds and domesticated camelids by this point in time.

Midway between the Lake Junin and Lake Titicaca basins, in the lower-elevation Ayacucho Valley, age profiles and the increasing abundance of camelids in sites indicates a shift from hunting to herding these animals by about 4000 B.P. Farther north, in the highlands and along the north coast of Peru, domesticated camelids show up by 3000 to 2500 B.P.

Given the evidence that is now available from the Lake Junin and Lake Titicaca basins, and from the Ayachucho Valley, we know that the herding of domesticated camelids had been established over a broad area of the south-central Andes by 4000 B.P. This suggests that there could well have been several independent centers of domestication, and that camelid herds could have come under increasing human control in a parallel manner from Junin in the north to Titicaca in the south. Whether the early herding of these animals centered on these two large lake basins, as is now suspected, or involved other areas as well, is still to be learned.

There is also still much to be learned about a second, much smaller, but still important Andean domesticate—the guinea pig.

Guinea Pigs

The domestication and early history of guinea pigs (*Cavia porcellus* and other species) seems in general to parallel that of the camelids. The distribution of wild guinea pigs extends in a broad arc through the Andes from Venezuela in the north to Argentina in the south, so it provides few clues as to where they were first domesticated, other than the high valleys of the Andes.

Wild guinea pigs were clearly an important food source for early (12,000 to 7500 B.P.) hunter-gatherer societies toward the northern and southern ends of their range, judging from their abundant representation among animal remains at sites near Bogotá, Colombia, in the north (Tequendama, El Abra) and the Ayacucho Valley in southern Peru (Ayamachay, Puente). In the intervening areas of northern Peru and Ecuador, the remains of guinea pigs are rare in human settlements.

So far, the only evidence for where and when *Cavia* made the transition from a much-hunted wild animal to a domesticated source of meat comes from sites in the Ayacucho Valley, which show a significant increase in guinea pig bones by 4500 B.P. This development parallels the emergence of camelid herding in highland valley settings in the south-central Andes, and quite likely indicates the initial domestication of *Cavia*. In the future, when specific morphological changes in guinea pig skeletons associated with domestication are identified, they should serve to confirm both when and where guinea pigs were domesticated in the central Andes, and establish whether or not these animals may also have been domesticated independently in the north Andean region, where they were such a prominent part of the hunter-gatherer's diet.

Though guinea pigs are not related to true pigs, they do share some attributes that make them attractive candidates for domestication. They have a very high reproductive rate, can be fed household refuse, and can easily be raised in confined quarters in houses. It has been suggested that they may have been particularly susceptible to domestication because they were drawn to the warmth, protection, and food scraps of human habitation sites. It is also possible that their domestication in the central Andes was encouraged by the parallel domestication of quinua, which would have provided a dependable food supply for them.

Brightly colored tubers of oca, ullucu, and mashua. Today these species are still important food crops in the Andes.

The Potato

At least four species of tubers were brought under domestication in the Andes. Three of them, though still important in Andean farming economies today, were never adopted to any extent into lowland diets: oca (*Oxalis tuberosa*), mashua (*Tropaeolum tuberosum*), and ullucu (*Ullucus tuberosus*). The fourth Andean tuber to be domesticated, in contrast, has become a major food crop throughout the world—the potato (*Solanum tuberosum*).

Archaeological studies have given us as yet only relatively limited information about the early history of this plant, but studies of present-day wild and domesticated potatoes point to an origin in the central Andes. The Lake Titicaca basin is today the center of genetic variability of cultivated potatoes in South America, and a strong candidate for the place where potatoes were first cultivated.

The cultivated species *Solanum stenotomum,* which grows today at high altitudes in southern Peru and Bolivia, is thought to be the modern representative of the earliest cultivated potato, from which the domesticates *S. tuberosum* subsp. *andigena* and *S. tuberosum* subsp. *tuberosum* were later derived. Introduced into Europe in the sixteenth century and from there distributed throughout the world, subsp. *andigena* would become an important crop in northern latitudes, only to be mostly killed when the late blight (*Phytophthora infestans*) arrived in Europe in the 1840s. The resultant famine was particularly severe in Ireland. The subspecies *tuberosum* was then introduced into Europe from Chile, and today these two subspecies are the forms cultivated around the world.

Based on both DNA analysis and physical resemblances to *S. stenotomum,* several wild Andean species of *Solanum,* grouped together into the *brevicaule* complex, have been identified as the likely pool from which the primary progenitor of domesticated potatoes came. These and other wild species were probably important food sources for early Andean hunter-gatherers, and their remains have been found in contexts dating to about 12,000 B.P. at the Monte Verde site in south-central Chile.

At present the best archaeological evidence comes not from the highland valleys and basins where potatoes are most likely to have been domesticated, but from the desert coast of central Peru. Twenty well-preserved, if desiccated and shrunken, *Solanum* tubers were recovered from midden deposits estimated to date between 4000 and 3200 B.P. in four sites at the mouth of the Casma Valley (Tortugas, Las Haldas, Huaynuma, Pampa de las Llamas-Moxeke). The tubers were analyzed in the early 1980s by Donald Ungent of Southern Illinois University, Carbondale, and Sheila and Thomas Pozorski of the Carnegie Museum.

The tubers' surface features and the shape of their starch grains enabled the researchers to identify them as potatoes rather than other Andean root crops. When examined under the microscope, these ancient potatoes were also seen to have broadly elliptical to ovate starch grains comparable in size and shape to those of modern cultivated potatoes, and dissimilar to the smaller, long-pointed starch grains of modern wild forms.

Ungent and the Pozorskis also examined the starch-grain morphology of five other tubers, which had been recovered during excavation of Tres Ventanas Cave, located far from the coast in the Chilca Valley. Though the starch grains in these tubers were not well preserved, they seemed to be more similar to the grains of modern cultivated potatoes than to

0   1   2 cm

Three of the shrunken, desiccated potatoes recovered from 4000- to 3200-year-old archaeological sites at the mouth of the Casma River valley in Peru. Along Peru's dry desert coast, plant remains and other archaeological materials are often remarkably preserved.

Just as maize spread southward from its Middle American heartland into Central and South America, this preeminent New World domesticate was also carried northward into what is now the United States. Maize reached the Southwest by about 1200 B.C., and from there it was apparently taken across the Great Plains and arrived in the eastern deciduous woodlands of North America by about A.D. 1 to 200. In each of these two widely separated and environmentally very different regions, maize eventually became the most important crop plant of Native American societies.

But there is much more to the story of agriculture's origins in North America besides the spread of maize. Research carried out since 1980 in both southwestern and eastern North America has dramatically changed our understanding of the development of agriculture, especially in the East, where we now know farming societies flourished more than 2000 years before maize or any other crop plant was introduced from outside the region. Here, more than in any other region of the world, investigators have brought innovations in technology and scientific instrumentation to bear on the question of agricul-

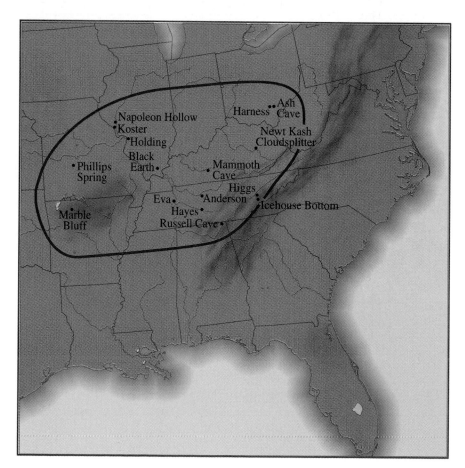

The location of archaeological sites that have provided evidence of the independent domestication of plants in eastern North America.

tural origins, and here they have most successfully integrated the analysis of archaeobiological materials with field and genetic studies of present-day plant populations. As a result, the development of agriculture is better documented in eastern North America than anywhere else in the world.

New approaches and direct radiocarbon (AMS) dating are also rewriting the history of Native American farming societies in the Southwest. This region vies with Europe to offer the clearest view of the complex ways in which hunter-gatherers adopt other societies' domesticates on their own terms, adding them into their established ways of life, meshing them with economics long shaped by the particular challenges and opportunities inherent in the local landscape.

Agriculture in the Eastern Woodlands

In the deciduous woodlands that stretch westward from the Atlantic Ocean to the eastern margin of the prairies and from the Gulf of Mexico north into Canada, Native Americans domesticated a variety of local seed plants. Though it went unrecognized for more than a century, the first evidence that eastern North America was an independent center of domestication was unearthed in 1876 by Ebenezer Baldwin Andrews when he excavated Ash Cave, in south-central Ohio.

Just as in Mexico and the south-central Andes, much of the evidence for early agriculture in eastern North America, from Andrew's time up until the 1960s, was recovered from caves and rock shelters. This is not because Native American societies in the eastern woodlands lived exclusively in caves—

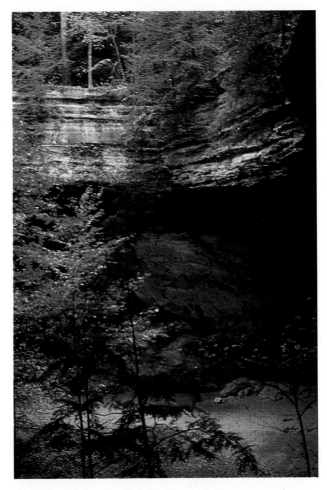

In 1876 Ebenezer Andrews excavated Ash Cave in south-central Ohio and discovered a 2000-year-old cache of seeds of *Chenopodium berlandieri,* now known to have been one of four plants domesticated in the eastern United States.

far from it. Their settlements are far more frequently found in river valley locations. Plant remains quickly decay away in the moist soils of the open-air river valley sites, however, unless they are accidently carbonized by partial burning. It was not

There are a rich variety of different species of *Chenopodium*. This illustration of a European species, *C. murale,* shows the numerous small seed clusters typical of wild chenopods, as well as the characteristic leaf pattern responsible for one of its common names—goosefoot.

until the 1960s that flotation recovery of such carbonized seeds from open-air sites in the East showed archaeologists that river valley settlements could provide clues regarding the shift to farming in the region. Up until then, the search for early domesticates was focused on rock shelters and the vestibules of caves, since in their dry soils uncarbonized plant remains can be remarkably preserved for thousands of years.

In Ash Cave, for example, Andrews uncovered a storage pit that contained what he estimated to be 6 gallons of small, sesame-sized black seeds. Andrews sent a sample of the seeds to the famous botanist Asa Gray, at Harvard University, who identified them as a species of *Chenopodium.* Also known as goosefoot or lamb's-quarter, a variety of species of *Chenopodium* today appear as weeds in gardens and fields across the East.

After he was through with them, Gray had the 25,000 *Chenopodium* seeds that Andrews had sent to him placed in a glass bottle and stored carefully away in Harvard's Peabody Museum collections. There the Ash Cave seeds remained for the next 108 years, largely undisturbed, until I traveled to Harvard in search of them. I had made a similar, though much shorter, journey the year before in hopes of locating another collection of ancient *Chenopodium* seeds, also long stored away in a museum. Climbing the stairs near my office, I had reached the attic of the National Museum of Natural History, where I sorted through materials excavated from Russell Cave, Alabama, in 1956. After several hours I came across what I had been looking for. Stored in a cigar box ("Tampa Nugget Sublimes") was a collection of about 50,000 *Chenopodium* seeds that had been found in a grass-lined storage pit in the cave.

The collections from Ash and Russell caves were the only large collections of well-preserved seeds of this plant known to have been recovered from storage pits. If, as I suspected, they represented the stored harvest of domesticated *Chenopodium* planted in field plots, they could provide an unmatched opportunity to look for morphological evidence of domestication.

Fortunately, *Chenopodium* had been independently domesticated in both South America (*Chenopodium quinoa*) and Middle America (*Chenopodium berlandieri* subsp. *nuttalliae*), where it is still grown today. Seeds from varieties now cultivated in Mexico provided a domesticated comparison for the Ash and Russell cave seeds, and modern wild populations of *Chenopodium berlandieri* in eastern North America provided a wild comparison. When viewed under a light microscope, seeds from both the Ash and Russell caves were found to exhibit a distinct netlike pattern of ridges on their tissue-thin outer

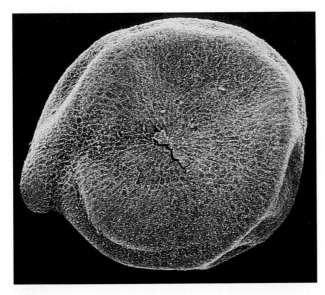

A scanning electron micrograph of one of the *Chenopodium berlandieri* seeds from Ash Cave. Along with a thin seed coat, one of the morphological markers of domestication in this species is the flattened (rather than rounded) seed margin, shown on the right edge, opposite the "beak."

pericarp layer. This patterning indicated that they belonged to the same species as the modern, wild, eastern North American populations of *C. berlandieri* that I had collected. But underneath this layer, the seed coat or testa of the archaeological seeds appeared much thinner than that of the modern wild chenopod. Such a thin seed coat represented a potential morphological marker of domestication. A thin-coated seed can sprout faster, and under cultivation those seeds that can sprout most quickly and shade out their neighbors will have a better chance of surviving to contribute to the harvest and next year's seed stock. Using one of the scanning electron microscopes at the National Museum of Natural History I confirmed my suspicions: the seeds from both Russell and Ash caves were from domesticated plants. Their seed coats were from 10 to 20 microns thick, much thinner than the testae of wild seeds, and comparable to those of modern domesticated forms. Direct AMS dates showed that the seeds from Ash Cave had been harvested and stored at around A.D. 230, those from Russell Cave about 390 B.C.

Accounts left by a French explorer, Le Page du Pratz, make it clear that this ancient domesticated chenopod was still being grown by the Natchez in the 1720s along the sandbanks of the Mississippi River. Its cultivation apparently ceased later in the eighteenth century, however, and today this domesticated seed plant is extinct. Once a clear morphological marker of domestication for this plant had been identified and its long historical presence in eastern North America was recognized, the next key question to be answered was when it was brought under domestication. The answer to this question, too, was found waiting in museum collections.

In 1929, archaeologists excavating the Marble Bluff shelter deep in the Arkansas Ozarks uncovered, in a crevice along the back wall, a large number of

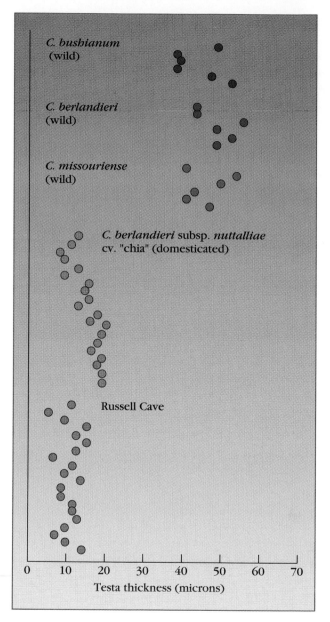

C. bushianum
(wild)

C. berlandieri
(wild)

C. missouriense
(wild)

C. berlandieri subsp. *nuttalliae*
cv. "chia" (domesticated)

Russell Cave

0   10   20   30   40   50   60   70

Testa thickness (microns)

Seed coat thickness in wild and domesticated *Chenopodium*. Unlike present-day wild *Chenopodium* species in eastern North America, which have seeds with thick testae (40 to 60 microns), the seeds from Russell Cave had seed coats less than 20 microns thick, comparable to the seed coats of a domesticated variety of *Chenopodium* grown today in Mexico.

This remarkably preserved 2000-year-old woven bag, from the Edens Bluff shelter in the Arkansas Ozarks, is likely to be similar to the one from Marble Bluff shelter found to contain 3000-year-old domesticated *Chenopodium berlandieri* seeds.

small seeds apparently originally stored in a woven bag, of which a few small fragments were also found. In the mid-1980s, after more than a half century of storage in the University of Arkansas Museum in Fayetteville, the seeds drew the attention of Gayle Fritz of Washington University in St. Louis. She found them to be a thin-testa, domesticated *Chenopodium*. A direct radiocarbon date of material from the bag indicated that it had been placed in the crevice of the Marble Bluff shelter about 3000 years ago.

Even earlier evidence of this species' domestication in the East was found when C. Wesley Cowan of the Cincinnati Museum of Natural History and I analyzed human paleofecal samples excavated from the Newt Kash and Cloudsplitter rock shelters of eastern Kentucky. Often well preserved in dry caves and rock shelters, human paleofeces frequently contain intact seeds that provide direct evidence of what people were eating thousands of years ago. The *Chenopodium* seeds extracted from the Newt Kash and Cloudsplitter paleofeces exhibited all of the morphological markers of domestication, and direct AMS dating revealed that they had been grown, harvested, and eaten about 3500 years ago. For reasons to be discussed a little later, it is likely that the date of *Chenopodium*'s domestication in the East will eventually be pushed back another five or ten centuries, to 4000–4500 B.P.

In this brief discussion of *Chenopodium* we see several of the most interesting aspects of the recent revolution in archaeobotanical research in eastern North America: the importance of remarkably preserved remains of plants recovered from their places of storage and from paleofeces in dry caves and rock shelters; the continuing value of carefully curated museum collections; and the recent application of advances in scientific technology such as AMS radiocarbon dating and scanning electron microscopy.

Chenopodium berlandieri was not the only indigenous seed plant brought under domestication in the East, nor was it the first to be identified and documented. The accounts of early travelers such as Le Page du Pratz prompted the anthropologist Ralph Linton to suggest in the 1920s that Native Americans may have been cultivating small seed crops in the East before the introduction of maize. Direct evidence for this possibility was reported in the 1930s, when the pioneering archaeobotanists Melvin Gilmore and Volney Jones of the University of Michigan analyzed assemblages of seeds and plant parts recovered from rock shelters in eastern Kentucky and the Arkansas and Missouri Ozarks.

Excavated by C. Wesley Cowan of the Cincinnati Museum of Natural History, Cloudsplitter rock shelter in eastern Kentucky has yielded some of the oldest evidence of domesticated plants in eastern North America.

Gilmore and Jones identified a number of local plants as possible domesticates on the basis of both the abundance and large size of their seeds found in rock shelter deposits. Three of their candidates have since been convincingly shown to be ancient domesticated crop plants: goosefoot (*Chenopodium berlandieri* subsp. *jonesianum*), marsh elder (*Iva annua* var. *macrocarpa*), and sunflower (*Helianthus annuus* var. *macrocarpus*).

The seeds of both marsh elder and sunflowers are enclosed in a hard outer shell, or achene. Soon after domestication both seeds and achenes became enlarged in response to selective pressures in the seedbed, which favored seeds with large food reserves that enabled seedlings to grow quickly and shade out their neighbors. Later the seeds became larger still as farmers deliberately selected plants that produced large seeds.

Napoleon Hollow, an open air site in the lower Illinois River valley northwest of St. Louis, has yielded the earliest evidence of the domestication of marsh elder. David and Nancy Asch, who analyzed material recovered from the midden deposits there, discovered 44 marsh elder achenes having an average length of 4.2 millimeters, considerably larger than the 2.5 to 3.2 millimeters average size recorded for achenes of modern wild marsh elder. One of these achenes yielded a direct accelerator date of 4000 B.P.—the earliest indication of the domestication of this eastern plant.

Until recently, the earliest evidence for domesticated sunflowers in the eastern United States came from northwestern Arkansas and eastern Tennessee in the form of achenes that were larger than those of modern wild sunflowers, which range in length from about 4.0 to 6.0 millimeters. The 2850-year-old carbonized sunflower achenes recovered from the Higgs site along the Tennessee River in eastern Tennessee averaged 7.8 millimeters in length, while

This wild sunflower in New Mexico, with its numerous small seed heads, is likely to be similar to the first domesticated sunflowers of 4200 years ago.

achenes of a similar age from the Marble Bluff rock shelter in northwest Arkansas were even larger, averaging 8.8 millimeters in length. The Marble Bluff and Higgs sunflower achenes were so much larger than achenes of modern wild sunflowers, in fact, that researchers expected evidence of even earlier domestication of this species to turn up eventually.

This expectation was realized when Gary Crites of the McClung Museum of the University of Tennessee analyzed six carbonized sunflower seeds from the open air Hayes site in the valley of the Duck River in central Tennessee. Here, deep and extensive midden deposits reflected a long sequence of occupational episodes. Flotation of midden soils yielded abundant plant remains, including the carbonized sunflower seeds, whose achenes can be estimated to have averaged 6.9 millimeters in length, clearly larger than the achenes of modern wild sunflowers. One of the seeds was directly dated by the AMS method, yielding a date of 4265 B.P. These sunflower achenes effectively pushed back the date of the sunflower's domestication more than 1300 years, and into close agreement with the domestication of marsh elder at about 4000 B.P. Sunflowers occupy an interesting position as an eastern domesticate: they are not native to these woodlands. The present-day range of wild sunflowers extends across the Great Plains and much of the western United States, but does not extend into the East. It appears that they were introduced into the East as camp-follower weeds or in the early stages of cultivation just before they were domesticated.

The excavations at Napoleon Hollow and the Hayes site were part of a shift toward excavation of river valley settlements that began in the 1960s. Just as in the Southwest, Mexico, and the central Andes, archaeologists looking for evidence of domestication had focused on dry caves and rock shelters at higher elevations rather than river valley settlements at lower elevations. This changed in eastern North America, however, when substantial federal funding was provided for excavating sites slated for destruction to make way for dams, highways, and other construction projects. The Napoleon Hollow site was excavated because it was in the right of way for a bridge over the Illinois River, and the Hayes site was scheduled to be flooded by a dam. As funding for research and analysis increased, flotation recovery became standard practice in the excavation of river valley sites, and the quantity and quality of seeds and other small plant parts recovered from archaeological deposits dramatically increased. A wealth of new information was uncovered regarding the origins of agriculture in the region, and the success of these excavations demonstrated that river valley settlements are as important a source of information as upland caves and rock shelters, not only in eastern North America, but throughout the Americas.

If AMS dating had been available to Gilmore and Jones in the 1930s, they would easily have recognized eastern North America as an independent center of plant domestication. They frequently found maize, too, in the dry rock-shelter deposits they analyzed, but could never confidently establish which came first, the introduction of maize or the domestication of local seed plants. The answer did not come until the 1980s, when for the first time it was possible to determine when maize arrived in the eastern woodlands. At the same time that AMS dating was establishing the time frame for the domestication of local seed plants, it was also demonstrating that much of the maize that was thought to be 3000 years old or older was actually much younger. The carbonized corn kernels from the Harness site in Ohio (A.D. 220), the Icehouse Bottom site along the Little Tennessee River in extreme eastern Tennessee (A.D. 175), and the Holding site in the American Bottom east of St. Louis (A.D. 1 to 150) now provide the earliest evidence for the introduction of this crop into the East, more than 2000 years after local seed plants had been domesticated.

At the same time, however, AMS dating was also casting a dark shadow across the idea that Native Americans had independently domesticated plants in eastern North America. Small carbonized fragments of rind, less than 2 millimeters thick and exhibiting the distinctive cellular cross section of the species *Cucurbita pepo,* were being found in flotation samples recovered from a number of river-valley sites in Illinois and Kentucky. These fragments yielded direct AMS dates of 7000 to 5500 B.P. Though *Cucurbita pepo* does include some wild gourds, it is far better known for its rich variety of domesticated pumpkins and squashes. It was also thought to have been domesticated in Mexico about 10,000 B.P., and no wild *C. pepo* gourds had ever been found in eastern North America north of Texas. The archaeological sites that had produced these early rind fragments were far to the north of the present-day range of the Texas wild gourd (*Cucurbita texana*), which grows in floodplain habitats along rivers of east Texas that flow into the Gulf of Mexico. The obvious conclusion was that domesticated squash had been introduced into the East, along with the concept of agriculture, as much as 2500 years before sunflowers, marsh elder, or chenopods were domesticated. The domestication of local plants, then, would have been a secondary, coattail process.

This scenario, however, has been overturned by an alternative explanation: that *Cucurbita pepo* was independently domesticated twice from different progenitor populations of wild gourds. It was domesticated both in Mexico, at a still undetermined place and time, and again in eastern North America, about 4500 years ago, at the same time that the other three eastern seed plants were domesticated.

The evidence from eastern North America strongly supports this explanation of multiple episodes of domestication. All of the early *Cucurbita* rind fragments are thin—less than 2 millimeters—rather than thick or fleshy, and could easily have come from indigenous wild gourds. The few seeds that dated earlier than 4500 B.P., from the Anderson site in Tennessee and the Cloudsplitter rock shelter in eastern Kentucky, were also small, within the range of modern wild gourds. The earliest morphological marker of *C. pepo*'s domestication in fact does not appear in the East until 4500 to 4300 B.P., about the same time that sunflowers and marsh elder were domesticated. More than sixty *C. pepo* seeds recovered from waterlogged deposits of the Phillips Spring site in west-central Missouri have an average length of 10.7 millimeters, larger than seeds produced by present-day wild *Cucurbita* gourds such as *Cucurbita texana.* Interestingly, the rind fragments and peduncles (where the vine attaches to the fruit) recovered from Phillips Spring closely resemble those of wild gourds, suggesting that domestication was just under way—so far only seeds showed morphological changes associated with domestication. The people who had begun to plant them had not yet started to select plants for larger and fleshier fruits.

Deena Decker-Walters, a botanist then at Texas A&M University and an authority on *C. pepo,* provided additional support for the two-center explanation in 1986. Her biochemical analysis revealed that this species comprised two ancient developmental lineages. The first contained all of the present-day Mexican land races of *C. pepo*; the second, apparently eastern North American lineage included the summer and acorn squashes.

The final, convincing piece of evidence came in the early 1990s, when the wild ancestor gourd of *C. pepo*'s eastern squash lineage was discovered growing deep in the Missouri and Arkansas Ozarks,

The Ozark wild gourd. Still suspended from the vine after an early frost has withered the leaves, striped fruits of the Ozark wild gourd will soon fall to the ground, to be carried away by the floodwaters of the following spring.

where it had been hiding in plain sight for more than 150 years. Distinct from its southern cousin the Texas wild gourd, this hardball-sized gourd had been occasionally recorded and collected in river valleys across the East, but was consistently viewed as not belonging to the natural flora. It was thought to be a human creation—a domesticated ornamental gourd that had escaped from the garden to become an agricultural weed, occasionally surviving in the wild for a year or two.

In an effort to test this garden-escape explanation, Wes Cowan of the Cincinnati Museum of Natural History and I began by asking whether garden gourds were actually being cultivated in the East by the time the plants were first mentioned as occurring in natural habitats. A survey of university and museum herbariums turned up a number of *C. pepo* gourds collected in the nineteenth century, with the earliest dating to the late 1840s and 1850s. These came from the St. Louis area, where several prominent botanists of the day considered them part of the local indigenous flora. Were they wild, or were they garden escapes? To try to determine when *C. pepo* gourds were first offered for sale in mail order catalogs, we consulted the extensive archive collection of seed catalogs in the National Agricultural Library in Beltsville, Maryland. If the catalogs didn't yet offer gourd seeds in the 1850s, then there would be no gourds in St. Louis gardens to escape into the wild. Gourd seeds, it turned out, were not consistently offered for sale in seed catalogs until the early 1870s. But we also found that a seed merchant in Philadelphia had offered *C. pepo* gourd seeds as early as 1805, so the door was still not fully closed on the garden-escape hypothesis. Stronger evidence of an indigenous eastern wild gourd was needed—living proof.

In the fall of 1990, Wes Cowan and I set out on a two-week survey of some of the sandbanks and gravel bars of remote Ozark watercourses to see if this mysterious gourd might be more than a weedy escape among cultivated plants. Suffering through day after difficult day of deep-blue skies, clear-flowing streams, and stunning fall foliage, we again and again found floodplain populations of *C. pepo* gourds flourishing far from any farms, in habitats where they could well have been long established as members of floodplain plant communities. The isolated Buffalo River in Arkansas provided some of the best evidence of *C. pepo* gourds growing in the wild. Even this documentation of gourds flourishing far from any evidence of human cultivation, however, was not enough to confirm the wild status of this floodplain plant unequivocally. Final proof came when Deena Decker-Walters and Terrance Walters, then at the Fairchild Tropical Garden in Miami, analyzed specific proteins of this Ozark wild gourd (*Cucurbita pepo* subsp. *ovifera* var. *ozarkana*). Their research confirmed that the gourd

found growing along streams and rivers in the Ozarks was a wild plant, not a garden escape. More important, they concluded that the wild Ozark gourd closely matched the profile of what one would expect for the wild ancestor of the eastern lineage of domesticated squashes.

We found that this wild Ozark gourd occupies a very interesting niche in river floodplain habitats. It is what can be called a floodplain weed—an aggressive colonizer of areas annually swept clear of plant life by the river's currents. Its small, hard-walled fruits are buoyant, and they are borne along on the rising floodwaters of spring until they are trapped in the willows and bushes of sandbanks and gravel bars. As the gourds break open, their cargo of a hundred seeds or more is released to colonize the open, sunny river's edge. Aggressive vines stretch up into trees and across the bare soil cleared by the flooding river.

Two of the other three species of plants domesticated in eastern North America today occupy the same floodplain niche as the Ozark wild gourd. The seeds of marsh elder are also dispersed by floodwaters, colonizing the still wet ground after the flood waters recede. Goosefoot (*C. berlandieri*), too, grows abundantly on the sandy banks and under the willows along the edge of rivers. Both marsh elder and *C. berlandieri* are essentially floodplain plants. Like the wild Ozark gourd, they have been shaped by thousands of years of evolution and selection along the streams of eastern North America. All three are finely tuned to flourish on naturally disturbed open soil.

As a result, these three floodplain weeds are also very aggressive colonizers of floodplain agricultural fields and other places where the soil has been disturbed by humans. Although he did not single out these three species or focus on eastern North America, Edgar Anderson of the Missouri Botanical Gar-

The exposed gravel bars and floodplain plant community of Gourd Island, along the Buffalo River in Arkansas, is a typical habitat for the Ozark wild gourd.

den proposed in the 1950s that in general such floodplain weeds were powerfully preadapted to domestication. Their proclivity for aggressive growth in open soil disturbed by either floodwaters or farmers probably played an important role in their initial domestication by Native Americans.

Hunter-gatherers harvested all three of these wild plants before 4500 B.P., so the plants were well positioned for domestication. They all produce an abundance of nutritionally rich seeds, so they would have been a valuable source of food before any plants were domesticated in the region. How, then, did they come to be grown in prepared seed plots? A good way of approaching this question is to consider when it was that hunter-gatherer societies in the East first began to create areas of disturbed soil that continued to be disturbed year after year and so provided good places for these floodplain weeds to colonize. In response to changes in climate and in the seasonal patterns of stream flow, plant and animal biomass levels appear to have increased dramatically in some river valleys in Illinois, Kentucky, Tennessee, and Alabama between 7000 and 5500 years ago. As resources became much more abundant in the river valleys than in the uplands, some hunter-gatherer groups became more sedentary and more firmly tethered to the valley's resources. River valley settlements became larger and more permanent. The small, short-term campsites that were scattered throughout the uplands and valleys in earlier times came to be supplanted by more substantial settlements, invariably close to oxbow lakes or to shoals where shellfish lived, where hunter-gatherers stayed throughout the warm season and perhaps year round. Over the years the refuse piled up. The deep midden deposits created by these settlers, along with their constant disturbance of the soil, provided the perfect opportunities for goosefoot, gourds, and marsh elder.

None of these more substantial river valley settlements that have been excavated—the famous Koster site along the lower Illinois River, the Black Earth site in southern Illinois, the Eva and other sites along the Tennessee River, and several sites along the Tombigbee River in northern Mississippi—have provided any clear overall community pattern or even any house outlines. Prepared clay floors sometimes suggest the locations of houses, and clusters of pits and tools indicate areas where various activities were carried out, but in general these settlements are difficult to re-create in overall plan. They are nonetheless impressive in their size, sometimes reaching a depth of several meters and

extending for 50 meters or more along the river's edge. Distinctive bone pins and stone spear points have been found distributed across much of the interior mid-latitudes of the East, telling us that the river valley communities exchanged ideas and materials over a broad area.

When these river valley settlers gathered seeds from stands of floodplain weeds and carried them home for storage and processing, they would have inadvertently dropped some of them onto disturbed soil where the plants could establish self-renewing colonies. Once established, these stands of floodplain weeds would have provided both a close-at-hand supplement to wild populations, and an opportunity for the settlers to experiment with intervening in the life cycle of the plants. Such simple steps as weeding these unintended gardens and scattering some of the harvested seeds over a broader area could eventually lead to the decisive step of deliberate planting. Once the cycle of fall harvest, storage of seed stock over the winter, and spring planting began, morphological change and domestication would have followed, probably within 50 to 100 years.

Deliberate planting of at least some of the four eastern seed plants had probably begun by 5000 B.P., and all four were probably being cultivated by 4500 B.P. Right now no single river valley can be identified as a heartland of plant domestication in the East. Rather, a good number of small, largely independent, and semi-isolated societies in stream and river valleys over a broad area appear to have experimented with domestication. They do not appear to have been strongly threatened by population growth, limited resources, or environmental decline. To the contrary, they seem to have been "affluent" and sedentary hunter-gatherers who lived in relatively rich environments. Fish, migratory waterfowl, and shellfish were important in their diets, as were whitetail deer, raccoons, turkeys, rabbits, and squirrels, along with hickory nuts, acorns, and other plant foods. Cultivated plants seem at first to have filled a small but significant role as an additional storable food reserve for winter and early spring.

Mortars and grinding stones attest to the processing of nuts and acorns, and the seeds of both wild and domesticated plants. Once the outer seed coat or testa of the sunflower, marsh elder, chenopod, or squash seed was cracked enough to allow digestion of its contents, it may not have been processed any further, but simply eaten as is. Human paleofeces recovered from caves often contain seeds of these domesticates that appear to have been simply chewed with little if any additional preparation. These seeds could also have been combined with other plant foods or meat and roasted or boiled in skin-lined pits (pottery had not yet been developed in the East).

Not for more than a thousand years, until about

Each of these circular earthen mounds covers a charnel house, where a Hopewell society cremated its dead about 2000 to 1800 years ago. Mound City National Monument, Ohio.

500 to 200 B.C., did farming become more important in the East. At this time, the seeds of cultivated plants, including the eastern domesticates and several other apparently cultivated plants such as erect knotweed (*Polygonum erectum*), maygrass (*Phalaris caroliniana*), and little barley (*Hordeum pusillum*), begin to appear in far greater abundance in river valley settlements and upland caves from eastern Tennessee to Arkansas and from northern Alabama to central Ohio and Illinois.

Probably the most dramatic evidence of this increased reliance on cultivated crops comes from Mammoth Cave in Kentucky. Here Patty Jo Watson of Washington University in St. Louis and Richard Yarnell of the University of North Carolina, Chapel Hill, have recovered and analyzed a large number of human fecal samples directly dated to

about 600 to 500 B.C. They consistently have found the paleofeces to contain large numbers of seeds from domesticated plants. Though it appears that this society relied heavily on field crops, it might also be the case that small groups brought along a supply of "trail mix" when they came to mine for minerals. Whether the Mammoth Cave evidence is of a specialized cavers diet, or reflects what people were eating more generally, there is clear evidence that peoples throughout the region had shifted to greater reliance on local seed plants by 200 B.C., before maize was introduced into the region.

This increase in the cultivation of seed crops in the eastern woodlands took place just as river valley societies were developing that became famous for their mortuary ceremonialism, large geometric earthworks, and remarkably beautiful artifacts, of-

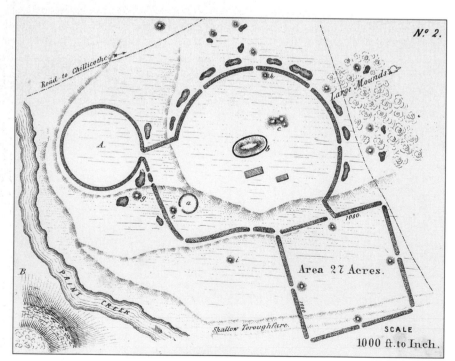

Hopewellian societies of eastern North America, who cultivated seven different species of seed plants, are renowned for their large geometrical earthwork constructions, many of which were carefully recorded in the mid-nineteenth century. (This illustration is Plate 21 in Squire and Davis's *Ancient Monuments of the Mississippi Valley,* 1848).

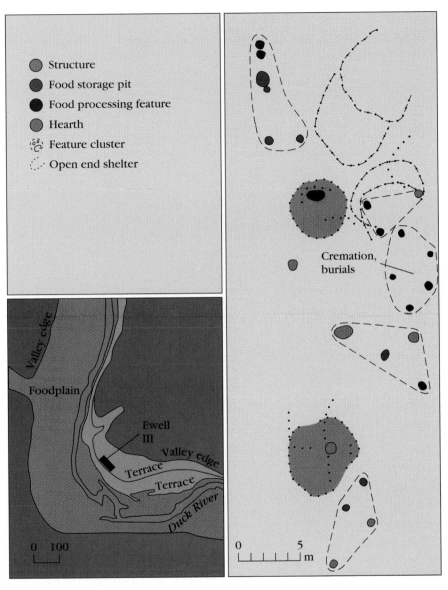

Legend:
- ● Structure
- ● Food storage pit
- ● Food processing feature
- ● Hearth
- ⊙ Feature cluster
- ⌒ Open end shelter

Valley edge

Foodplain

Ewell III

Valley edge

Terrace

Terrace

Duck River

0 100

Cremation, burials

0   5
⌐ ⌐ ⌐ ⌐ ⌐ m

Hopewellian farmers lived in small single-family settlements, such as the Ewell III site, along the Duck River in central Tennessee.

ten made out of raw materials obtained from great distances. The Hopewell societies of south-central Ohio are the best known of these farming groups. Much of what we know about them and about the Hopewellian cultures in other parts of the East comes from their ceremonial centers and burial mounds rather than from where they actually lived. In recent years, however, archaeologists have located and excavated a number of their settlements, which turn out to be not large villages but single-family farmsteads dispersed across the landscape within a day's journey of a ceremonial and mortuary center. These single-family farmsteads, located in stream or river valleys, consisted of a house or two, nearby refuse deposits, and clusters of storage pits, cooking pits, and hearths. Caves and rock shelters were also occupied by Hopewellians, sometimes as long-term settlements such as at Russell Cave, but more frequently for only short periods of time, such as at Ash Cave. Three of these Hopewellian settlements—Holding, Harness, and Icehouse Bottom—provide the earliest evidence for the arrival of maize in the eastern woodlands.

Curiously, even though eastern North American societies that adopted maize had already been cultivating local seed crops for more than 2000 years, and would have been, one would think, well prepared to take advantage of its agricultural potential, they did not do much with it for another 800 to 900 years. It was not until about A.D. 900 to 1000 that maize-centered agriculture emerged in eastern North America and rapidly came to dominate economies from southern Georgia to southern Ontario and from the Atlantic coast to Minnesota. Corn is found only rarely in eastern archaeological deposits dating before A.D. 800 to 900, an indication that even in those areas where it was grown, it was a minor crop.

Direct evidence of that minor role comes from the analysis of stable carbon isotopes in human bone. All of the indigenous wild and domesticated plants that were important in the diets of eastern Native Americans share a particular photosynthetic pathway (C-3) to transform sunlight into energy, whereas maize has a different photosynthetic pathway (C-4). As a result, we can ascertain the amount of corn these people ate by analyzing skeletal samples to determine the relative occurrence,

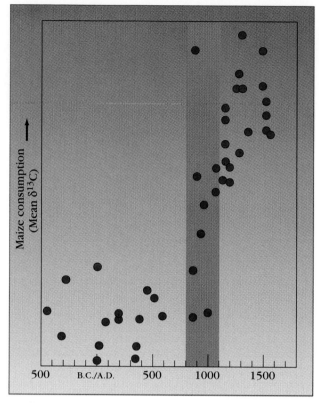

At about A.D. 900, maize became much more important in the diet of agricultural societies from southern Ontario to northern Florida, as shown by the abrupt change in $\delta^{13}C$ values of human bone.

or ratio, of two isotopes of carbon, ^{12}C and ^{13}C. Detailed analyses of burial populations up through time agree with the archaeobotanical record: we find a clear pattern of low consumption of C-4 plants (corn) across the East up until A.D. 900 or so, when maize consumption dramatically increases. Although many speculations have been offered, we still cannot explain why maize remained in such a minor role for so long, or why after such a long time it became so important so rapidly. We find the same puzzle in the Southwest, where maize remained relatively unimportant for a full thousand years after it arrived.

The Southwest

At an elevation of 2021 meters above sea level, high in the Mogollon Mountains of west-central New Mexico, Bat Cave occupied a prominent place for forty years in the story of the transition to farming in the American Southwest. Herbert Dick excavated down through the complex stratigraphy of this dry cave in 1948, and in the lowermost deposits made a surprising discovery: well-preserved maize cobs and kernels. When charcoal fragments also recovered from this lowest layer were dated by the then

new radiocarbon method, they yielded an age of 6000 to 4000 B.P. The discovery of the Bat Cave maize spurred investigation in half a dozen nearby caves over the next decade, and they too yielded early evidence of maize and squash. By the early 1960s, these early agricultural sites in the mountains of the central Southwest formed the basis of our understanding of when and where Southwestern societies adopted Middle American crop plants. It appeared that agriculture had entered the Southwest along mountain ranges, and at first was limited to the highlands, which received more rainfall. Only after 2000 to 4000 years did the cultivation of maize, squash, and beans extend down out of the Mogollon Highlands to lower altitudes.

As early as the 1960s, however, there were doubts about the very early dates of the maize from

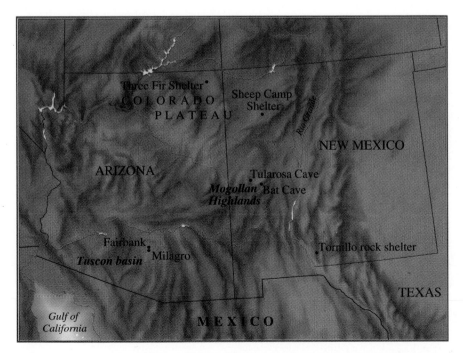

Archaeological sites in New Mexico and Arizona have yielded early evidence of the adoption of Middle American domesticated crops by Native American societies in the Southwest.

Bat Cave. The next oldest corn found in the region, at nearby Tularosa Cave, was 2000 to 4000 years more recent. It was not until the mid-1980s, however, that W. H. Wills, of the University of New Mexico, excavated at Bat Cave again and found that the charcoal that produced the early dates was not contemporaneous with the maize recovered from the cave's lowest levels. A series of direct AMS dates on the Bat Cave corn effectively cut its age in half, from 6000 to about 3000 years B.P. The four earliest AMS

dates on maize from Bat Cave fall between 3200 and 2800 B.P. In addition, a squash (*Cucurbita pepo*) seed from Bat Cave provided a direct AMS date of 2980 B.P.

At the same time that Wills's research significantly shortened the antiquity of crop plants in the Mogollon Highlands, both conventional large-sample and AMS radiocarbon dates were being obtained on early maize and squash from elsewhere in the Southwest. This broad-scale application of AMS dat-

Meticulous reexcavation and reanalysis of Bat Cave, carried out by W. H. Wills of the University of New Mexico, along with AMS dating, showed the Bat Cave maize to be only 3200 years old, about half as old as first thought.

ing showed that in these areas, too, maize and squash made their appearance in the same four-century span from 3200 to 2800 B.P. South of the Mogollon Highlands, in the arid desert and semi-arid grasslands of south-central New Mexico, Tornillo rock shelter near Las Cruces produced maize dating to 3175 B.P., and the Fairbank and Milagro sites near Tucson, Arizona, yielded maize that is 2800 years old. Similarly, a squash seed from Sheep Camp Shelter in Chaco Canyon, north of the Mogollon Highlands, has been AMS dated to 2900 B.P., and maize from Three Fir Shelter on Black Mesa has been directly dated to 2880 B.P. Beans may have entered the Southwest a bit later than squash and maize. The earliest beans found there, in Tularosa Cave in the Mogollon Highlands, date to 2470 B.P.

The ceramics and other tools found in association with these early crop plants show a clear continuity with earlier southwestern materials. This continuity indicates that agriculture was not brought north from Mexico by colonizing farmers. Rather, the rapid and widespread appearance of maize and squash across the Southwest represents the adoption by resident hunting-and-gathering societies of introduced crop plants, with seed stock perhaps carried north along the river valley corridor of the Rio Grande.

The speed and apparent ease with which maize and squash were adopted in the Southwest has led to the suggestion that perhaps, as in the East, one or more local seed plants—perhaps chenopod, amaranth, or little barley—had already been cultivated by the time maize arrived, smoothing the way for its acceptance. It is certainly possible that these local plants were important food sources, and southwestern societies may well have encouraged and manipulated them, but we have yet to see clear evidence of any morphological changes in their seeds that would indicate that these species had been deliber-

ately planted and domesticated. Even in her impressive analysis of a well-preserved assemblage of seeds and other parts of little barley (*Hordeum pusillum*) dating much later, for example, Karen Adams of the Crow Canyon Archaeological Center recognized none of the key morphological markers of domestication so well documented for cereal grains in the Fertile Crescent—no nonbrittle rachises, no increase in grain size, no loss of glumes. In the absence of any indication that these people cultivated any plants at all before they acquired domesticated plants from outside their region, the Southwest seems to provide an intriguing opportunity to see how hunter-gatherers adjusted to introduced crop plants and made the best use of them.

One of the most interesting aspects of this situation is that the various Native American societies of the Southwest that added squash and maize (and later beans) to their foraging economies inhabited a number of environmental zones. From the arid grasslands and deserts of the south to the Mogollon Mountains and on into the Colorado Plateau, these Middle American crop plants were accepted by hunter-gatherer groups that had adapted in various ways to different landscapes and depended on different wild plants and animals.

In each of these places the Native Americans appear to have added maize and squash to their local adaptations in much the same way that hunter-gatherers along the southwestern coast of Europe selectively added sheep to their economies. The first domesticates in both regions produced no immediate, wholesale revamping of life. Societies in the Southwest and in southern Europe used the domesticates to supplement the food they collected from wild resources while maintaining their long-standing patterns of seasonal movement. It was not until about A.D. 1, more than a thousand years after maize and squash were first introduced, that any southwestern Native Americans began to rely heavily on the plants they cultivated.

It is interesting, however, that as southwestern Native American societies intensified their use of maize, they had to solve a problem that had existed for more than a thousand years. From the moment maize and squash arrived in the arid Southwest, Native Americans faced the challenge of ensuring enough water to keep these plants alive and growing until they produced a successful harvest. The earliest solution to this problem, perhaps throughout the Southwest and certainly in the low-elevation, low-rainfall landscapes south of the Mogollon Rim, where Hohokam farmers much later would construct irrigation canals and catchment dams, was to rely not on rainfall but on groundwater. In this regard, the cultivation of maize, the preeminent New World cereal, closely paralleled the first experiments with cultivating Old World cereals in the Fertile Crescent. Early farmers of the Levantine corridor established their settlements close to springs and lakes, where a high water table ensured adequate moisture through the growing season. Some of the earliest farmers in the Southwest, too, settled in areas where the water table was high.

The best record of the early use of groundwater in cultivating maize in the Southwest comes from an area just south and east of Tucson, Arizona. Here a series of parallel alluvium-filled river valleys empty into the Tucson basin from the surrounding mountain ranges. In the process of cutting steep-sided arroyos down through the alluvial deposits of these valleys, the San Pedro, Tanque Verde, and Santa Cruz rivers and their tributaries have exposed deeply buried archaeological deposits, which provide a record of the long human occupation of the Tucson area. Since the 1930s archaeologists from the University of Arizona have been investigating these ancient settlements, and since the 1980s interest has

focused on early farming sites dating between 3000 and 2000 B.P. Sometimes exposed for 50 meters or more along arroyo banks and ranging up to half a meter or more thick, sites of this time period lack pottery but contain numerous storage pits, earth ovens, and associated fire-cracked rock, as well as small circular house structures, burials, and grinding stones for processing plants. As far as artifacts and architectural features are concerned, these sites do not seem to differ significantly from the pre-agricultural sites exposed in the arroyo cutbanks. But maize is abundantly represented in flotation samples from these settlements, indicating the success with which corn was grown in this region of low rainfall but a high water table.

Noting the unbroken similarity of these early farming settlements up through time, Bruce Huckell of the University of Arizona believes that these maize-growing societies sustained a stable and successful adaptation for a thousand years or more, from 3000 to 2000 B.P. These early river-valley farming settlements, each occupied for perhaps 200 years or more, were probably base camps from which groups could set out in search of the seasonally abundant wild plants and animals of both the valley floor and the surrounding uplands.

This stable way of life combined cultivation with the use of a variety of wild plants and animals, including mesquite, cacti, grasses, agave, pinyon, mountain sheep, mule deer, and pronghorn antelope. In many ways there was not much of a change from the hunting-and-gathering life of the people who lived here earlier. Importantly, though, maize did make for a more stable life. By cultivating corn near river-valley base camps, the people of these farming communities could remain in their settlements for longer periods of the year. Judging from the remarkable continuity in their settlements and land-use patterns over the thousand years that followed their decision to supplement their foraging and hunting with the cultivation of crops, maize provided a key element in the formation of a sustainable, stable adaptation to the Tucson region.

Thus the introduction of crop plants to these people's long-established hunting-and-gathering economies has important parallels with the origins of agriculture in the Levantine corridor. Although major cereal crops were independently domesticated in one region and introduced in the other, in both regions they supplemented long-established and quite successful broad-spectrum hunting and gathering economies. Crops could be cultivated without much modification of age-old lifeways, but they did provide an important measure of security, a reduction of risk, by offering a dependable and storable source of food. And in both regions, those first harvests, modest though they surely were, held the promise of the dramatically larger yields that in the intervening years have changed the face of the earth.

EPILOGUE

THE SEARCH FOR EXPLANATIONS

The emergence of agriculture marks a major turning point in human history, so it is no wonder that scholars have long sought to understand and explain it. Most interested biologists and archaeologists have focused their research on particular domesticates or certain world areas: these scientists have identified the wild ancestors of domesticates and the evidence for their domestication; they have found out where and when domestication took place; and they have learned how hunter-gatherers actually transformed wild species into domesticates. Each of these individual discoveries does not in itself provide an overall account of agricultural origins. The discoveries do, however, represent what could be thought of as the building blocks of a solid foundation from which such an explanation may be constructed. But is the foundation alone enough? Does our growing understanding of where, when, and how agriculture emerged provide an adequate explanation, or is it necessary to go further—to explain *why* human societies made the transition from hunting and gathering to an agricultural way of life?

Over the years, a variety of theories have been proposed that attempt to pinpoint human motivations and to identify the underlying causes of the emergence of agriculture. Whatever the nature of the theories, they have all had to contend with the ever-accumulating mass of information regarding plant and animal domestication. As this foundation of knowledge is constantly added to and strengthened, it places constraints on the kinds of causal explanations that it can support. Those theories that are not firmly connected to this foundation will be easily knocked down. The challenge for any researcher, then, is to add to the basic foundation of knowledge—the what, when, where, and how of agricultural origins—while also perhaps building up from it a firm anchored causal explanation that can withstand the test of time.

Before considering what kind of causal explanations might be built on the foundation of understanding that now exists, let's first briefly look at this foundation itself, considered by many researchers to be the core of any proposed explanation. After all, explanations that attempt to get at ultimate causes and human motivations are often rather speculative, flimsy affairs, only partially supported by available evidence and all too prone to collapse.

In contrast, evidence of how, where, and when plants and animals were domesticated is more solid and dependable, as are explanations of how hunter-gatherers transformed wild plants and animals into domesticates.

Take, for example, the landmark research of Jack Harlan and J. M. J. de Wet: they not only detailed the morphological changes that take place in seed plants as they are transformed from wild to domesticated forms, but they have also identified the specific human actions that produced those changes. Similarly, Gordon Hillman has identified which specific harvesting methods are necessary to transform a field of wild wheat having brittle rachises into a field of domesticated plants having tough rachises, and how long the transformation would take. Even though Hillman, Harlan, and de Wet do not attempt to explain why barley and wheat were domesticated, they nonetheless have impressively illuminated the pathway that leads from wild to domesticated.

Consider, too, the success of John Doebley, of Paul Gepts, and of Deena Decker-Walters and her colleagues: they have identified the wild ancestors of maize, beans, and squash and have determined the likely areas of the Americas in which these plants were domesticated. Researchers have also recognized the important attributes that predispose species to starring roles as domesticates, and this knowledge has led to a clear understanding of why certain plants and animals were domesticated and others weren't. Such profiles go a long way toward explaining the roster of domesticates in different regions of the world. In many ways, then, biological research on present-day plant and animal populations has provided a firm foundation on which to construct theories that consider the causes of agricultural origins.

Archaeological research, too, has contributed to this foundation. Through the analysis of plant and animal remains from ancient settlements and the identification of distinctive markers of domestication, archaeologists like Hans-Peter Uerpmann, Brian Hesse, and Carol Nordstrom have been able to pinpoint with greater accuracy where various species were first domesticated. In addition, direct AMS radiocarbon dating now enables archaeologists to answer with accuracy the key question of when human societies first created particular domesticates.

This assemblage of knowledge, then, is what can be thought of as the basic foundation for understanding the emergence of agriculture—knowing when and where plant and animal species were domesticated, the identity of their wild ancestors, the markers of domestication evident in the archaeological record, and the specific categories of human behavior that led to domestication, such as the deliberate planting of stored seed stock. To the scholars constructing the theories of ultimate causes, this foundation represents the necessary but preliminary research that allows them to address the key question of *why* hunting-and-gathering societies first domesticated plants and animals and developed a farming way of life.

While these theories all focus on finding the causes of agriculture, they differ from one another in a number of ways. Some are proposed to explain the emergence of agriculture in a particular region of the world, while others are universal in their application. Some focus on a single cause, while others propose several. Some see the causes of agriculture as originating outside of human society in nature, while others propose that agriculture owes its origins to cultural changes within hunter-gatherer societies. Did human societies first domesticate plants and animals as an adaptive response to some external pressure like population growth or climate change, or did domestication take place in the absence of outside stress, as the result of changes in the organization and integration of the societies themselves? Did agriculture arise out of need or opportunity?

Population growth has long been the "external," noncultural force most often proposed as the impetus that led hunter-gatherer societies to develop agriculture. In the 1960s Lewis Binford of Southern Methodist University theorized that human population growth pressured societies in the Fertile Crescent to domesticate plants and animals and shift to a farming way of life. In the 1970s Mark Cohen of the State University of New York at Plattsburg developed a similar, but universally applicable, causal explanation in which human societies worldwide were forced to turn to agriculture as a solution to problems of overpopulation on a global scale. These and other explanations citing population pressure as a single cause have since been set aside as explanations focused on particular regions have come to the fore. These newer explanations consider population growth as only one of a number of potential contributing factors in the origin of agriculture.

More recently, other proposed universal explanations have identified internal or cultural causes for the emergence of agriculture, but these too lack much supporting evidence. In 1992, for example, Brian Hayden of Simon Fraser University theorized that domestication was the direct result of competitive feasting, which would have spurred individuals or families to focus on creating delicacies that would increase their social standing. Hayden's argument that the first species domesticated throughout the world were delicacies rather than staple foods, however, is directly contradicted in every region of the world that we have considered. In these regions, early domesticates were invariably important foods in the diets of the societies making the transition to a farming way of life. Similarly,

although Hayden has cited a level of complex cultural development, of social hierarchies and strong status differentiation, as being necessary for competitive feasting and the emergence of agriculture, such a level of development has yet to be documented as present when plants and animals were first domesticated in Asia, Africa, and the Americas.

Other researchers have turned away from universal explanations and have chosen instead to address the question of causality within a single region. Their regional explanations tend to differ from universal explanations in several ways. They recognize how diverse independent centers of domestication are in environment, timing of domestication, and the species involved. Such regionally focused explanations, as a result, are much more firmly anchored to the evidence that now exists regarding the emergence of agriculture in particular regions of the world. In addition, these regional explanations often recognize that the transition from hunting and gathering can frequently be broken down into a sequence of related developmental puzzles. Take, for example, the Fertile Crescent, where the domestication of cereals, the domestication of goats, and the subsequent development of strong mixed agricultural economies were all part of a complex and long-term transformation.

In addition, regional-scale explanations are often more likely to consider the historical context of domestication. Rather than proposing a simple prime mover as a single cause, they often identify a combination of preconditions or contributing factors, both internal and external, that together might have led to the domestication of plants and animals in that particular region. In earlier chapters a number of such regionally tailored causal explanations have been discussed for settings as diverse as the Levantine corridor, the eastern woodlands of North America, the southern Sahara, and the Oaxaca Valley in Mexico.

I thought if might be interesting to conclude our worldwide review of the emergence of agriculture by taking another brief look at these regional explanations to see to what extent they might be similar. How far might it be possible to go in recognizing a common set of contributing factors for the emergence of agriculture in different regions of the world? Let's begin by considering the Levantine corridor, southern Sahara, and eastern North America. These three regions have more in common than you might expect.

First, in all three regions the species brought under domestication were seed plants rather than root crops or animals: barley, einkorn wheat, and emmer wheat in the Levantine corridor; millet, sorghum, and African rice in the southern Sahara; marsh elder, sunflower, chenopod, and squash in the eastern United States. Second, in all three regions the wild ancestors of these domesticates appear to have been important food sources before their domestication, and the human societies in question had developed an efficient technology for harvesting and processing seeds. Third, in all three regions the people who domesticated these seed plants lived in relatively large, permanent communities occupied throughout most if not all of the year. These were not small bands of hunter-gatherers who frequently relocated their temporary camps at different seasons of the year, but rather affluent societies leading a sedentary way of life.

Fourth, these societies can be considered relatively affluent not just because they enjoyed a broad spectrum of wild plants and animals in their diets, but perhaps more importantly because they had access to the resources of rich aquatic habitats. For in the Levantine corridor, the southern Sahara, and the eastern United States, the large permanent settlements poised to make the transition to farming were tied to permanent water sources and their associated plant and animal life.

Fifth, researchers have proposed that in each of these three regions the seed plants in question were first cultivated nearby lakes or rivers, where a predictable groundwater supply could ensure dependable harvests. Floodplain weeds of eastern North America and wild African rice were already well adapted to such settings, while barley, wheat, sorghum, and millet were brought in from other habitats.

Sixth, although the societies of all three regions enjoyed the security of a lakeside or riverside environment offering plentiful resources, their communities were bounded both in time and space by far less secure environments. In the Levantine corridor, the Younger Dryas climatic downturn brought cooler temperatures for 200 to 300 years between 11,000 and 10,000 B.P., not long before the domestication of cereal crops. Even after the Younger Dryas had ended, the wild food resources available to hunter-gatherers would have dropped off significantly the farther away one went from the lakes and springs of the Levantine corridor. Similarly, in eastern North America a change in climate during the Middle Holocene (8000 to 4000 B.P.) led to a proliferation of enriched aquatic habitat zones, including oxbow lakes and shoals, in river valleys, but also reduced the capacity of upland zones to support human hunter-gatherers. At about the same time, in the southern Sahara, the severe climatic downturn that produced a massive southward expansion of the desert was well under way by 5000 B.P. and had intensified by 4000 B.P., increasing the contrast between rich habitat zones at lake and marsh edges and the poorer habitats of the outlying savannah. In all three areas, climate change had contributed to a steepening of the environmental gradients between rich waterside habitat areas and outlying dryer zones less able to sustain hunter-gatherer societies, especially sedentary ones.

The societies of these richly endowed areas may have been culturally as well as environmentally circumscribed. By this I mean simply that the human landscape was relatively full, and the affluent societies situated in rich resource zones were boxed in to some extent by the presence of other societies on the boundaries of their territories. It is difficult to know accurately just how limited their access to the game and wild plants of outlying areas was. We do not know exactly how large their resource territories were, or how flexible the boundaries between neighboring groups, or to what extent groups cooperated or competed across territorial boundaries.

In summary, it would seem that, in these three areas, seed plants were domesticated by affluent societies living in sedentary settlements adjacent to rivers, lakes, marshes and springs, locations that would have offered both abundant animal protein—in the form of fish and waterfowl, for example—and well-watered soils for secure harvests. These societies also seemed to have been circumscribed by the presence of other societies and by environmental zones that were poorer in resources. In each case, of the many wild species likely being auditioned for further experimentation and manipulation, those showing the most promise were apparently already important dietary staples. These promising species were preadapted to domestication: they presented few barriers to successful cultivation and likely produced impressive and reliable harvests in their lake-margin and river-valley fields.

If this speculative comparison of the factors contributing to seed plant domestication in the southern Sahara, eastern United States, and Levantine corridor is accurate, what does it say regarding the causes of the shift to a farming way of life? Did agriculture arise out of need or out of opportunity? Were the causes or contributing circumstances external, internal, or both?

Clearly, plant domestication was not carried out by societies living in marginal zones, where limited resources would have restricted group size and made permanent settlements unlikely. But even though seed plants were domesticated in zones of plentiful resources by relatively affluent societies, the transition to a farming way of life was not entirely stress-free. Climatic pressures and population growth appear to have contributed to the process, at a distance, by producing resource gradients and hardening cultural boundaries around rich resource zones. It wouldn't have been easy to simply move to a better location when times were hard; these societies would have needed a way of dealing with the possibility of hard times right where they were. Within these zones, too, population growth or other factors might have heightened the ever-present fear of resource shortfall, even in times of abundance, pushing societies to increase the yield and reliability of some food resources, and pointing the way to domestication. This scenario is similar, in a way, to that proposed by Kent Flannery for the valley of Oaxaca, where even during the good years hunter-gatherer societies would have been motivated by the expectation of lean years to experiment with ways of increasing storable food surpluses.

It is not so much the immediate threat of going hungry that spurs domestication, or even the constant reality of a marginal existence. An agricultural way of life appears to have emerged where societies were not immediately threatened, but nonetheless were encouraged by surrounding circumstances to search widely for ways of reducing long-term risk. One strategy would have been to experiment with ways of increasing the yield and reliability of promising species.

The affluent societies of these rich resource zones may also have been pulled toward plant domestication by their changing structure. A newly sedentary people living in larger settlements would need new forms of social integration and interaction and new rules for the ownership and control of land and its resources. These changes may have encouraged the production of a greater harvest surplus, if such a surplus could have been used to establish and maintain contracts of social obligation between families or larger kinship groups such as lineages and clans. Food surpluses may have served to cement social contracts in a variety of ways: they could have been lent out to relatives or neighbors in times of need, offered up for community celebrations, or paid out as a dowry or brideprice when a marriage formed a new alliance between families. There are, then, a variety of social forces, other than competitive feasting, that could have encouraged family groups to invest more of their time manipulating seed plants in an effort to increase harvest yields and storable surplus. Thus both need and opportunity may well have been important, to varying degrees, in the initial domestication of plants in these regions.

Interestingly, other regions of the world seem to fit this general pattern, at least to some extent. As the likely heartland of rice domestication, for example, the Yangtze Valley corridor, with its vast landscape of lakes and marshes, would have offered China's earliest farmers a well-watered, secure setting for cultivation. Indeed, the earliest documented rice farmers of the Yangtze—in both the Hupei basin and around Hang-chou Bay—were certainly living in permanent, long-established communities adjacent to rivers and lakes. These farmers belonged to affluent societies that relied on a broad spectrum of wild species, especially those from aquatic habitats. As a result I do not think it would be too surprising if, when Chinese archaeologists eventually uncover the settlements of the preceding Yangtze societies that first domesticated rice, these earlier societies turn out to be similar in important ways

to the well-documented rice-farming communities of later times. These earliest rice farmers, too, will be found to have lived in permanent, sedentary settlements adjacent to watercourses and lakes, on prime real estate for having access to wild rice and for cultivating domesticated varieties, and they too will have enjoyed a broad variety of resources from the nearby lakes, marshes, rivers, and their margins, including wild rice as a staple food.

In northern China, the millets first cultivated along the Yellow River may also have been domesticated in a generally similar context. Here, as in the Levantine corridor, wild plants growing naturally at higher elevations were moved down into better-watered valleys. And just as in the southern Sahara, where the drought-resistant plants sorghum and pearl millet were brought in from outlying dryer savannah, so too were the Chinese millets both drought-resistant species relocated from adjacent grasslands. These drier upland savannahs to the west and north of the center of millet farming provide another point of similarity with the pattern we have seen in other regions: they represent a zone of more marginal resources that borders and partially circumscribes the heartland of millet domestication in the river valleys. Here, too, the earliest documented settlements are large permanent villages whose inhabitants exploited a wide range of wild plants and animals, and it is highly likely that, when eventually discovered, the earlier settlements of the first millet farmers will prove to be sedentary river-valley communities and their inhabitants will have shown a broad reliance on local floodplain species as well as the wild millets and other resources of the upland savannah.

Somewhat surprisingly, the south-central Andes might also fit this pattern, even though it is a high-elevation center of domestication where a distinctive mixed agricultural economy emerged that was based on both root and seed crops (potatoes, quinua) and animals (guinea pig, llama, alpaca). Although much of the evidence to date for the domestication of Andean plants and animals comes from caves and rock shelters high in the sierra, the south-central Andes center of domestication is anchored at both ends by river and lake environments at lower elevations—its north end is marked by the Lake Junin basin and the south end by the Lake Titicaca basin. The remains in these caves, I believe, were from species originally brought under domestication at lower elevations, in lake basins and river valleys. The earliest agricultural economies of the region were developed, I would suggest, along the margins of Lake Junin and Lake Titicaca and the lower courses of the rivers that fed into them, as well as in other intermontaine river valleys between Junin and Titicaca such as Ayacucho. Once again, the first farmers would have been affluent hunter-gatherers relying on a variety of wild species, including the wild progenitors of the domesticates.

A long-lasting climatic downturn in the central Andes preceded the domestication of plants and animals between 5000 and 4000 years ago. It would have increased the difference in resource availability between lake basins and river valleys on the one hand and higher-elevation environmental zones on the other. The result would have been a zone of relatively abundant resources circumscribed by poorer zones, similar to the situation noted in other regions. As yet there is of course no evidence to support this speculative scenario for the south-central Andes, but that may change as Mark Aldenderfer of the University of California, Santa Barbara, and other researchers now turn their attention to these lake basins and their tributary river systems in the search for early agricultural settlements.

Finally, I would suggest that Mexico too could fit this pattern and that, as is the case in eastern North America and the south-central Andes, the evidence of domestication recovered from higher-elevation cave sites such as those in Tamaulipas and Tehuacán reflects a transition to a farming way of life that took place largely in lower-elevation river valley settings rich in resources. There is as yet no archaeological evidence for this view, but the present-day distribution of the wild progenitors of maize and the common bean point to the Balsas River and other watercourses flowing west into the Pacific. Here archaeologists should eventually uncover the settlements of the earliest, no doubt sedentary, farming societies of the region.

It would appear, then, that in many regions of the world, experiments leading to seed plant domestication and, eventually, agriculture were carried out in a common set of conditions. The experimenters were hunter-gatherer societies that had settled by lakes, marshes, or rivers—locales so rich in wild resources that these societies could establish permanent settlements and rely to a considerable extent on local plant and animal communities. Thus a sedentary way of life, supported by the plentiful resources of an aquatic zone, seems to have been an important element in early experiments with domestication. Moreover, lake- and river-margin settings offered soils moist and fertile enough to ensure that early cultivated fields produced dependable harvests. Such a guarantee of success could have reassured people that they could safely commit time to experimentation, while the confining presence of neighboring groups focused their efforts at risk reduction in that direction. As we have seen, all hunter-gatherer societies experiment with wild food resources in order to increase yield and reliability, but in these particular settings—rich but circumscribed resource zones—these experiments were channeled in certain very productive directions. Of key importance, too, was the presence of wild species with star quality preadaptations to domestication. Finally, a sedentary way of life would have created new opportunities for social alliance and integration, and hence new motivations for trying to expand the production of storable food reserves.

While the different regions of the world in which agriculture emerged may well have shared a number of these contributing factors, it is important not to carry the search for similarities too far, or to invest it with too much explanatory authority. The danger is that in rendering down the long and complex developmental histories of different regions into a simple set of shared characteristics, we may lose sight of the rich diversity that exists between the various centers of origin. In each of the widely separated regions of the world considered in this book, the transition from a hunting-and-gathering existence to an agricultural way of life was accomplished by human societies with very different cultures, who created domesticates out of a rich variety of candidate species, and who altered their own existence in distinctive ways. Searching for common elements and common causes across these centers of origin can provide insights about the general nature of the transition to agriculture, and illuminate new directions that research should take in particular regions. But the keys to gaining a better understanding of the emergence of agriculture rest in each of the different regions of origin, where biologists and archaeologists with a wide range of interests are continuing to refine and expand our knowledge of this revolutionary turning point in the history of our planet.

FURTHER READINGS

BOOKS AND ARTICLES EASILY READ BY THE
GENERAL READER

Kathleen Kenyon, 1957, *Digging Up Jericho*. London: Benn.

Stephen Budiansky, 1992. *The Covenant of the Wild: Why Animals Chose Domestication*. New York: William Morrow.

Juliet Clutton-Brock, 1981. Domesticated Animals from Early Times. London: British Museum (Natural History) and Heinemann.

Jack R. Harlan, 1992. Crops and Man. 2d ed. Madison, Wisc.: American Society of Agronomy.

Charles G. Heiser, Jr., 1990. Seed to Civilization. Cambridge, Mass.: Harvard University Press.

Jefferson Chapman, Hazel Delcourt, and Paul A. Delcourt, 1989. "Strawberry Fields, Almost Forever." *Natural History* (September).

Robert E. M. Hedges and John A. J. Gowlett, 1986. "Radiocarbon Dating by Accelerator Mass Spectroscopy." *Scientific American* 244:82-89.

Ofer Bar-Yosef and A. Belfer-Cohen, 1989. "The Origins of Sedentism and Farming Communities in the Levant." *Journal of World Prehistory* 3:477-498.

Jack R. Harlan, 1967. "A Wild Wheat Harvest in Turkey." *Archaeology* 20:197-201.

Theya Molleson, 1994. "The Eloquent Bones of Abu Hureyra." *Scientific American* 271:70-75.

Andrew Moore, 1979. "A Pre-Neolithic Farmers' Village on the Euphrates." *Scientific American* 237:62-70.

Charles Redman, 1978. *The Rise to Civilization*. New York: W. H. Freeman.

Graeme Barker, 1985. *Prehistoric Farming in Europe*. Cambridge: Cambridge University Press.

Thomas W. Jacobson, 1976. "17,000 Years of Greek Prehistory." *Scientific American* 234:76-84.

Robert J. Rodden, 1965. "An Early Neolithic Village in Greece." *Scientific American* 212:81-92.

Kwang-chih Chang, 1986. *The Archaeology of Ancient China*. 4th ed. New Haven, Conn.: Yale University Press.

Bruce D. Smith, 1991. "Harvest of Prehistory." *The Sciences* (May/June).

C. Wesley Cowan and Bruce D. Smith, 1993. "The Wild Gourd of the Ozarks." *The World & I* (October).

SCHOLARLY REFERENCES

CHAPTER 1

Braidwood, Linda, Robert Braidwood, Bruce Howe, Charles Reed, and Patty Jo Watson (eds.), 1983. *Prehistoric Archaeology along the Zagros Flanks.* The University of Chicago Oriental Institute Publications Volume 105. Chicago.

Vavilov, Nikolai I., 1992. *The Origin and Geography of Cultivated Plants.* Cambridge: Cambridge University Press.

Young, T. Cyler, Philip E. L. Smith, and Peder Mortensen (eds.), 1983. *The Hilly Flanks: Essays on the Prehistory of Southwestern Asia Presented to Robert J. Braidwood.* Studies in Ancient Oriental Civilizations 36. Chicago: The Oriental Institute, University of Chicago.

CHAPTER 2

Bretting, Peter K. (ed.), 1990. *New Perspectives on the Origin and Evolution of New World Domesticated Plants.* Economic Botany 44 (Supplement).

Clutton-Brock, Juliet, 1989. *The Walking Larder.* London: Unwin Hyman.

Cowan, C. Wesley, and Patty Jo Watson, 1992. *The Origins of Agriculture: An International Perspective.* Washington, D.C.: Smithsonian Institution Press.

Galton, F., 1865. *The First Steps Towards the Domestication of Animals.* Transactions of the Ethnological Society of London 3:122-138.

Harlan, Jack R., J. M. J. de Wet, and E. Glen Price, 1972. "Comparative Evolution of Cereals." *Evolution* 27:311-325.

Harris, D. R., and G. C. Hillman, 1989. *Foraging and Farming: The Evolution of Plant Exploitation.* London: Unwin Hyman.

Meadow, Richard H., 1989. "Osteological Evidence for the Process of Animal Domestication." In Juliet Clutton-Brock (ed.), *The Walking Larder,* pp. 80-90. London: Unwin Hyman.

CHAPTER 3

Delcourt, Paul A., Hazel Delcourt, Patricia A. Cridlebaugh, and Jefferson Chapman, 1986. "Holocene Ethnobotanical and Paleoecological Record of Human Impact on Vegetation in the Little Tennessee River Valley, Tennessee." *Quaternary Research* 25:330-349.

Gowlett, John A. J., 1987. "The Archaeology of Radiocarbon Accelerator Dating." *Journal of World Prehistory* 2:127-170.

Smith, Bruce D., 1988. "SEM and the Identification of Micro-morphological Indicators of Domestication in Seed Plants." In Sandra Olsen (ed.), *Scanning Electron Microscopy in Archaeology,* pp. 203-213. British Archaeological Reports International Series. Oxford.

Watson, Patty Jo, 1976. "In Pursuit of Prehistoric Subsistence: A Comparative Account of Some Contemporary Flotation Techniques." *Midcontinental Journal of Archaeology* 1:77-100.

CHAPTER 4

Bar-Yosef, Ofer, and M. E. Kislev, 1989. "Early Farming Communities in the Jordan Valley." In David Harris and Gordon Hillman (eds.), *Foraging and Farming,* pp. 632-642. London: Unwin Hyman.

Bar-Yosef, Ofer, Avi Gopher, Eitan Tchernov, and Mordechai Kislev, 1991. "Netiv Hagdud: An Early Neolithic Village Site in the Jordan Valley." *Journal of Field Archaeology* 18:405-424.

Hillman, Gordon, 1990. "Domestication Rates in Wild-Type Wheats and Barley Under Primitive Cultivation." *Biological Journal of the Linnean Society* 39:39-78.

Hillman, Gordon, S. M. Colledge, and D. R. Harris, 1989. "Plant-food Economy during the Epipaleolithic Period at Tell Abu Hureyra, Syria." In David Harris and Gordon Hillman (eds.), *Foraging and Farming,* pp. 240-268. London: Unwin Hyman.

Hole, Frank, Kent V. Flannery, and James A. Neely (eds.), 1969. *Prehistory and Human Ecology of the Deh Luran*

Plain. Memoirs of the Museum of Anthropology, University of Michigan 1. Ann Arbor: University of Michigan Press.

Meadow, Richard, 1995. "The Development of Animal Husbandry in the Near and Middle East." In Anne B. Gebauer and T. Douglas Price (eds.) *The Transition to Agriculture.* Santa Fe: School of American Research.

CHAPTER 5

Bogucki, Peter, 1988. *Forest Farmers and Stockherders: Early Agriculture and its Consequences in North-Central Europe.* Cambridge: Cambridge University Press.

Clark, J. Desmond, and Steven A. Brandt (eds.), 1984. *From Hunters to Farmers: The Causes and Consequences of Food Production in Africa.* Berkeley: University of California Press.

Dennell, Robin W., 1992. *"The Origins of Crop Agriculture in Europe."* In C. Wesley Cowan and Patty Jo Watson (eds.), *The Origins of Agriculture,* pp. 71-100. Washington, D.C.: Smithsonian Institution Press.

Geddes, David S., 1985. "Mesolithic Domestic Sheep in West Mediterranean Europe." *Journal of Archaeological Science* 12:25-48.

Harlan, Jack, Jan M. J. de Wet, and Ann Stemler (eds.), 1976. *Origins of African Plant Domestication.* The Hague: Mouton Publishers.

Harlan, Jack R., 1992. "Indigenous African Agriculture." In C. Wesley Cowan and Patty Jo Watson (eds.), *The Origins of Agriculture,* pp. 59-70. Washington D.C.: Smithsonian Institution Press.

Keeley, Lawrence H., 1992. "The Introduction of Agriculture to the Western North European Plain." In Ann B. Gebauer and T. Douglas Price (eds.), *Transitions to Agriculture in Prehistory,* pp. 81-95. Madison, Wisc.: Prehistory Press.

Muller, Johannes, and John Chapman, 1990. "Early Farmers in the Mediterranean Basin: The Dalmatian Evidence." *Antiquity* 64:127-134.

CHAPTER 6

Crawford, Gary, 1992. "Prehistoric Plant Domestication in East Asia." In C. Wesley Cowan and Patty Jo Watson (eds.), *The Origins of Agriculture,* pp. 7-38. Washington D.C.: Smithsonian Institution Press.

Higham, C., and Bernard Maloney, 1989. "Coastal Adaptation, Sedentism, and Domestication: A Model for Socio-economic Intensification in Prehistoric Asia." In David Harris and Gordon Hillman (eds.), *Foraging and Farming,* pp. 650-666. London: Unwin Hyman.

Li, Hui-lin, 1983. "The Domestication of Plants in China: Ecographic Considerations." In D. N. Keightley (ed.), *The Origins of Chinese Civilization,* pp. 21-63. Berkeley: University of California Press.

Wenming, Yan, 1991. "China's Earliest Rice Agriculture Remains." *Indo-Pacific Prehistory Association Bulletin* 10:118-126.

Zhao, Songquiao, and Wu Wei-Tang, 1986. "Early Neolithic Hemodu Culture along the Hangzhou Estuary and the Origin of Domestic Paddy Rice in China." *Asian Perspectives* 27:29-34.

Zhimin, An, 1989. "Prehistoric Agriculture in China." In David Harris and Gordon Hillman (eds.), *Foraging and Farming,* pp. 643-649. London: Unwin Hyman.

CHAPTER 7

Aldenderfer, Mark, 1995. *Montane Foragers: Asana and the South-Central Andean Archaic.* Iowa City: University of Iowa Press.

Benz, Bruce F., and Hugh Iltis, 1990. "Studies in Archaeological Maize 1: The 'Wild' Maize from San Marcos Cave Reexamined." *American Antiquity* 55:500-511.

Browman, David, 1989. "Origins and Development of Andean Pastoralism: an Overview of the Past 6000 Years." In Juliet Clutton-Brock (ed.), *The Walking Larder,* pp. 256-267. London: Unwin Hyman.

Byers, Douglas S., 1967. *The Prehistory of the Tehuacan Valley.* Volume 1: Environment and Subsistence. Austin, Texas: University of Texas Press.

Doebley, John, 1990. "Molecular Evidence and the Evolution of Maize." In Peter K. Bretting (ed.), *New Perspectives on the Origin and Evolution of New World Domesticated Plants,* pp. 6-28. Economic Botany 44 (Supplement).

Flannery, Kent V., 1986. *Guila Naquitz.* New York: Academic Press.

Gepts, Paul, 1990. "Biochemical Evidence Bearing on the Domestication of *Phaseolus* (Fabaceae) Beans." In Peter Bretting (ed.), *New Perspectives on the Origin and Evolution of New World Domesticated Plants,* pp. 28-38. Economic Botany 44 (Supplement).

Long, Austin, Bruce F. Benz, J. Donahue, A. Jull, and L. Toolin, 1989. "First direct AMS dates on early maize from Tehuacan, Mexico." *Radiocarbon* 31:1035-1040.

MacNeish, Richard S., 1958. *Preliminary Archaeological Investigations in the Sierra de Tamaulipas, Mexico.* Transactions of the American Philosophical Society 48-5-170.

Pearsall, Deborah, and D. R. Piperno, 1990. "Antiquity of Maize Cultivation in Ecuador: Summary and Reevaluation of the Evidence." *American Antiquity* 55:324-337.

Ugent, D., S. Pozorski, and T. Pozorski, 1982. "Archaeological Potato Tuber Remains from the Casma Valley of Peru." *Economic Botany* 38:417-432.

Wheeler, Jane, 1984. "On the Origin and Early Development of Camelid Pastoralism in the Andes." In Juliet Clutton-Brock and Caroline Grigson (eds.), *Animals and Archaeology: Early Herders and Their Flocks,* pp. 395-410. British Archaeological Reports International Series 202.

Wilson, Hugh D., 1988. "Quinua Biosystematics I: Domesticated Populations." *Economic Botany* 42:461-477.

Wing, Elizabeth, 1986. "Domestication of Andean Mammals." In F. Vuilleumier and M. Monasterio (eds.), *High Altitude Tropical Biogeography,* pp. 246-264. Oxford: Oxford University Press.

CHAPTER 8

Cowan, C. Wesley, and Bruce D. Smith, 1993. "New Perspectives on a Wild Gourd in Eastern North America." *Journal of Ethnobiology* 13:17-54.

Decker-Walters, Deena, Terrance Walters, C. Wesley Cowan, and Bruce D. Smith, 1993. "Isozymic Characterization of Wild Populations of *Cucurbita pepo.*" *Journal of Ethnobiology* 13:55-72.

Smith, Bruce D., 1992. *Rivers of Change: Essays on Early Agriculture in Eastern North America.* Washington D.C.: Smithsonian Institution Press.

Wills, W. H., 1988. *Early Prehistoric Agriculture in the American Southwest.* Santa Fe, N.M.: School of American Research.

————, 1992. "Plant Cultivation and the Evolution of Risk-Prone Economies in the Prehistoric American Southwest." In Anne B. Gebauer and T. Douglas Price (eds.), *Transitions to Agriculture in Prehistory,* pp. 153-175. Madison, Wisc.,: Prehistory Press.

SOURCES OF ILLUSTRATIONS

CHAPTER 1

Page facing 1: (*background photo of corn*) Art Wolfe Inc.; (*hoe blades*) From James A. Brown, Richard A. Kerber, and Howard D. Winters, "Trade and the evolution of exchange relations at the beginning of the Mississippian period." In Bruce D. Smith (ed.), *The Mississippian Emergence.* Washington and London: Smithsonian Institution Press, 1990, p. 266, Fig. 85.

Page 1: Diego Rivera, 1950. National Palace, Mexico City. Giraudon/Art Resource.

Page 2: Ofer Bar-Yosef.

Page 5: Novesti Press Agency.

Page 6: Adapted from N. I. Vavilov, *Origin and Geography of Cultivated Plants.* New York: Cambridge University Press, 1992, p. 209.

Page 7: Adapted from N. I. Vavilov, *Origin and Geography of Cultivated Plants.* New York: Cambridge University Press, 1992, p. 430.

Pages 8 and 9: Oriental Institute, University of Chicago.

CHAPTER 2

Page 14: (*background photo of rice*) Ian Lloyd/Black Star; (*bone hoes*) From Mou Yung-hang, Proceedings of the Annual meeting of the Archaeological Society of China, Peking, 1, 1980, p. 99. Reprinted in Kwang-chih Chang, *The Archaeology of Ancient China,* 4th ed. New Haven, Conn.: Yale University Press, 1986.

Page 15: Art Wolfe, Inc.

Page 16: Penny Tweedie/Woodfin Camp & Assoc.

Page 19: Chip Clark.

Page 22: From Hugh D. Wilson, "Domesticated *Chenopodium* of the Ozark Bluff dwellers," *Economic Botany* 35(2): 233–239, 1981.

Page 24: Musee de l'Homme, Paris. Erich Lessing/Art Resource.

Page 26: Joe Rodriguez/Black Star.

Page 28: Phillippe Lafond.

Page 29: Melinda Zeder.

Page 30: Adapted from Frank Hole, Kent V. Flannery, and James A. Neely (eds.), *Prehistory and Human Ecology of the Deh Luran Plain: An Early Village Sequence from Khuzistan, Iran*. Memoirs of the Museum of Anthropology, No. 1. Ann Arbor: University of Michigan Press, 1969, Fig. 117.

Page 32: Chip Clark.

Page 33: Catherine Karnow/Woodfin Camp & Assoc.

CHAPTER 3

Page 34: (*background photo of wheat*) Lance Nelson/The Stock Market; (*sickle blades*) From Frank Hole, Kent V. Flannery, James A. Neely, *Prehistory and Human Ecology of the Deh Luran Plain: An Early Village Sequence from Khuzistan, Iran*. Memoirs of the Museum of Anthropology, No. 1. Ann Arbor: University of Michigan Press, 1969, Fig. 26.

Page 35: Gil Stein.

Page 36: Museum of Anthropology, University of Michigan, Ann Arbor.

Page 37: Gil Stein.

Page 38: Adapted from John A. J. Gowlett, "The archaeology of radiocarbon accelerator dating," *Journal of World Prehistory* 2:127–170, 1987.

Pages 41 and 42: Bruce Smith.

Page 43: Joan Nowicke/Smithsonian Institution.

Page 45: Adapted from John Doebley, "Molecular evidence and the evolution of maize." In Peter K. Bretting (ed.), *New Perspectives on the Origin and Evolution of New World Domesticated Plants. Economic Botany 44* (Supplement): 6–28, 1990.

Page 46: (*left*) Hugh Iltis; (*right*) Tony Stone Images.

CHAPTER 4

Page 48: (*background photo of wheat*) Lance Nelson/The Stock Market; (*sickle blades*) From Frank Hole, Kent V. Flannery, James A. Neely, *Prehistory and Human Ecology of the Deh Luran Plain: An Early Village Sequence from Khuzistan, Iran*. Memoirs of the Museum of Anthropology, No. 1. Ann Arbor: University of Michigan Press, 1969, Fig. 26.

Page 49: Archaeological Museum, Istanbul. Erich Lessing/Art Resource.

Page 52: Barry Iverson/Woodfin Camp & Assoc.

Page 57: (*top three graphs*) Adapted from D. Helmer, "Le development de la domestication au Proche-Orient de 9500 a 7500 BP: Les nouvelles donnees d'el Kowm et des Ras Shamra." *Paleorient* 15: 111–145, 1979; (*bottom four graphs*) Adapted from Hans-Peter Uerpmann, *Probleme der Neolithisierung des Mittelmeerraums*. Tubinger Atlas des Vorden Orients, Reihe B, 1979, Nr. 28. Dr. Ludwig Reichert, Wiesbaden. All seven graphs reprinted in Richard Meadow, "The development of animal husbandry in the Near and Middle East." In Anne B. Gebauer and T. Douglas Price (eds.), *Last Hunters, First Farmers*. Santa Fe: School of American Research, 1995.

Page 58: Laurie Campbell/Natural History Photographic Agency.

Page 60: (*right*) Adapted from Brian C. Hesse, "Evidence for husbandry from the early neolithic site of Ganj Dareh in western Iran" (Ph.D. dissertation, Columbia University, 1978). University Microfilms International 78-9905, Ann Arbor, Fig. 1.

Page 61: (*top three graphs*) Adapted from D. Helmer, "Le development de la domestication au Proche-Orient de 9500 a 7500 BP: Les nouvelles donnees d'el Kowm et des Ras Shamra." *Paleorient* 15: 111–145, 1979; (*bottom six graphs*) Adapted from Hans-Peter Uerpmann, *Probleme der Neolithisierung des Mittelmeerraums*. Tubinger Atlas des Vorden Orients, Reihe B, 1979, Nr. 28. Dr. Ludwig Reichert, Wiesbaden. All nine graphs reprinted in Richard Meadow, "The development of animal husbandry in the Near and Middle East." In Anne B. Gebauer and T. Douglas Price (eds.), *Last Hunters, First Farmers*. Santa Fe: School of American Research, 1995.

Page 62: Chip Clark.

Page 66: Louvre, Paris. Erich Lessing/Art Resource.

Page 67: Adapted from Caroline Grigson, "Size and sex: Evidence for the domestication of cattle in the Near East." In Annie Milles, Diane Williams, and Neville Gardner, *The*

Beginnings of Agriculture. Symposia of the Association for Environmental Archaeology, No. 8, British Archaeological Reports International Series 496, 1989. Reprinted in Richard Meadow, "The development of animal husbandry in the Near and Middle East." In Anne B. Gebauer and T. Douglas Price (eds.), *Last Hunters, First Farmers.* Santa Fe: School of American Research, 1995.

Page 73: Adapted from Gordon Hillman, S. M. Colledge, and D. R. Harris, "Plant-food economy during the Epipaleolithic period at Tell Abu Hureyra, Syria." In David Harris and Gordon Hillman (eds.), *Foraging and Farming.* London: Unwin Hyman, 1989, pp. 240–268.

Page 75: From Ofer Bar-Yosef et al., "Netiv Hagdud: An early neolithic village site in the Jordan Valley," *Journal of Field Archaeology* 18: 405–424, 1991.

Page 76: M. Nir-Barazani, CRFJ. Courtesy of Ofer Bar-Yosef.

Page 77: Dagon Agricultural Collection, Haifa. Erich Lessing/Art Resource.

Page 78: From Ofer Bar-Yosef et al., "Netiv Hagdud: An early Neolithic village site in the Jordan Valley," *Journal of Field Archaeology* 18:405–424, 1991.

Page 80: (*top left*) Deutsche Verlagsanstalt/Bild der Wissenschaft; (*bottom right*) Ashmolean Museum, Oxford.

Page 82: Gil Stein.

Page 84: From Frank Hole, Kent V. Flannery, and James A. Neely, *Prehistory and Human Ecology of the Deh Luran Plain: An Early Village Sequence from Khuzistan, Iran.* Memoirs of the Museum of Anthropology, No. 1. Ann Arbor: University of Michigan Press, 1969.

Page 87: Gil Stein.

CHAPTER 5

Page 90: (*background photo of wheat*) Lance Nelson/The Stock Market; (*stone tools*) From Jacquetta Hawkes, *The Atlas of Early Man.* New York: St. Martin's Press, 1978 (reprinted and revised, 1993), p. 75.

Page 91: Saint Romain-en-Gal, Musee des Antiquites Nationales, St. Germain-en-Laye, France. Erich Lessing/Art Resource.

Page 95: Musee de l'Homme, Paris. Erich Lessing/Art Resource.

Page 97: Indiana University Classical Archaeology Archives.

Page 98: Pitt Rivers Museum, Oxford.

Page 100: Adapted from Robert J. Rodden, "An early Neolithic village in Greece," *Scientific American* 212: 81–92, 1965.

Page 101: From Alasdair Whittle, *Neolithic Europe: A Survey.* Cambridge: Cambridge University Press, 1985, p. 45.

Page 102: Erwin Keefer. Württembergisches Landesmuseum, Stuttgart.

Page 103: Adapted from Peter Bogucki, *Forest Farmers and Stockherders: Early Agriculture and its Consequences in North-Central Europe.* Cambridge: Cambridge University Press, 1988.

Page 105: From Lawrence H. Keeley, "The introduction of agriculture to the western North European plain." In Anne B. Gebauer and T. Douglas Price (eds.), *Transitions to Agriculture in Prehistory.* Monograph in World Archaeology, No. 4. Madison, Wis.: Prehistory Press, 1992.

Page 107: Milan Horacek/Bilderberg.

Page 109: Art Wolfe Inc.

Page 110: Chip Clark.

Page 111: Tony Stone Images.

CHAPTER 6

Page 114: (*background photo of rice*) Ian Lloyd/Black Star; (*bone hoe*) From Mou Yung-hang, Proceedings of the Annual meeting of the Archaeological Society of China, Peking, 1, 1980, p. 99. Reprinted in Kwang-chih Chang, *The Archaeology of Ancient China,* 4th ed. New Haven, Conn.: Yale University Press, 1986.

Page 115: Tony Stone Images.

Page 117: Reinhart Wolf/Bilderberg.

Page 122: Luca Invernizzi Tettoni/Photo Bank.

Page 126: Adapted from Mou Yung-hang, Proceedings of the Annual

Meeting of the Archaeological Society of China, Peking, 1, 1980, p. 99. Reprinted in Kwang-chih Chang, *The Archaeology of Ancient China,* 4th ed. New Haven, Conn.: Yale University Press, 1986.

Page 129: Adapted from Institute of Archaeology, Chinese Academy of Sciences, *Archaeological Discoveries and Studies in New China.* Peking: Wen-wu Press, 1984, Fig. 41. Reprinted in Kwang-chih Chang, *The Archaeology of Ancient China,* 4th ed. New Haven, Conn.: Yale University Press, 1986.

Page 130: From *K'au-ku (Archaeology)*1: 22, 1983. Reprinted in Kwang-chih Chang, *The Archaeology of Ancient China,* 4th ed. New Haven, Conn.: Yale University Press, 1986.

Pages 131 and 132: Richard S. Mac-Neish, Andover Foundation for Archaeological Research.

Page 134: From the Centre for East Asian Cultural Studies, Unesco, *Recent Archaeological Discoveries in the People's Republic of China.* Paris: The United Nations Educational, Scientific, and Cultural Organization, 1984.

Pages 137 and 138: John Eastcott and Yva Momatiuk/Woodfin Camp & Assoc.

Page 139: From Institute of Archaeology, Chinese Academy of Social Sciences, *Archaeological Discoveries and Studies in New China.* Peking: Wen-wu Press, 1984. Reprinted in Kwang-

chih Chang, *The Archaeology of Ancient China,* 4th ed. New Haven, Conn.: Yale University Press, 1986.

Page 140: Adapted from *Hsi-an Pau-p'o.* Peking: Wen-wu Press, 1963.

Page 141: Kal Muller/Woodfin Camp & Assoc.

Page 143: Alister Marshall, courtesy of Jack Golson.

CHAPTER 7

Page 144: (*background photo of corn*) Art Wolfe Inc.

Page 145: Martin Rogers/Woodfin Camp & Assoc.

Page 146: Ramiro Matos.

Page 147: Diego Rivera, *The Great Tenochtitlan,* detail, The Selling of Corn, 1945. National Palace, Mexico City. Giraudon/Art Resource.

Page 150: Robert S. Peabody Museum of Archaeology.

Page 151: (*top*) Robert S. Peabody Museum of Archaeology; (*bottom*) Adapted from Douglas S. Byers, *The Prehistory of the Tehuacan Valley, Vol. 1: Environment and Subsistence.* Austin, Tex.: University of Texas Press, 1967.

Page 152: Quesada/Burke.

Page 154: Adapted from John Doebley, "Molecular evidence and the evolution of maize." In Peter K. Bretting (ed.), *New Perspectives on the Origin and Evolution of New World Domesticated Plants. Economic Botany 44* (Supplement): 6–28, 1990.

Page 156: John Doebley.

Page 158: Dolores Piperno, Smithsonian Institution Tropical Research Institute.

Page 160: Paul Gepts.

Page 164: Michael Nee, New York Botanical Garden, Bronx.

Page 165: Thomas Andres, New York Botanical Garden, Bronx.

Page 168: Kent V. Flannery, *Guila Naquitz.* New York: Academic Press, 1986, Fig. 5.27.

Page 169: Kent V. Flannery, University of Michigan.

Page 171: Steven R. King.

Page 172: Steven R. King.

Page 174: John Rick/Stanford.

Page 175: Art Wolfe Inc.

Page 176: David Brownell/Image Bank.

Page 178: Steven R. King.

Page 179: Donald Ugent.

Page 180: (*top left, top right, and bottom left*) Donald Ugent; (*bottom right*) National Research Council.

CHAPTER 8

Page 182: (*background photo of corn*) Art Wolfe Inc.; (*hoe blades*) From James A. Brown, Richard A. Kerber, and Howard D. Winters, "Trade and the evolution of exchange relations at the beginning of the Mississippian period." In Bruce D. Smith (ed.), *The Mississippian Emergence*. Washington and London: Smithsonian Institution Press, 1990, p. 266, Fig. 85.

Page 183: Engraving by Theodore De Bry, plate 21, 1591 (made after a painting by Jacques le Moyne de Morgues). Reprinted in Stefan Lorant (ed.), *The New World*. New York: Duell, Sloan & Pearce, 1946.

Pages 185, 186, and 187: Bruce D. Smith.

Page 188: (*left*) Adapted from Bruce D. Smith, *Rivers of Change: Essays on Early Agriculture in Eastern North America*. Washington, D.C.: Smithsonian Institution Press, 1992; (right) The University Museum, University of Arkansas. Catalog no. 32-3-391. Slide no. 88133.

Pages 189, 190, 193, and 195: Wes Cowan.

Page 197: Van Bucher/Photo Researchers.

Page 198: Squier and Davis, 1848, plate 21.

Pages 199 and 200: Adapted from Bruce D. Smith, *Rivers of Change: Essays on Early Agriculture in Eastern North America*. Washington, D.C.: Smithsonian Institution Press, 1992.

Page 202: Wirt Wills.

INDEX

OTHER BOOKS IN THE SCIENTIFIC AMERICAN LIBRARY SERIES

POWERS OF TEN
by Philip and PHylis Morrison and the office of Charles and Ray Eames

SUN AND EARTH
by Herbert Friedman

ISLANDS
by H. William Menard

DRUGS AND THE BRAIN
by Solomon H. Snyder

EXTINCTION
by Steven M. Stanley

EYE, BRAIN AND VISION
by David H. Hubel

SAND
by Raymond Siever

THE HONEY BEE
by James L. Gould and Carol Grant Gould

ANIMAL NAVIGATION
by Talbot H. Waterman

SLEEP
by J. Allan Hobson

FROM QUARKS TO THE COSMOS
by Leon M. Lederman and David N. Schramm

SEXUAL SELECTION
by James L. Gould and Carol Grant Gould

THE NEW ARCHAEOLOGY AND THE ANCIENT MAYA
by Jeremy A. Sabloff

A JOURNEY INTO GRAVITY AND SPACETIME
by John Archibald

SIGNALS
by John R. Pierce and A. Michael Noll

BEYOND THE THIRD DIMENSION
by Thomas F. Banchoff

DISCOVERING ENZYMES
by David Dressler and Huntington Potter

THE SCIENCE OF WORDS
by George A. Miller

ATOMS, ELECTRONS, AND CHANGE
by P. W. Atkins

VIRUSES
by Arnold J. Levine

DIVERSITY AND THE TROPICAL RAINFOREST
by John Terborgh

STARS
by James B. Kaler

EXPLORING BIOMECHANICS
by R. McNeill Alexander

CHEMICAL COMMUNICATION
by William C. Agosta

GENES AND THE BIOLOGY OF CANCER
by Harold Varmus and Robert A. Weinberg

SUPERCOMPUTING AND THE TRANSFORMATION OF SCIENCE
by William J. Kaufmann III and Larry L. Smarr

MOLECULES AND MENTAL ILLNESS
by Samuel H. Barondes

EXPLORING PLANETARY WORDS
by David Morrison

EARTHQUAKES AND GEOLOGICAL DISCOVERY
by Bruce A. Bolt

THE ORIGIN OF MODERN HUMANS
by Roger Lewin

THE EVOLVING COAST
by Richard A. Davis, Jr.

THE LIFE PROCESSES OF PLANTS
by Arthur W. Galston

IMAGES OF MIND
by Michael I. Posner and Marcus E. Raichle

THE ANIMAL MIND
by James L. Gould and Carol Grant Gould

MATHEMATICS: THE SCIENCE OF PATTERNS
by Keith Devlin

A SHORT HISTORY OF THE UNIVERSE
by Joseph Silk